ADOLESCENCE

Founded by KARL MANNHEIM

The International Library of Sociology

THE SOCIOLOGY OF
YOUTH AND ADOLESCENCE
In 12 Volumes

ADOLESCENCE

Its Social Psychology: with an Introduction to
recent findings from the fields of
Anthropology, Physiology, Medicine,
Psychometrics and Sociometry

by

C. M. FLEMING

First published in 1948 by
Routledge and Kegan Paul Ltd

Reprinted in 1998 by
Routledge
11 New Fetter Lane, London EC4P 4EE

Printed and bound in Great Britain

British Library Cataloguing in Publication Data
A CIP catalogue record for this book
is available from the British Library

Adolescence
ISBN 0-415-17658-1
The Sociology of Youth and Adolescence: 12 Volumes
ISBN 0-415-17828-2
The International Library of Sociology: 274 Volumes
ISBN 0-415-17838-X

CONTENTS

FOREWORD

Young people are educable. Young people are worth educating. Upon their wise handling depend the issues of ultimate harmony or conflict in the home, in workshop or factory, and among the nations. Many current methods of treatment find, however, their justification only in the somewhat mythical descriptions of past centuries. For most of these there is little support in the more careful studies of recent years.

In the pages which follow an attempt is made to bring together in accessible form relevant findings from long-term studies of human development, from anthropological records of differing social patterns, and from observation of the therapeutic effects of group membership in schools, in the armed forces and in industry. All these have a contribution to make to the understanding of the nature and the needs of adolescents; and a full appreciation of their significance seems likely to lead to rather remarkable modifications of current procedures in industry, in international relationships, in schools and in homes.

London, 1947.

FOREWORD TO THE SECOND EDITION

Adolescents are more like adults than adults have often been tempted to suppose. They share all human longings and encounter all human problems. Their development like that of adults is continuous, variable and disharmonious. When shut out from adult companionship they reject those things which their elders hold most dear. When admitted to the fellowship of religious awareness they mature with unexpected grace. Psychological research in the last fifteen years has brought further confirmation of these findings; and in this revised edition an attempt has been made to assess relevant evidence on these and other issues.

London, 1963.

CHAPTER I

OF ADOLESCENTS AND OTHERS

A compartment full of people in a suburban train. My nearest neighbour reads *David Copperfield* with absorbed attentiveness. More passengers enter. He gives up his seat. He sways with the movement of the train, and his face comes into view. He is young. He continues to read with firm concentration. He is as tall as many men but not a man. He is obviously not the contemporary of the adults near him. In what does the difference consist?

A group of nurses in a hospital. One face and figure stands out among the others. In height, in dress, in performance, she conforms to the Institution's pattern; but her uniform does not conceal her age. The others are mature women. She is still a girl.

A half-empty bus. Two at the far end very elegantly attired. High heels, coquettish hats, plucked eyebrows, lipstick, handbags. Highly decorative. Very vivacious. Then, on a closer view, one is little more than a child. The other an old woman.

Two cricket pitches in a park. Two games being played with comparable concentration. Figures are of similar height. One group at a glance can, however, be described as consisting of boys and the other as undoubtedly composed of men.

A class of boys and girls—of ages between thirteen and fourteen. Schooling has been almost identical. Attitude, gesture and performance are quite observably divergent. Alec in the corner has still the body of a child. Robert in the front is almost a man in height. Jean has the fragility of a little girl. Beth is a healthy tomboy. Alice has a matronly maturity of manner and the physique of a well-grown woman. Yet all have in common the attribute of youth. All belong to the group that is commonly described as adolescent. Some among them are scarcely distinguishable from children. Others would appear to be fully adult were it not for the subtle bloom of their youthfulness.

Adolescents cannot be said to form a homogeneous group. It is, however, possible to differentiate between adolescents and adults and also to distinguish adolescents from children. What, then, are the characteristics of the adolescent? Allowing for the

I

infinite variety of social relationships and the wide range of human reactions, what observations can reasonably be made on those to whom that descriptive term can justly be applied?

In the first place, it may be noted that the word "adolescent" is commonly used with more than one connotation. In its simplest sense, it is applied to those within the age-group which is developing from childhood to adult status. The term as so used is somewhat elastic but it refers roughly to young people of chronological ages between, say, twelve and twenty, or, more accurately, to those who are physiologically old enough to have experienced puberty but not yet sufficiently mature to have developed the physical stability of adult life.

The word, however, is also employed to describe personal characteristics often found among such physiological adolescents—wherever those attributes may be found. It is possible, therefore, to speak of an elderly woman as being adolescent in her attitude to life or of a middle-aged man as retaining the social immaturity of his adolescence. The word is not a mere equivalent of puberal. Puberty among quite normal children has been reported to occur at all ages between eight or nine and eighteen or nineteen; and both precocious and delayed puberty are more common than is generally believed. The word adolescent carries with it social as well as physiological implications. It refers not merely to the years of physiological maturing but to the period of social and personal development which is commonly (though not always) contemporaneous with that time of physical change.

In the second place it may be observed that, as these examples suggest, adolescence may be studied from many aspects. It may be described from the point of view of physique, of intellect or of personal development; but, since human beings live in communities, no one of these is profitably considered except in relation to the groupings in which adolescents are found—the home, the school, the factory, the club, the college or the street. Of these, the first and probably the most formative is the home. Adolescents, then, may be considered in their relationship to those others who, with them, form a home.

PART I

THE ADOLESCENT AT HOME

CHAPTER II

Bodily Changes

Adolescents at home, probably more frequently than anywhere else, commonly fail to win recognition of their entry upon this stage of growth. Tom is so obviously the same person who not long ago was a toddler and Rosemary seems still a nimble child to the parents and relatives who see her every day. It is therefore difficult for parents to realise that Tom is rapidly approximating to adult height and strength and that Rosemary is a fully mature woman who is physically, if not socially, ready for adult responsibilities.

The realisation of a change of some kind very often comes first to the adolescents themselves. It may happen in various ways. There are certain alterations in appearance to which attention may be drawn by the casual comments of their contemporaries or their seniors. There are changes of shape or function which are at first apparent to themselves alone. There are modifications of wishes and ambitions of which also they only may be aware. There are variations in interests and changes in attitudes which may puzzle or alarm the adolescents or their friends.

Each of these is sufficiently important to warrant further discussion; but each is significant only in its relationship to the past history of the adolescents, to their present attitudes and wishes and to their expectations for the future. Each in turn also derives its effect from the nature and the attitude of the groups of which the adolescents find themselves members. In some circles, development towards maturity may be linked with more or less acute anxiety. In others, there may be an absence of fear or distress which permits the changes to take place with no accompanying mental disturbance or emotional strain.

For this reason the reactions both of adolescents and of adults to the manifestations of growth can be observed to vary from family to family, from district to district and from country to country as well as from one generation to another.

What, then, are these phenomena of growth?

Changes in physical development may profitably be considered at this point,[1] since it is first of all in the home that adolescents commonly notice such modifications.

Growth in itself is not a new experience to children. It has been one of the accompaniments of living from their earliest days. Puberty is, however, preceded by a definite acceleration of rate, and this is accompanied by changes in structure which are greater than anything of which adolescents have any recollection. The developmental changes of comparable extent which occurred during intra-uterine life or in the first months after birth have not only been forgotten but their social significance was also very different from that of the alterations which startle them as they change from relatively small children to adults in bodily proportions, facial appearance and physical power.

Perhaps the most surprising of their experiences is that they become aware of the fact that they are not only changing rapidly in certain scarcely specified directions, but that they are now recognisably different from their nearest associates. Such individual differences were undoubtedly also observable in childhood, but their range was smaller and their social importance was less. Adolescents are often exposed more continuously than little children to social pressure from parents and friends who wish them to excel; and in response to this they begin to pay more attention to the bewildering variety of human appearance which is exemplified by themselves and their contemporaries.

Differences in bodily proportions and physique have attracted the interest of investigators for many centuries, and many attempts have been made to simplify their description by suitable classifications. Hippocrates, four hundred years before Christ, proposed a division of human beings into those with a habitus apoplecticus (short and thick) and those with a habitus phthisicus (long and thin); and an Aristotelian delight in such analyses has since appeared in modern guise in distinctions[2] based upon dominant functions (cerebral, digestive, respiratory and muscular), upon habitual diet (herbivorous or carnivorous), or upon descriptions of relative length and breadth such as linear and lateral,[3] leptosome or asthenic (slender), pyknic (broad) and athletic (muscular).[4] More recent studies accompanied by increasingly accurate measurements with specially constructed instruments have, however, cast doubt upon the existence of a small number of clearly defined and discrete types. Sheldon, for example,[5] describes three main physical patterns: endomorphic (thick-set, with a tendency to lay on fat), mesomorphic (muscular, with broad shoulders and hips) and ectomorphic (thin with light bones and poorly developed muscles); but he recognises that the variations in relative proportions are so many that a subsidiary classification into seventy-six combinations of seven differing degrees of these primary bodily components is barely sufficient to account for all the varieties of bodily build observable in the adult population.

No two bodies are exactly alike, and the ways in which two physiques may differ are endless. Even a mesh of seventy-six holes is admittedly too coarse to provide adequate means of describing the measurable variations in human structure. The attempt to classify human beings into two or three physical types has, therefore, aptly been said to be comparable to trying to build a language with three adjectives. Careful anthropometric measurements provide no support for a belief in the existence of a small number of discrete kinds of people except in so far as these are regarded as the extremes of a continuous distribution of physiques. As in other descriptive systems, the path of progress has been from the notion of two-fold and three-fold classifications to the concept of variations along differing dimensional axes.

The existence of such varying assortments of physical dimensions renders very complicated any attempt at description of the incidence of changes which occur during adolescence. There is a wide range of variations at each age for each bodily dimension which has been studied, as well as great diversity in the combination of all physical characteristics. Some are fat. Some are thin. Some are muscular. Some are fragile. Some have sturdy bodies and ineffective hands or feet. Some are short in the legs. Some are long in the trunk. Some are deep chested. Some are wide in the waist. These diversities have been included in the deliberate calculation of indices devised to express the ratio of hip width to height, the relationship between chest circumference or shoulder width and total stature, or the relative proportions of the length of the head and the trunk as compared with that of the legs. The full description of an individual is now known to require the use of several such indices. It needs also to be supplemented by indications as to the texture, pigmentation and hairiness of the skin, the relative harmony of bodily development and the degree of approximation to the physical characteristics of the opposite sex.[6]

The importance of such findings for the student of adolescence lies less in the exact information they give than in their emphasis upon the infinite variety of types of bodily appearance and in their reminder of the need to prepare adolescents for the fact that their rate of development, and the resulting relationships of their height to their width or their weight, are unlikely to be quite like those of any other young person whom they know. Adolescents differ in the age at which their growth spurt occurs and in the rate at which they develop just as much as grown-up people differ in size, shape and physical proportions. The parent who can casually draw attention to this variety, and who is convinced of its relative unimportance for the future happiness of his child, will do much to calm the fears of an adolescent who imagines himself to be as remarkably unattractive and different from his fellows as the ugly duckling was in the fairy tale.

It is important to note that early reports on growth and development were for the most part based either on anecdotal illustrations of personal impressions (in the style since popularised by Piaget) or on averages obtained from cross-sectional studies—measurements in these being taken from different boys and girls at different ages. These averages were often reported without any indication as to the variations which they obscured* and an illusory impression of regularity of growth was conveyed by the graphs which portrayed the findings of such measurements of different groups. When, for example, graphs were constructed which showed the average heights of groups of boys and girls at different ages from one year to twenty, there was a temptation to forget that an average represents merely the central tendency of a set of findings and that there are necessarily many normal girls and boys whose actual dimensions differ very considerably from those of the average of their group. Observation of the graphs showed marked acceleration at certain ages; and statements were made which implied an expectation of the uniform appearance of increased growth at these periods—about the age of ten and a half for girls and twelve and a half for boys. There was a tendency to label as abnormal the development of those boys and girls in whom it failed to appear and also a tendency to exaggerate the extent of the differences between members of the groups of girls and members of the groups of boys. Both interpretations have had important social and educational sequels; and conclusions based

* A convenient way of indicating the scatter of test results is through calculation of the standard deviation—a measure of the extent of deviation from the average. Early reports neglected to record this.[7]

upon them still find an echo in current discussions of adolescence. They have to be read with extreme caution and interpreted with a knowledge of their definite limitations.

There are, however, certain quite useful generalisations which can be drawn from these earlier reports. The years of adolescence are characterised by a period of more rapid physical growth than has appeared in the latter years of childhood; and this is followed by a gradual slowing down of the rate of development. Older reports tended, by their method of presentation, to over-emphasise the sameness of this sequence. If, however, a calculation is made of the extent of variation from the mean of these measurements at each age, it is more easy to realise both the degree of overlapping in actual dimensions from one year to another and the wide differences at each age between the most fully developed child and the least mature. The recognition of this overlapping and these differences is probably the most important finding of the last fifty years.

A similar anticipation of regularity was encouraged by the analysis sometimes made of the same type of evidence in terms of average yearly increments in growth. When this was done it was shown, in the case of height, for example, that the average height (length) of boys is somewhat greater than that of girls at birth, that it increases at approximately the same rate to about the age of eight, that the rate for girls then begins to exceed that of boys and that this relatively larger increase maintains itself for approximately five yearly measurements. About the age of ten, therefore, the average height of girls equals that of boys. From the ages of eleven to fourteen their yearly increment is greater than that of boys, but from ages thirteen to nineteen their annual increment decreases steadily to such an extent that by the age of fifteen the boys on the average have again become somewhat taller.

An even more spectacular difference in the relative increment of growth is reported in the girls' increase in weight about the age of eleven and the boys' spurt about the age of fourteen. Such curves and the histograms which represent the same findings in columnar form served in the past to lend additional support to comments upon the differences between boys and girls.[8] The average height of girls is slightly less than that of boys except between the ages of eleven to fourteen years, when the average of the girls exceeds that of the boys. The average weight of girls in similar fashion exceeds that of boys between the ages of twelve to

B

fifteen years. This does not, however, imply, as sometimes used to be supposed, that all girls are taller and heavier than all boys for three or four years during adolescence; or that all girls mature earlier than all boys; but it means, in terms of human relationships, that very tall and strongly built girls are likely to be found among children aged eleven to fifteen, and that markedly short and undeveloped boys may appear in any home among the age-groups eleven to fourteen. The importance of these divergencies in size and strength will depend upon current expectations and attitudes; and in districts where tradition favours tall vigorous boys and slight slender girls there is inevitably some degree of social handicap in the experience of the girl who happens to be large for her age and the boy who chances to be small.

The existence of variety in development is rendered more obvious by "long-term" studies which report data obtained from successive measurements of the same individuals over a period of years.[9] One of the most comprehensive of these was undertaken in 1922 in connection with the Psycho-Educational Clinic of the Harvard Graduate School of Education.[10] More than 3,500 pupils entering the first grade of three cities of the metropolitan area of Boston were tested annually for as long as they remained in school; and completed records for approximately half that number of pupils were available after twelve testings. Data were obtained in terms of detailed physical measurements of various types, intelligence test results (both verbal and non-verbal), and records of scholastic achievements, personal attributes and family history.

With information of this kind it is possible to avoid many of the errors of interpretation which result from the selective use of anecdotes or from misunderstandings of the findings of cross-sectional research. In long-term studies it has, for example, been demonstrated beyond doubt that all adolescents do not experience their period of maximum growth at the same age.[11] If girls are grouped according to the six-monthly period in which their greatest growth occurs the range is between a time of maximum growth as early as ten and a half years and one whose most rapid increase is in the six-monthly period round about age fourteen and a half.

For boys the corresponding differences are between those who grow most rapidly at about twelve and a half years and those whose most swift growth is postponed to nearly seventeen years. If children are grouped according to their age of maximum growth in height, there is therefore a wide range of differences in the average height of groups of girls between eleven and fourteen years and a similarly extensive range for boys between about thirteen and sixteen years. The difference in average of these same groups at ages six or seven or at eighteen or nineteen years is very much less; and consequently the citation of a single average height for all girls or boys during the years of adolescence gives a much less representative picture of the total group than does a single such average reported in childhood or after the attainment of adult dimensions. Pronouncements upon the physical attributes of adolescents in terms of group averages and comparisons of individuals with the average measurements of their contemporaries are therefore now recognised as being even more hazardous and misleading than is such a use of averages in early childhood, or in adult life.

To this recognition of the extent of variations from the mean among quite normal adolescents, long-term studies have added evidence as to the degree of variability in the development of individual boys and girls.* When measurements are made of the dimensions in height or weight of pupils of identical initial or final size, their changes in relative position from year to year are remarkable. Each seems to follow his own pattern of growth in relation to the average of the group.[12] Efforts to produce greater similarity by organised exercise or additional feeding are in most cases foredoomed to failure and merely increase the difficulties of adolescents who are already sufficiently burdened with the complications attendant upon their endeavour to adjust their ways of living to their own changes in bodily structure.

Long-term studies of individuals have also drawn attention to other differences between early and late maturing adolescents. It is not, of course, easy to determine the most satisfactory criteria of physical maturity. Popular opinion commonly accords most importance to the appearance of strong facial hair among boys and the establishment of menstrual discharges and enlarged breasts among girls. These have probably the greatest social significance. They have, however, certain disadvantages as indicators of adult physical development. Extensive variations in the degree of male hirsutism without accompanying variations in masculinity render

* The author has pleasure in thanking Professor Walter F. Dearborn and Professor John W. M. Rothney for permission to reproduce four figures illustrative of this from their book *Predicting the Child's Development.*

mere growth of moustache or beard an unsatisfactory measure of maturity. Abundant facial hair of an adult type is also sometimes found among girls, and an increase in the size of the breasts occasionally appears in boys. The frequent irregularity of menstruation in the first few years after its appearance and the fact that it is a criterion which does not apply to boys make it less useful than other criteria such as skeletal age[13] (determinable from X-ray photographs of the growing areas of the bones in the hand or the knee) or the simpler measure obtainable from recording the middle

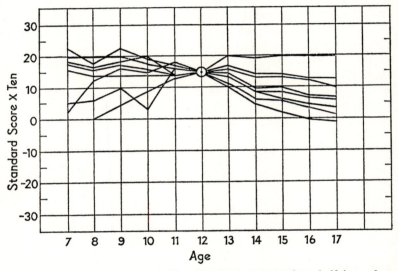

FIG. I. Changes in relative status of eight girls who were one and one-half sigma above the mean stature of two hundred and sixty-six girl subjects of the Harvard Growth Study at the age of twelve (from Dearborn and Rothney).

of the six-monthly period in which a child shows the most rapid growth in bodily size. This latter indicator can very conveniently be compared with other physiological variables if careful anthropometric measurements are being made at regular intervals. It has therefore been employed in certain extensive long-term studies.

Early maturing children attain adult proportions very quickly, and have therefore a longer period in which to make the social adjustments which are expected from them before entry upon adult responsibilities. They may need to pass through a period of considerable loneliness until their contemporaries develop to their level, but the prestige of such girls and boys is high, and they tend to show greater confidence and stability and to establish better personal relationships with adults than their more retarded peers. Boys who mature early tend to become large broadly built men. Late-maturing boys tend to be tall but more long-legged and slender. Among girls less distinct differences in bodily proportions have been noted between the two groups; but there is a more definite tendency for late-maturing girls to be taller than early maturing girls.

Developmental rate, of course, is not uniform in all bodily organs. The tall girl of fourteen may be immature in other respects and may feel herself at a disadvantage as compared with her friends whose organic balance is better than her own. She may also suffer from the fact that adults expect from her a degree of maturity which she is unable to display.

The origin and the extent of such discrepancies have been the subject of extensive studies in the last few decades. There has in consequence been a considerable increase in knowledge of the endocrine changes which are believed to be involved in growth and development. These are characterised by an increased secretion of the pituitary gland which produces not only growth hormones of the general type (which enable a healthy child to attain its maximum size), but gonad-stimulating hormones which lead to the liberation of increased amounts of male and female sex hormones. These direct the growth of the sex organs and determine the appearance of secondary sexual characteristics such as increased size of breasts, voice changes and the like. It is now known that every individual is bi-sexual and secretes from an early age both male and female sex hormones.[14] These sex hormones increase in quantity as children approach puberty; and after the age of eleven or twelve (on the average) the secretion of female sex hormones can be shown to increase markedly in the case of most girls and that of male sex hormones in most boys. These hormones not only influence the development of sexual characteristics and functions but they seem to act also upon the pituitary gland and to cause a reduction in its production of the growth hormone. Premature sexual development is therefore followed by premature cessation of bodily growth. On the other hand, in cases where sexual development is too long delayed, the growth of the limbs continues to a disproportionate extent.

Boys and girls are, of course, not aware of such endocrine

changes. They do notice, however, the larger alterations in bodily proportions both in themselves and their contemporaries. These are obvious first in the early and rapid growth of the girls in height and in width of hips. This is followed at a somewhat later date by the boys' increase in height, in width of shoulder and in size of feet and hands. Meanwhile more intimate changes are occurring, such as the swelling of the breasts in girls (and occasionally in boys), the appearance of pigmented pubic hair and later of hair under the arm-pits in both boys and girls, voice changes and a more or less sturdy growth of facial hair in boys (and sometimes in girls).

In the case of all these, the surprise of the uninitiated adolescent is increased by the fact that, as has been indicated above, there are such individual variations in rate of development that no two out of a normal group of adolescents may prove to be experiencing quite the same rate or incidence of growth. Even more startling to adolescents is the appearance of menstrual or seminal discharges in the case of girls and of boys respectively and the less obvious accompanying variations in pulse rate, blood pressure and basal metabolism. Of the secondary consequences of these they may become aware through unusual fatigue, muscular weaknesses and failure to exhibit the physical stamina expected of them by their contemporaries or their seniors.

Evidence as to the actual date of first occurrence of seminal emissions is much more scanty than the corresponding information as to the age of appearance of menstrual discharges.[15] There is reason, however, to believe that individual variations in age of onset are at least as great; and analyses of the evidence also seem to indicate that the average difference in age as between these comparable experiences for boys and for girls approximates to not more than about six months—that type of maturation appearing in girls on the average six months earlier than in boys.[16]

When a less satisfactory criterion, such as the breaking of the voice, is used as the criterion of sexual development in boys the difference between median age of maturing has been reported as about nine months; but if appearance of the first pigmented pubic hair is taken as the physical development in boys which corresponds in maturation to the onset of menstruation in girls, it would appear that boys and girls reach comparable stages of adolescence at approximately the same age.[17]

No one of these alterations in functioning is by itself indicative of the attainment of complete physical maturity or procreative power; but all form part of the pattern of change which complicates the adolescent's attempt to adjust his increased dimensions to the expectations and the claims of the adult world. Physiological changes are less easily studied than the more obvious alterations in physical characteristics, such as height, weight or bodily outline. Pulse rate shows an average decrease of about eight beats per minute over the adolescent period but the rate of girls remains from two to six beats faster than that of boys at each age. Blood pressure, on the contrary, rises with age; and after about the age of thirteen the pressure in boys rises more rapidly than in girls and becomes significantly higher. Basal oxygen consumption decreases to the adult level in girls by about seventeen years and in boys by eighteen or nineteen. With increasing age there is also evidence of a slower rate of physiological recovery after severe exercise; but estimation of the degree of an adolescent's physical fitness is complicated again by marked individual differences in rate and direction of maturing as well as by the difficulty of applying the necessary tests under ordinary conditions. The adolescent is unaware of the nature of these changes, but may become relatively disinclined for active exercise at the time that he is experiencing a somewhat lower blood pressure and diminished ability to raise the pulse rate after exertion.

With the establishment of menstruation, there comes in girls a stabilising of physiological functions and an approach to adult levels—a relative cessation of the rise in blood pressure, a decline in pulse rate and a fall in basal oxygen consumption. These are often accompanied by a somewhat rapid approximation to adult types of preference in relation to physical activities and choice of games.[18] Such modifications of attitude seem, however, to be only remotely related to the physiological changes of adolescence.[19] In attempting to assess their origins it is important to note that there are in many family circles marked differences in the expectations entertained by the adult group in relation to girls as compared with boys, as well as definite suggestions as to the desirability of rapid conformity to adult customs, both in the choice of activities and in the motivation acknowledged. It is at present therefore impossible to say what differences would be found in the relative physical performances of boys and girls and of adolescents and young adults, if the social pressure of adult groups were to be extensively modified. (Some inkling of possible alterations may, however, be obtained from a study of the changes in individual behaviour resulting from recent changes in public demands.)

The social consequences of these changes in genital structure and functioning depend very much on the attitudes and expectations of the group in which the adolescent grows to maturity. The adolescent is himself aware that his body is changing; but he is often uncertain of his social status. He knows that he is growing up, but he is, in many respects, treated as if he were still a child. There may be parental blindness to the alterations that are taking place. There may be parental unwillingness to admit that a new adult is joining the family circle. The years of adolescence are years of physiological learning in which certain physical adjustments are effected by the inescapable processes of bodily development. They are also years of social learning—in which the child gradually awakens to an understanding of the social meaning of maturity. Where encouragement and sympathy are shown by the adults in the intimate circle of the home, the experience of such growth may be relatively uneventful. Where there is opposition or parental blindness the adolescent may suffer acutely from conflicting wishes and may show obvious symptoms of personal and social insecurity. This emotional distress renders much more difficult the period of transition in which social adaptations have to be made— both by adolescents and by their seniors. The adolescent may be sensitive as to his position. He may dread social slights. He may be irritated by trifling restrictions. He may show aggressiveness in unexpected fashions. Parents who are aware of the social origin of such behaviour can, however, view such symptoms of immaturity with an absence of distress which does much to smooth the path of their children. If they are also conscious of the wide variations in the normal age of onset of genital maturation they can, by the serenity of their attitude, simplify still further the experiences of those in whom such alterations are long delayed (with consequent shortening of the period of socially approved uncertainty and physiological learning).

The same comments may be made in connection with the reactions of adolescents to their growth changes in bodily build, facial outline and distribution of fat.[20] Their responses appear to correspond less to differences in sex or in age than to differences in the suggestions and the social pressure to which they have been subjected. The outline of the forehead of many boys and a few girls, for example, begins in late adolescence to show the receding hair curves of the adult male. The nose becomes more prominent and the chin assumes its adult dimensions. If great emphasis has been laid upon the beauty of the boy he may pass through a time of acute distress when his mirror reveals that the childish features which were once admired are no longer to be seen. The un-healthiness of skin which often accompanies such changes may at the same time be the subject of thoughtless comment from friends and relatives. "He used to be such a good looking boy." "She is very much changed." "She was a lovely baby." Facial blemishes and spots are not commonly recognised by parents as of probable glandular origin, and a deep sense of physical unworthiness may follow upon misguided attempts to remove them by superficial treatment or to obscure them by the use of cosmetics. This sense of inferiority may be increased by comments on the disproportion-ate over-development of feet or hands which results in clumsiness and awkwardness which are socially annoying—especially in the small overcrowded houses to which many adolescents require to adapt their changing bodily dimensions.

The burden of this dependence upon adult expectations is aggravated by the fact that, accompanying all these physical and physiological changes, there is more or less consciously in all adolescents an awareness of the need to make progress, to grow, to meet new experiences and to do fresh things. This complicates their problem; but, like bodily changes, it is not an experience which is peculiar to them as adolescents. It characterises every stage of living; but, in adolescence, as has been indicated above, it is sharpened by social pressure. Boys and girls are continually reminded by much that they see and hear that they are expected to become grown up and that maturity brings with it certain privileges. To a greater or lesser degree, dependent on the nature of other past suggestions, they accept this as inevitable and de-sirable and prepare themselves for adult status.

REFERENCES

[1] For useful summaries see:
Bayley, N., and Tuddenham, R. D., Adolescent Changes in Body Build, in Jones, H. E., *et al.*, Adolescence, *Forty-Third Yearbook, Nat. Soc. Study Educ.* Part I. Chicago: Univ. of Chicago, 1944.
Bayley, N., Individual Patterns of Development. *Child Dev.*, 27, 45-74, 1956.
Tanner, J. M., *Growth at Adolescence*. Oxford: Blackwell, 1955.
Tanner, J. M., *Education and Physical Growth*. London: Univ. of London Press, 1961.
Tanner, J. M., (ed.), Human Growth, *Syn. Soc. Hum. Biol.*, 3. London: Pergamon Press, 1961.
[2] For a summary of such classifications of constitutional types, see: Sheldon, W. H., *The Varieties of Human Physique: An Introduction to Constitutional Psychology*. New York: Harper, 1940.
[3] Stockard, C. R., *The Physical Basis of Personality*. London: Allen & Unwin, 1931.
[4] Kretschmer, E., *Physique and Character*. New York: Harcourt, Brace, 1925.
[5] Sheldon, W. H., loc. cit. [2].
[6] For a further elaboration of this in relation to accompanying differences in temperament, see:
Sheldon, W. H., and Stevens, S. S., *The Varieties of Temperament. A Psychology of Constitutional Differences*. New York: Harper, 1942.
Rees, W. L., Physical Constitution, Neurosis and Psychosis, *Proc. Roy. Soc. Med.*, XXXVII, 635-638, 1944.
[7] For discussion of statistical terms applicable to educational research, see:
Vernon, P.E., *The Measurement of Abilities*. London: Univ. of London Press, 1940 and 1956.
Lindquist, E. F. (ed.), *Educational Measurement*. Washington, D.C.: Amer. Council on Educ. 1951.
Thomas, R. M., *Judging Student Progress*. New York: Longmans, 1954.
Thorndike, R. L., and Hagen, E., *Measurement and Evaluation in Psychology and Education*. New York: Wiley, 1955 and 1961.
[8] As, for example, in:
Harris, H. A., *Memorandum on the Anatomical and Physiological Characteristics and Development of Children between the Ages of Seven and Eleven*. Consult. Committee on Primary School. London: H.M.S.O., 1931. Appendix II.
[9] Greulich, W. W., Physical Changes in Adolescence, in Jones, H. E., *et al.*, loc. cit. [1].
Ames, V. C., and Flory, C. D., Physical Growth from Birth to Maturity, *Rev. Educ. Res.*, XIV, 5, 1944.
See also:
Thompson, H., Physical Growth, in Carmichael, L. (ed.), *Manual of Child Psychology*. New York: John Wiley, 1946 and 1954.
Jensen, K., Physical Growth and Physiological Aspects of Development, *Rev. Educ. Res.*, XX, 390-410, 1950.
Staton, W. M., The Adolescent: His Physical Growth and Health, *Rev. Educ. Res.*, XXIV, I, 19-29, 1954.

Jensen, K., Physical Growth, *Rev. Educ. Res.*, XXV, 5, 369–414, 1955, and XXVIII, 5, 375–391, 1958.

Strang, R., *The Adolescent Views Himself*. New York: McGraw-Hill, 1957.

[10] Dearborn, W. F., et al., *Predicting the Child's Development*. Cambridge: Sci-Art Publishers, 1941.

On long-term studies see also:

Simmons, K., The Brush Foundation Study of Child Growth and Development, *Monogr. Soc. Res. Child Dev.*, IX, 1, 37, 1944.

Moore, T., Hindley, C. B., and Falkner, F., A Longitudinal Research in Child Development and some of its Problems, *Brit. Med. J.*, II, 1132–1137, 1954.

Moore, T. W., Studying the Growth of Personality, *Vita Humana*, 2, 65–87, 1959.

Falkner, F. (ed.), *Child Development: An International Method of Study*. Basel: Karger, 1960.

[11] Shock, N. W., Physiological Changes in Adolescence, in Jones, H. E., et al., loc. cit. [1].

See also:

Hahn, L., The Relation of Blood Pressure to Weight, Height and Body Surface Area in Schoolboys ages 11 to 15 years. *Arch. Dis. Childh.*, 27, 131, 43–53, 1952.

Tanner, J. M., 1955. loc. cit. [1].

For other details of the California Study see:

Jones, H. E., The California Adolescent Growth Study, *J. Educ. Res.*, XXXI, 8, 561–567, 1938.

Shock, N. W., Physiological Aspects of Development, *Rev. Educ. Res.*, XIV, 5, 1944.

[12] Dearborn, W. F., et al., loc. cit. [10].

[13] For relevant findings from the California Adolescent Growth Study see:

Bayley, N., Skeletal Maturing in Adolescence as a Basis for Determining Percentage of Completed Growth, *Child Dev.*, 14, 1, 1–46, 1943.

Bayley, N., Size and Body Build of Adolescents in Relation to Rate of Skeletal Maturing, *Child Dev.*, 14, 2, 47–90, 1943.

[14] For discussion on this see:

Greenhill, J. P., *The 1944 Year Book of Obstetrics and Gynecology*. Chicago: Year Book Publishers, 1945.

Kinsey, A. C., et al., *Sexual Behavior in the Human Female*. Philadelphia: Saunders, 1953.

Anastasi, A., *Differential Psychology*. New York: Macmillan, 1958.

[15] For evidence as to genital maturation in groups of adult men see:

Heath, C. W., et al., *What People Are. A Study of Normal Young Men*. Cambridge, Mass.: Harvard Univ. Press, 1945.

Kinsey, A. C., et al., *Sexual Behavior in the Human Male*. Philadelphia: Saunders, 1948.

[16] Brooks, F. D., *The Psychology of Adolescence*. Boston: Houghton Mifflin, 1929.

See also:

Campbell, E. H., The Social-Sex Development of Children, *Genet. Psychol. Monogr.* 21, 461–552, 1939.

[17] Horrocks, J. E., The Adolescent, in Carmichael, L. (ed.), *Manual of Child Psychology*. New York: John Wiley, 1954.

See also:

Scott, J. A., *Report on the Heights and Weights (and other Measurements) of School Pupils in the County of London in 1959*. London County Council, 1961.

[18] Stone, C. P., and Barker, R. G., The Attitudes and Interests of Pre-menarcheal and Post-menarcheal Girls, *J. Genet. Psychol.* 54, 27–71, 1939.

Jones, M. C., and Bayley, N., Physical Maturing among boys as related to behaviour, *J. Educ. Psychol.*, 41, 129–148, 1950.

Horrocks, J. E., loc. cit. [17].

Davidson, H. H., and Gottlieb, L. S., The Emotional Maturity of pre- and post-menarcheal girls, *J. Genet. Psychol.*, 86, 261–266, 1955.

Mussen, P. H., and Jones, M. C., Self-Conceptions, Motivations, and interpersonal attitudes of late- and early-maturing boys, *Child. Dev.*, 28, 242–256, 1957.

Mussen, P. H., and Jones, M. C., The Behavior-inferred motivations of late- and early-maturing boys, *Child. Dev.*, 29, 61–67, 1958.

Jones, M. C., and Mussen, P. H., Self-Conceptions, Motivations and interpersonal attitudes of early- and late-maturing girls, *Child. Dev.*, 29, 491–501, 1958.

Faust, M. S., Developmental Maturity as a determinant in prestige of adolescent girls, *Child Dev.*, 31, 173–184, 1960.

[19] Meek, L. H., *The Personal-Social Development of Boys and Girls with Implications for Secondary Education.* New York: Progressive Education Association, 1940.

Terman, L. M., *et al.*, Psychological Sex Differences, in Carmichael, L., (ed.) loc. cit. [9].

See also:

Anastasi, A., loc. cit. [14].

Stolz, H. R., and Stolz, L. M., *Somatic Development of Adolescent Boys.* New York: MacMillan, 1951.

[20] For discussion of relevant findings from the California Adolescent Growth Study see:

Stolz, H. R., and Stolz, L. M., Adolescent Problems related to Somatic Variations, in Jones, H. E., *et al.*, loc. cit. [1].

CHAPTER III

REACTIONS TOWARDS ADOLESCENCE

Up to this point there is reason to believe that these observations apply with considerable exactitude to adolescents in general. Markedly physiological changes occur in all young people in the period of physical development from childhood to adult status. Identical characteristics are not shown by all adolescents; but the sequence of bodily growth indicated by these findings appears to be more or less universal. Puberty and the transition to physical maturity are accompanied by these phenomena in widely separated districts, in very different types of homes, and under very diverse climatic conditions.

Wide individual differences are observable both in the date and the extent of such changes; but the differences are not consistently explicable in terms of climate, of race or of social status. Reliable evidence is admittedly difficult to obtain—partly because of differences in the criteria used to determine levels of maturity and partly because of the absence of accurate recording and the reliance of many investigators on adult recollections of childhood experiences. From data available from Scandinavian countries and from the United States of America there is some indication of an earlier median occurrence of menstruation over the period 1850–1950; but more recent London studies with more reliance on direct records cast doubt on the continuance of this trend. The matter is further complicated by the use of different methods of statistical analysis. This in itself makes comparison hazardous; but in general it may be said that it is not now believed that the onset of menstruation or the beginning of seminal discharges is uniformly earlier in the tropics than in more temperate zones. It is not considered that there are significant discrepancies in the development of different racial groups and it is not thought that there is a consistent relationship between genital maturing and nutrition or socio-economic level nor between age of sexual maturity and intelligence or personality in adult life.[1]

There seems also little reason to suppose that in these respects there has been much change throughout the centuries of man's

recorded history. Human beings everywhere have similar biological characteristics. In neural organisation, muscular capacity
and glandular functions the basic processes are alike in all.

Reactions towards these experiences do not, however, share this
universality; and for this reason generalisations as to changes in
ambitions, wishes, interests or attitudes as well as comments upon
modifications in the expression of emotions or alterations in social
behaviour have to be made with extreme caution and with an
awareness that what is reported is not necessarily an attribute of
adolescence as such, but rather of adolescence in a certain family
circle in a given country at a specified period of its history.

The personal reactions of young people and the difficulty they
experience in adaptation are, for example, even within British
family circles, directly related to the treatment they have received
in earlier years.[2] In homes in which the metaphysical questionings of
the child of four or five were treated with sympathy and answered
honestly, the parents continue to receive the confidence of the
adolescent boy or girl. Relations of easy friendliness established
prior to adolescence increase in depth of understanding[3] when the
adolescents' questions as to the surprising personal experiences
now being encountered are in turn treated with respect and
answered in man-to-man fashion.

Where parental friendliness is lacking the adolescent will at this
stage turn more definitely away from his home; and the rift which
was somewhat concealed in early or later childhood will become
evident through visible estrangement of greater or lesser extent.
An unfortunate consequence of this is that interpretations of
changes in bodily structure are then often sought from ill-informed
contemporaries who may not only fail to reassure the growing
child but may produce much unhappiness through instilling quite
unfounded fears.[4]

The reactions of adolescents to the experiences of growth vary
still more widely with the nature of the society in which their
homes are to be found—its economic condition, its stage in industrial development and its cultural pattern.

In the simpler society of earlier centuries in Europe there is every
reason to believe that adolescents found that their increase in
height and in muscular strength was met by an immediate demand
for services which they could render with very little training. Customs did, of course, alter to some extent from one generation to
another and vary from country to country; but physical maturing

was almost at once followed by an opportunity of taking a place as an adult in fighting, fishing, farming, hunting or house-work. Relatively little alteration in status thereafter occurred until effectiveness was reduced by decrepitude and senility. The skills which had to be learnt were simple and definite; and adolescents quickly attained the stability consequent on acceptance as valuable members of the group of which they formed a part. Sexual maturing was in similar fashion followed by recognition of adult status and by encouragement in the discharging of adult functions. Life was short.[5] Its average expectancy at birth was less than twenty-five years and early marriage was customary in all ranks of society. The emotional instability, discontent and quarrelsomeness which characterised some young people inside their homes did not come to public knowledge; and the problems incidental to growth were rarely of sufficient interest to win discussion in contemporary writings.

Adolescence as a period of development and of greater or lesser willingness to mature was, of course, an observable phenomenon through the Middle Ages, the Renaissance and the earlier generations of the industrial revolution; but very little notice appears to have been taken of it until an accelerated rate of change in ways of living and fairly widespread prolongation of the period of economic dependence accentuated the problems both of the adolescent and his parents.

A like absence of any special interest in the experiences of young people is an observable characteristic of similar simpler societies to-day. By common consent the transition from youth to maturity is there thought of as an important happening which may be marked by ceremonial initiation into the accepted behaviour of the adult group.[6] It is believed to occur at a specific time and its consummation is followed by admission to the privileges of adult life. Little attention is paid to the wishes or the variabilities of individuals; but on the other hand there is commonly in such societies no prolonged period in which a physiologically mature youth is debarred from full functioning as a member of the group.

The nature of this functioning varies under differing cultural conditions.[7] In some communities there is, for example, little emphasis on distinctions between men and women either in social activities or group behaviour. Boys and girls (as is reported by Mead[8] in a description of the Arapesh tribe) play the same games and children are brought up as much by the fathers as by the mothers. Sex relationships are as likely to be initiated by women as by men. There is no stress on leadership, competition or dominance; and children are not hurried to maturity but are kept from knowledge of adult problems. Few children show temper-tantrums. There is little emphasis on private property and little evidence of stealing or lying. Violence and aggression among men and women are regarded as signs of maladjustment; and loss of affection is considered to be a penalty for such aggressiveness.

In other communities (such as the Mundugumor tribe) both men and women are expected to be violent and aggressive. Love affairs are hasty and passionate. Rejection of children is common. There is intense hostility and conflict for power between siblings, between parents and children and between husbands and wives. Punishment is severe. There is strong emphasis on possessions and prestige and all children are prodded towards maturity.

In other communities it may be that (as in the Tchambuli tribe) girls are urged on to maturity while boys are not. Women may then become self-reliant, aggressive and efficient. They may own the property and do the most important work while the men give their attention to art and ceremonial and the care of children. The men in such tribes are reported to be shy, timid and inferior in status. They are thought of as being the less highly sexed. They wait for favours from women and their corporate life is observed to be characterised by petty gossip, spying, quarrelling and back-biting. Gentle women and actively-sexed or aggressive men are looked upon as maladjusted.

In other parts of the world there may be an emphasis on measured kindliness and tolerance comparable to that described by Benedict[9] in the matrilineal groupings of the Pueblos of New Mexico. In some places there may be as fierce a sense of ownership and as omnipresent ill-will and treachery as she portrays in the island of Dobu; and in other circles there may be something akin to the self-glorification and fear of insults which darkens existence among the Kwakiutl of the North-West Coast of America.

In comparable fashion, differences in social organisation lead to differences in expectations as to the part to be played by adoles-cents as well as in the attitude of adolescents towards their own experiences of growth.

Coming of age in Samoa is accompanied by different experi-ences from growing up in New Guinea, in Germany, in the United States of America or in England. The same series of physical developments may in one society be met with an apparent absence of conflict or distress and in another be the occasion for acute shame or fear.

In Samoa,[10] where the child from an early age shares in the life of a large number of households and where age rather than relationship gives disciplinary authority, life is a much more casual matter than it is in the more highly emotionalised tiny family of western civilisation. In the first months of life the baby in Samoa is handed carelessly from one woman to another; as an infant it is cared for by older boys and girls of six or seven; and each child in turn, as it matures, is disciplined through its responsibility for a still younger one. At eight or nine small boys learn to co-operate in reef-fishing; and as soon as girls become strong enough to carry heavy loads they are set to work on the plantations, to carry food-stuffs down to the village or to join in long fishing expeditions. In all these activities adolescents share in the work of the adult community—but without any encouragement towards precocity. They have a part to play among their relatives; but they must not be too efficient, too outstanding or too eager to assume responsibility. Boy and girl relatives are separated by taboos at an early age, and strong preferences even within the family circle are discouraged.

Disagreements between parents and children are settled by the children going to the home of another relative. Unofficial experimentation in sexual relationships is permitted by common consent; and no particular prestige is accorded to married women in distinction from unmarried ones. (All unmarried girls past puberty are classified with the wives of untitled men in the ceremonial organisation of the village.)

Boys and girls and men and women are all familiar with the sight both of birth and of death; and it is taken for granted that all will of necessity have complete knowledge of the human body and its functions. At the same time, the impersonality of the contacts of little children with their large number of adult relatives is continued in the comparative absence of strong affectional ties among adults. There is little interest in or appreciation of individual differences and there seems to be little experience of jealousy, rivalry and emulation. Little pressure is put upon the adolescent to behave in a prescribed fashion at a given age. It matters little whether sexual maturing is delayed or accelerated, for all can play a part in the life of the village according to their physical size and strength.

c

The tempo of life as a whole is slow. Wars and cannibalism have long since passed away. The climate is favourable and food is plentiful. No one feels anything very strongly. Defeat is taken lightly and young people early learn to accept with a smile the customs and traditions which still are adequate for the requirements of life in a simple and homogeneous community.

In such a society there is little marked difference of behaviour between the group which is experiencing puberty and the groups which are two or three years younger or older. The sudden bodily changes of adolescence do not appear to be accompanied by personality changes other than those following upon those social expectations of sexual functioning which are expressed in the random teasing of adolescents by adults. Boys and girls of sixteen or seventeen are interested in one another. The girl's shamed avoidance of older boy-relatives and the antagonism towards younger ones, which were fostered by taboos at an earlier age, are replaced in public by a pleasurable shyness and embarrassment; but there seems an absence of anxiety, distress or fear. Arrangements will be made for marriage at the recognised time; but in the meanwhile there is neither an urgency to grow up nor a special premium set upon remaining young. The adolescents think of themselves as youthful. "Laititi a'a." "I am but young." There is time for experiment and tacitly approved opportunities for amorous adventures alongside the responsible contribution which they are now admittedly making to the life of the community. Strong personal affections and allegiances are not expected to appear; and they seem rarely to be desired. When one adventure is over another may be expected to begin. Adolescence does not appear to be a period of storm, anxiety and strain. Bodily changes attract no particular attention beyond the casual acceptance of the fact that another group of boys and girls is approaching marriageable age. When marriages are arranged they will be accepted in an impersonal fashion and the contribution to community living begun in childhood and adolescence will be continued by another group of men and women whose interests and activities will in turn escape interruption by unduly violent sexual preferences or emotional entanglements.

Somewhat different is the picture, seen by the same observer, of young people who are growing up in New Guinea.[11] There, in houses built upon piles in the lagoons of the Admiralty Islands, is a community whose adults live by trading and fishing. The children take no part in the activities of grown-up people. They spend their days in undirected and unimaginative play—rolling and wrestling upon the mud banks or propelling their small canoes. They have no property of their own, and they take no interest in the activities of the adults, who, in turn, expect from them no co-operation, no contribution to the corporate life, no deference and no obedience. They are early taught the physical alertness and resourcefulness necessary for those whose homes are balanced precariously above the waters of a lagoon. Respect for the property of adults is enforced; and an early introduction is given to the elaborate system of taboos under whose shadow the community lives. When very small they learn to be ashamed of their bodies and their bodily functioning. They come to understand that they must not eat in the presence of certain relatives and that they may not be seen uncloaked by certain others; but accompanying this there is complete freedom for play. They may be aggressive, obstreperous, vociferous and insatiable in their demands upon the subservient mothers who prepare food for them when they wish to eat or the fathers who handle them tenderly and share in their childish games. From the age of eleven or twelve girls perform some household tasks; but boys take no part in adult activities until about the age of twenty.

For girls there are initiation ceremonies at the time of their first menstruation, and before that date most of them have already been betrothed. Their free play begins to be restricted by taboos and special costumes from the time that the choice of their husband is determined; but the onset of puberty is the signal for the final abandoning of the games and joyous companionship of other girls and boys in the village. A time of waiting then begins in which no new responsibilities are undertaken, and no fresh adventures are possible. For three or four years the adolescent girl matures physically in slow and uneventful fashion under the close supervision of older women.

In the case of boys there is a family feast of blessing at some point between the ages of twelve and sixteen when decorative piercing of the ears is performed in public. During this festival boys are, however, given no instruction. They meet no fresh taboos and they are not made to feel any more grown up. After it they still live unhampered by social or economic duties and their general insubordination and unco-operativeness remain unmodified.

For neither boys nor girls do the years immediately after puberty appear to be a time of storm, stress or conflict. For girls they are a period of enforced passivity. For boys they bring a further extension of the earlier years of scornful and careless impertinence. For both they represent the last years of greater or lesser liberty before the expected shadow of married life falls upon them. Marriage is anticipated with shame or with fear; and it brings to both young men and young women a sudden transition to a position of poverty-stricken dependence upon the whims of rich relatives. The boy has to work for the uncles or older brothers who have bought him his wife. The girl becomes a person of no importance in the home of the relatives of a young man who associates with her in a spirit of shamed hostility and distaste. No interest is taken in the wishes or the contentment of either the boy or the girl. Both turn fiercely to the competitive activities of adult trading which will bring to them, if successful, the right to make their voices again heard in public and to give way once more to fierce vituperations or to uncontrolled hysterical rages.

The transition from the irresponsibility of childhood to the obligatory diligence of adult status takes place at a clearly defined point and in quite definite fashion. It follows the pattern set by the community and the variations appear merely to be those corresponding to the greater or lesser aggressiveness and energy of the young people themselves. The period of adolescence assumes no special significance for the adults of the community. There is no sign of any special concern with problems specific to the sexual adjustments which in other cultural settings are thought of as consequent upon puberty.

In civilisations nearer home there are differences of emphasis almost as marked as those between Samoa and Peri. In the typical patriarchal homes of Europe the father was the stern law-giver. He controlled the destinies of the mother and the children. Women were trained exclusively for work in the home—as mothers, household servants or governesses. Children were kept in dependence upon the father—the girls as his domestic assistants and the boys as apprentices to his profession or trade. The family circle was an enclosed one; and fierce hostilities often developed against the father as the dominant male who was not merely a dictator but an ever-present rival for the attention and the caresses of the mother.[12] The adolescent boy and girl dreaded to grow up and venture forth into the dangerous outside world; and at the same time they rebelled against the continuance of control and supervision. They struggled between their feelings of insignificance and powerlessness and their desire to be independent and strong. They longed to be free and at the same time they feared the consequences of freedom. With the prolongation of the period of economic dependence this personal conflict became increasingly acute. It was not an inescapable concomitant of adolescence. It was, however, a characteristic of much adolescent experience in the traditional setting of western Europe and the eastern states of North America at the end of the nineteenth century.

In Germany under the Nazis this pattern was continued with the further complication that the father was not merely overbearing and dictatorial at home but might be seen to cringe to his immediate party superiors out of doors. The prestige of custom and tradition had been lowered by national defeat, and the economic power of the parents had been reduced by the losses of the inflation. The closed family-circle was to a considerable extent broken and the boys were deliberately encouraged in overt aggressiveness with its tacit stimulation of homosexual practices, while girls were as carefully trained in continued domestic docility and passivity.[13] Great emphasis was put on physical strength for boys and on fertility among women; and strong social pressure was exerted on those in whom development in these directions was delayed. Both boys and girls were at an early age taken into membership of semi-military clubs and organisations. Extreme importance was attached to conformity with the customs of these groups—to physical endurance and to loyalty to the state. Such attitudes led to encouragement of rapid maturing in the activities useful in war and to a depreciation of intellectual or artistic development in favour of physical prowess of the type favoured for men or for women.

In the United States of America the pattern of social expectation meanwhile continued to develop on lines more closely akin to those observable in other parts of Europe. There was great tolerance and more companionship between parents and children; but American children, especially in the more recently populated parts of the United States, were very often in the position of showmen or guides to their elders. They were Americans by birth. Their parents or grandparents were not. They attended American schools; and they were familiar with the electrical devices and the personal luxuries which were unknown in the simpler societies from which their parents came. In consequence, they talked while their elders listened. They exhibited their prowess—both physical and mental—and, to a greater degree than in Europe, they organised their social life through "dates" and "petting parties" which were largely independent of the activities of their homes. Such separation of parents and children has increased with the development of large towns in certain parts of North America; and the "adolescent society" of school or club has taken over much of the social education which was formerly a prerogative of the home. Prestige in the eyes of other boys and girls has come to mean more than the approval of parents whose working contacts with their families are few and whose leisure activities are organised in adult groups from which children are excluded.[14]

This does not mean that within either tribes or nations there are no deviations from the accepted pattern. The general absence of conflict observable in Samoa was concomitant with some homes in which distress and strain at adolescence were observable. In New Guinea there were some aggressive adolescent girls and some timid boys. In Nazi Germany there were families in which democratic tolerance, open-mindedness and kindliness were still practised. There are breakfast tables in the United States of America where the father talks and the adolescent children listen with as great apparent attentiveness as in the most traditional setting of more feudal England. There are boys and girls in Europe who instruct their parents and organise their own social developing with little regard for the suggestions of their home or school; and there are wide divergencies between American schools in the degree of rejection of the social values of parents or teachers. It remains, however, true to say that the experiences of adolescents do differ in definite fashions in different cultural settings in different parts of the world as well as at different periods of history. These experiences in turn react upon the personal development of the adolescents and determine their attitude to the sequences of their physical maturing.

It remains also true to say that, on the whole, problems (both social and personal) specifically describable as those of adolescence have increased in complexity with the general lengthening of the period of postponement of adult status and with the reduction in the prestige of custom and tradition which is also a characteristic of twentieth-century living in the Western World. The conflict between family loyalties and military requirements in Nazi Germany was reflected in excessive anxiety and tension on the part of adolescent boys and girls. Discrepancies between the expectancies of immigrant parents or grandparents and the habits of Americans of the second or third generations led to undue storm and stress in the years when these differences came to mean more to the developing child. Postponement of recognition as adults and lack of experience of the satisfactions associated with responsible contributing to the welfare of a group resulted in discontent, self-disparagement and unhappiness and these (in any country) do much to render the period of adolescence a time of strain. These difficulties appear to be part of the price which is being paid for education for the greater complexities of modern life. They accompany the lengthened social infancy in which protection from economic independence provides opportunities for such fuller education. The form they take varies somewhat from one country to another and even from one home to another; but it seems true to say that in all modern industrialised states the years of preparation for this more diversified living are making ever greater demands upon the skill of the educator and the co-operative acquiescence of the adolescent.

REFERENCES

[1] Greulich, W. W., Physical Changes in Adolescence, in Jones, H. E., *et al.*, Adolescence, *Forty-Third Yearbook Nat. Soc. Study Educ.* Chicago: Univ. of Chicago, 1944.

Thompson, H., Physical Growth, in Carmichael, L. (ed.), *Manual of Child Psychology*. New York: Wiley, 1946 and 1954.

Wilson, D. C., and Sutherland, J., The Age of the Menarche, *Brit. Med. J.*, 2, 130–132, 1949.

Ibid., Age at Menarche, *Brit. Med. J.*, 1, 1267, 1950.

Ibid., Further Observations on the Age of the Menarche, *Brit. Med. J.*, 2, 826–866, 1950.

Ibid., The Age of the Menarche in the Tropics, *Brit. Med. J.*, 2, 607–608, 1953.

Tanner, J. M., *Growth at Adolescence*. Oxford: Blackwell, 1955.

Novak, E., *et al.*, *Textbook of Gynaecology*. Fifth Edition. London: Baillière, Tindall and Cox, 1956.

Anastasi, A., *Differential Psychology*. New York: Macmillan, 1958.

Bell, G. H., *et al.*, *Textbook of Physiology and Bio-Chemistry*. London: Livingstone, 1961.

Thoma, A., Age at Menarche, *Obst. and Gynecol. Survey*, 16, 4, 539–541, 1961.

Scott, J. A., *Report on the Heights and Weights (and other Measurements) of School Pupils in the County of London in 1959*. London: L.C.C., 1961.

[2] For an accessible summary of home influences see:

Fleming, C. M., *The Social Psychology of Education*. London: Kegan Paul, Trench, Trubner, 1944, 1959 and 1961.

[3] See case studies in:

Sheldon, W. H., and Stevens, S. S., *The Varieties of Temperament. A Psychology of Constitutional Differences*. New York: Harper, 1942.

Leonard, E. A., *Problems of Freshman College Girls. A study of Mother-Daughter Relationships and Social Adjustment of Girls Entering College*. New York: Teachers College, 1932.

Jersild, A. T., *The Psychology of Adolescence*. New York: Macmillan, 1957.

Strang, R., *The Adolescent Views Himself*. New York: McGraw Hill, 1957.

Gallagher, J. R., *Emotional Problems of Adolescents*. New York: Oxford Univ. Press, 1958.

[4] For some discussion of this see:

Bibby, C., *Sex Education*. London: Macmillan, 1944 and 1957.

Hacker, R., *Telling the Teenagers*. London: Andre Deutsch, 1957.

[5] For figures relative to the lengthening of the period of dependency, see:

Landis, P. H., *Adolescence and Youth. The Process of Maturing*. New York: McGraw-Hill, 1945 and 1952.

[6] Malinowski, B., *Sex and Repression in Savage Society*. London: Kegan Paul, Trench, Trubner, 1927.

Miller, N., *The Child in Primitive Society*. London: Kegan Paul, Trench, Trubner, 1928.

[7] For summaries of evidence on different societies see:

Sargent, S. S. (ed.) *Culture and Personality*. New York: Viking Fund, 1949.

Whiting, J. W. M., and Child, I. L., *Child Training and Personality*. New Haven: Yale Univ. Press, 1953.

Mead, M., and Wolfenstein, M., *Childhood in Contemporary Cultures*. Chicago: Univ. of Chicago, 1955.

Kaplan, B. (ed.), *Studying Personality Cross-Culturally*. Evanston: Row Peterson, 1961.

Hsu, F. L. K., Watrous, B. G., and Lord, E. M., Culture Pattern and Adolescent Behavior, *Internat. J. Soc. Psychiat.*, VII, 1, 33–53, 1960–61.

[8] Mead, M., From the South Seas, *Studies of Adolescence and Sex in Primitive Societies*. New York: William Morrow, 1939.

[9] Benedict, Ruth, *Patterns of Culture*. London: George Routledge & Sons, 1935. See also:

Kardiner, A., *The Psychological Frontiers of Society*. New York: Columbia Univ. Press, 1945.

[10] Mead, M., loc. cit., 1939 [8].

[11] ibid.

[12] For discussion of this see:

Dell, Floyd, *Love in the Machine Age*. London: George Routledge & Sons, 1930.

Fromm, Erich, *The Fear of Freedom*. London: Kegan Paul, Trench, Trubner, first published in England, 1942.

[13] See:

Siemsen, H., *Hitler Youth*. London: Lindsay Drummond, 1940. This may be compared with Benedict, R., loc. cit. [9].

Fromm, Erich, loc. cit. [12].

[14] Bateson, G., Morale and National Character, in Watson, G. (ed.), *Civilian Morale*. Boston: Houghton Mifflin, 1942.

Coleman, J. S., *et al.*, *Social Climates in High Schools*. Washington: Co-operative Res. Monogr. 4, 1961.

Coleman, J. S., Johnstone, J. W. C., and Jonassohn, K., *The Adolescent Society*. Glencoe: Free Press, 1961.

See also:

Schneiders, A. A., *Personality Development and Adjustment in Adolescence*. Milwaukee: Bruce Publishing Company, 1960.

Hess, R. D., The Adolescent: His Society, *Rev. Educ. Res.*, XXX, 1, 5–12, 1960.

Hsu, F. L. K., Watrous, B. G., and Lord, E. M., loc. cit. [7].

CHAPTER IV

THEORIES ABOUT ADOLESCENCE

Recognition of individual and social problems specific to adolescence appears to be of relatively recent growth. A brief survey of its development is of some relevance here. Recorded discussions of education among Egyptians, Jews and Greeks in pre-Christian times carried memories of the rituals of primitive initiation ceremonies; and their expectation of uniform and sudden maturing was re-echoed through many later centuries by writers who had little to say beyond an emphasis on the discreteness of the different periods of childhood and an assumption that there was a clearly-defined and swift transition to adult status at some point at which wise admonition could profitably be directed by a parent to a child or by a teacher to a pupil.

It was assumed by the more philosophic of these early thinkers[1] that there were distinct stages in individual development—a blossoming of the body, followed by a maturing of the emotions or appetites and terminated by the growth of the intellect. What is now called early adolescence was associated with the second of these and later adolescence with the third. Echoes of such Aristotelian classifications may be found in more modern guise in the assumption made by Vives in the sixteenth century that the course of learning is from the senses to the imagination and from that to the mind. It reappeared in the next century in the suggestion of Comenius in his Great Didactic that schooling should be divided into four six-yearly periods in which teachers should exercise first the senses, then the memory and imagination, next the understanding and the judgment and finally the harmonising will; and it attained dignified elaboration in Rousseau's pronouncement that "each age and condition of life has a perfection and maturity of its own".

Rousseau combined the earlier emphasis on discrete stages of development with the suggestion that there was a correspondence between the growth of the individual and what he took to be the history of the race. He also assumed in a fashion reminiscent of Locke that childhood was a period of mental passivity from which there was a gradual escape to mental activity through a successive maturing of faculties. From birth to the age of two he conceived a child to be "to all intents and purposes an animal—in a state of undifferentiated feeling, scarcely more conscious of himself than in pre-natal life". In the years from two to twelve the child reached the level of savage man. His mind was dominated by the senses and he lacked any proper power of reasoning. He was oblivious to moral considerations, and his only law was that of physical necessity. The third period of childhood was that of pre-adolescence which lasted from twelve to fifteen. A boy* was then capable of living a self-sufficient life. He experienced an increase of physical strength. Intellect made its appearance and he became able to regulate his actions with a view to future consequences. Conscience, however, was still undeveloped and personal utility was the sole motive in his behaviour. The fourth period was that of adolescence, extending from fifteen to the time of marriage at about twenty-five. During these years the sex functions awakened, the youth underwent a new birth, and true social life began. Soul was now added to intellect and sense; and beauty, goodness and truth acquired a personal value. Conscience ruled life and virtue became possible.

These theories were elaborated in great detail in Rousseau's story of the boy Emile, to whose upbringing a devoted tutor dedicated many diligent years. They exercised a strong influence upon educational thinking in many countries; and, after more than a hundred and fifty years, their echoes are still to be heard in popular pronouncements upon the stages of childhood and the education suited to differing age-groups. It is, however, important to note the source of the theories and to realise that they are of the type which can fairly be described as more akin to philosophic fiction than to observations based upon actual experiment or research. Rousseau was neither a successful teacher, a devoted parent nor a genuine student of child development. He did, however, succeed in drawing attention to the need for basing educational provision upon the nature of the child; and he exercised a further direct influence upon European and American thinking through the effect he produced on writers such as Kant, Pestalozzi

---

* The word "boy" is deliberately used here by Rousseau. In all his discussions he assumed that since men and women "are not and ought not to be constituted alike in character or temperament, it follows that they ought not to have the same education". Boys are to be trained to be complete human beings with world-wide interests. Girls are to be educated exclusively for wifehood and motherhood.

and Seguin. His hypothesis of a correspondence between individual and racial stages in development found echoes in Froebel and Ziller; and at the beginning of this century it passed into current educational discussions through the work of Stanley Hall and his collaborators in the Child Study Movement of America.

Stanley Hall stands half-way between the philosophic fiction of past centuries and the controlled observation and experiment of the present. He was influenced by the nineteenth-century doctrine of evolution and he sought to transfer to the study of education the scientific exactness of the developing physical sciences. He explored children's minds and attitudes through the reminiscences which adults set down in response to his questionnaires and he analysed the self-expression of children through essays and directed interviews.

To investigations of this type he added a very careful analysis of the results of nineteenth-century studies in physiology, anthropology and experimental psychology. Present refinements of educational measurement were then unknown. The results which he reported were in terms of mere averages and percentages; but his work did much to lay the foundations for the scientific study of child behaviour.

At the same time his books contained echoes of earlier musings. "By looking inward, we see for the most part only the topmost twigs of the buried tree of mind. The real ego is a spark struck off from the central source of all being . . . freighted with meanings that, could we interpret them, would give us the salient facts of its development history. Its essence is its processes of becoming. It is not a fixed, abiding thing, but grew out of antecedent soul states as different from its present form as protoplasm is from the mature body. . . . Every element has shaped and fashioned it. Its long experience with light and darkness, day and night, has fashioned its rhythm indelibly. . . . Cloud forms have almost created the imagination. Water and a long apprenticeship to aquatics and arboreal life have left as plain and indelible marks upon the soul as upon the body. Sky, stars, wind, storms, fetishism, flowers, animals, ancient battles, industries, occupations and worship have polarized the soul to fear and affection, and created anger and pity. The soul is thus a product of heredity. . . . It is still in the rough and . . . full of contradictions. . . . Where most educated and polished externally, it still has inner veins where barbaric and animal impulses are felt."[2]

His contribution to the study of adolescence can best be understood in the light of his views as to the relation of adolescence to the preceding period of childhood.

"The years from about eight to twelve constitute an unique period of human life. The acute stage of teething is passing, the brain has acquired nearly its adult size and weight, health is almost at its best, activity is greater and more varied than ever before or than it ever will be again, and there is peculiar endurance, vitality and resistance to fatigue. The child develops a life of its own outside the home circle, and its natural interests are never so independent of adult influence. Perception is very acute, and there is great immunity to exposure, danger, accident, as well as to temptation. Reason, true morality, religion, sympathy, love and esthetic enjoyment are but very slightly developed. Everything, in short, suggests the culmination of one stage of life as if it thus represented what was once, and for a very protracted and relatively stationary period, the age of maturity in some remote, perhaps pigmoid, stage of human evolution, when in a warm climate the young of our species once shifted for themselves independently of further parental aid." "The child revels in savagery. . . .

"Insight, understanding, interest, sentiment, are for the most part only nascent . . . but the senses are keen and alert, reactions immediate and vigorous, and the memory is quick, sure and lastng, and ideas of space, time, and physical causation, and of many a moral and social licit and non-licit, are rapidly unfolding. Never again will there be such susceptibility to drill and discipline, such plasticity to habituation, or such ready adjustment to new conditions. It is the age of external and mechanical training. . . . The method (of teaching used with such children) should be mechanical, repetitive, authoritative, dogmatic . . . with the least amount of explanation or coquetting for natural interest."

In contrast with this, "adolescence is a new birth, for the higher and more completely human traits are now born. . . . The child comes from and harks back to a remoter past; the adolescent is neo-atavistic and in him the later acquisitions of the race slowly become prepotent. Development is less gradual and more saltatory, suggestive of some ancient period of storm and stress when old moorings were broken and a higher level attained. . . . Important functions previously non-existent arise. . . . Every step of the upward way is strewn with wreckage of body, mind and morals. . . . Sex asserts its mastery in field after field, and works its havoc in the form of secret vice, debauch, disease and enfeebled heredity, cadences the soul to both its normal and abnormal rhythms, and sends many thousand youths a year to quacks, because neither parents, teachers, preachers or physicians know how to deal with its problems. . . . There are new repulsions felt toward home and school, and truancy and runaways abound. The social instincts undergo sudden unfoldment and the new life of love awakens. It is the age of sentiment and of religion, of rapid fluctuation of mood, and the world seems strange and new. Interest in adult life and in vocations develops. Youth awakes to a new world and understands neither it nor himself. . . . Character and personality are taking form, but everything is plastic. Self-feeling and ambition are increased, and every trait and faculty is liable to exaggeration and excess. It is all a marvellous new birth."

To these echoes of the past he added a detailed description of the difficulties of the adolescent in the United States of America in the first decade of this century. "Sedentary life is reducing the vigor and size of our lower limbs. . . . Industry is . . . now specialised, monotonous, in closed spaces, bad air and perhaps poor light. . . . The diseases and unrest bred in the young by life in shops, offices, factories and schools increases . . . the thin limbs, collapsed shoulders or chests, the bilateral asymmetry, weak hearts, lungs, eyes, puny and bad voices, muddy or pallid complexions, tired ways, dyspeptic stomachs. . . . Now, instead of head-hunting, winning a new name, wrestling alone with spirits or other of the drastic initiations of savages, the civilised and more sedentary youth must vent his intensification of personal feeling in dreams of greatness. . . . At its best, metropolitan life is hard on childhood. . . . Civilisation with all its accumulated mass of cultures and skills, its artifacts, its necessity of longer and severer apprenticeship and specialisation, is ever harder on adolescents."

Along with this emphasis on discrete periods of development and on the stress and strain of adolescence Stanley Hall presented a very comprehensive summary of the research findings of the latter part of the nineteenth century. He brought together the contributions then made by experimental psychology, by physiology, anthropology, sociology and literature to the understanding of adolescent development in its relation to social life, to sexual maturing, to crime, to religion and to education. His writings had much influence upon educational thinking in the first decades of the twentieth century, and echoes of his opinions are still heard in many popular books on youth and in current educational discussions of the treatment required by young people.[3]

Their chief weaknesses lie in their failure to allow for the effect of social relationships, their apparent unawareness of individual differences, and the consequent absence of adequate interpretation of those cases which deviate from the average of a group. He reports in great detail the results, for example, of measurements of the height and weight of many thousands of adolescents; but he records only averages and percentage increments. As a consequence, he tends to assume that these averages are fully representative of each group; and he passes from a careful analysis of such figures to conclusions such as those in his chapters on education where he states that co-education during adolescence is unwise, since girls are then so much nearer to maturity than boys.

This neglect of the range of individual differences and forgetfulness of the overlapping of measurements for boys and girls was combined with an acceptance of the contemporary nineteenth-century viewpoint as to the attributes and relative functions of men and women. It was also accompanied by the assumption (in spite of a careful collection of current anthropological evidence as to differences of behaviour in different cultural settings) that his interpretation alone was true to the facts of human nature.

Man "before he lost the soil and piety", was therefore, according to Stanley Hall,[4] not only woman's protector and provider, but her priest. His superiority has, however, been somewhat damaged by modern civilised existence. "The more exhausted men become, whether by over-work, unnatural city life, alcohol, recrudescent polygamic inclinations, exclusive devotion to greed and pelf; whether they become weak, stooping, blear-eyed, bald-headed, bow-legged, thin-shanked, or gross, coarse, barbaric, and bestial, the more they lose the power to lead woman or to arouse her nature, which is essentially passive."

On these grounds it is especially undesirable for boys to be outshone at school by girls, or for girls to be educated in close proximity to boys whom they may learn to despise because of their smaller size and lesser prowess. The girl being "riper in mind and body than her male classmate and often excelling him in the capacity of acquisition he seems a little too crude and callow to fulfil the ideals of manhood normal to her age . . . and so she often suffers mute disenchantment. . . . The boy is correct in feeling himself understood and seen through by his girl classmates to a degree that is sometimes distasteful to him, while the girl finds herself misunderstood by and disappointed in men. . . . There is a little charm and bloom rubbed off the ideal of girlhood by close contact, and boyhood seems less ideal to girls at close range. . . ." Co-education for all these reasons was, therefore, in his opinion both retrogressive and unwise.

A comparable dependence upon current methods of statistical analysis and current views as to human nature render many of his other findings suspect in the light of fuller evidence.

A somewhat similar perpetuation of the old is to be found in the writings of Sigmund Freud,[5] who has probably been second only to Stanley Hall in his influence upon twentieth-century discussions of adolescence.[6] Freud, like Stanley Hall, attained prominence in the first decade of the century. He was one of the group of writers of that period who won recognition through their formulation of the importance of redirecting attention to the complete personality of the patient, the child or the pupil. Nineteenth-century philosophy had interpreted human nature from the point of view of the intellect. Emphasis in the early twentieth century had, therefore, to be put on the part played by feeling, by emotional development and by bodily satisfactions.

Freud was a physician in Vienna for the formative years of his maturity; and he himself and many of his patients came from the homes of prosperous middle-class families in that cosmopolitan city.[7] He shared Stanley Hall's attachment to past theories and he assumed a complete discrepancy in the characteristics of men and women, boys and girls. His conception of masculinity was in similar fashion paralleled by an acceptance of the patriarchal structure of society exemplified in the social life of Vienna at the turn of the century.[8] This was taken to be universal and inevitable as well as desirable; and his whole interpretation of human nature was based upon the consequences which followed from an explanation of social functioning in terms of the rivalry (or co-operation) of brothers for the overthrowing of the father in his possession of the mother.

While accepting this contemporary framework and remaining apparently unaware of the local nature of its cultural pattern, Freud did not, however, agree with Stanley Hall that the sexual instinct had its birth at puberty.

"That children should have no sexual life—sexual excitement, needs and gratification of a sort—but that they suddenly acquire these things in the years between twelve and fourteen would be, apart from any observations at all, biologically just as improbable, indeed, nonsensical, as to suppose that they are born without genital organs which first begin to sprout at the age of puberty. What does actually awake in them at this period is the reproductive function, which then makes use for its own purposes of material lying to hand in body and mind."[9]

Much of his discussion was still, nevertheless, in terms of clearly defined periods—an infancy in which the sexual life of the child consisted entirely in "organ-pleasure", in "the activities of a series of component-instincts (the sadistic and the anal) which seek for gratification independently of one another, some in his own body and others already in an external object", a latency period from the sixth or eighth year onwards when these desires were repressed and forgotten, and the time of puberty when reproductive or normal sexual functioning became possible.

In his description of the latter period he also repeated certain of the metaphors of the nineteenth century. "It is indeed one of the most important social tasks of education to restrain, confine and subject to an individual control (itself identical with the demands of society), the sexual instinct when it breaks forth in the form of the reproductive function. In its own interests, accordingly, society would postpone the child's full development until it has attained a certain stage of intellectual maturity, since educability practically ceases with the full onset of the sexual instinct. Without this the instinct would break all bounds and the laboriously erected structure of civilization would be swept away. Nor is the task of restraining it ever an easy one." Experience has taught educators "that the task of moulding the sexual will of the next generation can only be carried out by beginning to impose their influence very early, and intervening in the sexual life of children before puberty, instead of waiting till the storm breaks". "Consequently almost all infantile sexual activities are forbidden or made disagreeable to the child."[10]

These activities, in Freud's use of the term, were, for the most part, sensuous satisfactions of ordinary bodily functioning in nutrition and excretion. Puberty brought a new strength to the selfish pleasure-seeking instinct which in childhood was satisfied in this fashion and made possible its subsequent gratification

D

through normal sexual functioning. To the sublimation of this united sexual impulse Freud attributed the artistic and scientific developments of civilisation. To its repression and frustration he ascribed its discontents.

This emphasis on the importance of "sex" and on the significance of its satisfactions served, in much popular discussion, to support Stanley Hall's pronouncements on the special characteristics of the period of adolescence and added to these a further emphasis on the distresses experienced by individuals who were faced with twentieth-century delays in authorised sexual gratification. Freud's work also strengthened still further the conception of an inevitable and catastrophic adolescent rebellion against parental standards and social conventions. "From the time of puberty onwards the human individual must devote himself to the great task of freeing himself from the parents; and only after this detachment is accomplished can he cease to be a child and so become a member of the social community."[11]

Echoes of both these points of view—the emphasis on discrete stages of development and the expectation of conflict and distress —are to be found in current parental discussions of adolescence to-day and have now to be reckoned with as part of the home background of many young people. "He is of course quite different now." "Young people nowadays are degenerate." "Children have no sympathy with their parents." "Parents can't expect to understand young people." "It's adolescence. You can do nothing about it." "It's a difficult age."

Much of this is, in popular acceptance, assumed to have a universality of application for which more recent investigations offer little support.

The process of growing up has undoubtedly in the twentieth century been accompanied in many parts of the world by conditions of considerable stress. These have been reflected in the behaviour both of adolescents and their parents.[12] Difficulties of adjustment have arisen which have stimulated earnest study of the nature of adolescence and the requirements of youth. In other districts under differing conditions where there has been an emphasis upon social values of other types, a greater freedom from strain appears to have been accompanied by an absence of observable conflict and by much greater ease in maturing. Evidence as to the extent of such variations is one of the chief contributions of research workers in the last few decades.

Adolescence is certainly a period in which rapid physical development occurs. The child at this period becomes able to pass from the exploration and the conquest of his home, his garden or his street to experimentation with the actualities of adult living. Doubt is, however, nowadays cast upon the supposition that this development requires to be described in terms of anything so speculative as a recapitulation of the evolution of the race. There is also considerable reason to suppose that the actual history of men through the ages was not quite so simple as was formerly thought and did not fall into the clearly discrete epochs postulated for it by the theorists. The life of the group which used to be called "savage" is now known to be both more complex and more varied than was assumed by the philosophers of the eighteenth or the nineteenth centuries. In similar fashion, as will be indicated in subsequent chapters, the development of the young human being is both more continuous, more complex and more highly differentiated than the psychologists of the past and the popular writers of to-day would lead one to suppose.

REFERENCES

[1] For a clear exposition of the development of theories on education see:
Boyd, W., *The History of Western Education*. London: A. and C. Black, 1921.

[2] Hall, G. Stanley, *Adolescence: Its Psychology and its Relation to Physiology, Anthropology, Sociology, Sex, Crime, Religion and Education*. New York: D. Appleton and Company, 1904 (*passim*).

[3] For a useful discussion of their relevance to the English Education Act of 1944, see:
Wheeler, O. A., *The Adventure of Youth*. London: Univ. of London Press, 1945.

[4] Hall, G. Stanley, loc. cit. [2] *passim*.

[5] For accessible translations, see:
Freud, S., *Introductory Lectures on Psycho-Analysis*. London: Allen & Unwin, 1922.
Freud, S., *New Introductory Lectures on Psycho-Analysis*. London: Hogarth Press, 1933.
Freud, S., *An Autobiographical Study*. London: Hogarth Press, 1935.
Freud, S., *The Psycho-Pathology of Everyday Life* (1901), translated into English in 1914 and reprinted. London: Penguin Books, 1938.

[6] For an example of orthodox psycho-analytic interpretations see:
Deutsch, H., *The Psychology of Women. A Psychoanalytic Interpretation*. Volume One: *Girlhood*. London: Research Books, 1946.

[7] A simple description of this life in Vienna in the opening years of the century is given in:
Bottome, P., *Alfred Adler: Apostle of Freedom*. London: Faber and Faber, 1939.

[8] For discussion of the social setting and historical background of Freudian theories, see:
Dell, Floyd, *Love in the Machine Age*. London: George Routledge & Sons, 1930.
Suttie, I. D., *The Origins of Love and Hate*. London: Kegan Paul, Trench, Trubner, 1935.
Horney, K., *New Ways in Psycho-Analysis*. London: Kegan Paul, Trench, Trubner, 1939.
Klein, V., *The Feminine Character*. London: Kegan Paul, Trench, Trubner, 1946.
Barbu, Z., The Historical Pattern of Psycho-Analysis. *Brit. J. Sociol.*, III, 1, 64–76, 1952.
Bennet, E. A., *C. G. Jung*. London: Barrie and Rockcliff, 1961.

[9] Freud, S., *Introductory Lectures on Psycho-Analysis*. London: Allen & Unwin, 1922.

[10] Ibid.

[11] Ibid.
Horney, K., *The Neurotic Personality of Our Time*. London: Kegan Paul, Trench, Trubner, 1937.

[12] See also, with special reference to the problems of adolescents:
Ausubel, D. P., *Theory and Problems of Adolescent Development*. New York: Grune and Stratton, 1954.
Wattenberg, W., *The Adolescent Years*. New York: Harcourt, Brace, 1955.
Coleman, J. S., Johnstone, J. W. C., and Jonassohn, K., *The Adolescent Society*. Glencoe: Free Press, 1961.

CHAPTER V

PSYCHOLOGICAL NEEDS AND ADOLESCENT ATTITUDES

Intimate changes in bodily functioning often come to the notice of adolescents first in the privacy of their homes. In similar fashion they may there first become aware of what appear to be changes in their wishes and consequent modifications in their attitudes towards parents and relatives.

Interpretations of such changes have altered in recent decades in fashions comparable to contemporary modifications of outlook upon the observable facts of physical growth. In the nineteenth century the study of human beings was thought of as one branch of an *a priori* philosophy. Attention was given primarily to discussions of sensation, perception, cognition, memory, imagination and reasoning; and behaviour was thought of as fully explicable in those terms. Current metaphors were those of the importance of "impressing" correct ideas upon the minds of the young. The dissemination of reliable information was expected to lead to the reform of all social ills. By 1900 it had been established that body as well as mind must be taken into account. Psychologists approached their topic from the standpoint of the biologist rather than the metaphysician. Metaphors borrowed from the study of animals became fashionable in the New Psychology; and differences in behaviour were attributed to differences in the strength of inherited "instincts"—whether those were thought of with Freud as two in number or whether the analogy was extended to include thirteen or more in the terminology of McDougall. This type of approach was contemporary with that of Stanley Hall's eloquent generalisations on the averages obtained by measuring, by counting heads or by collecting replies to questionnaires. It encouraged the acceptance as inevitable and universal of the pattern of behaviour then observable in California, in Vienna or in London; but the frontiers of knowledge have since extended, and it is now recognised as an inadequate description of the differences in activities and attitudes which can be noted among people in societies of varying types.

Recent observers have therefore become more conscious of the fact that human beings are neither chiefly intellectual nor chiefly physical in their functioning, but that they are also initially and continuously social in their nature—members of groups and conditioned to such membership. Individuals cannot, therefore, be described fully either in terms of prevalent mental state or of dominant bodily impulse. They require to be interpreted also in their relationship to other human beings and in the light of the effect upon them of these others.[1]

This emphasis upon group membership (like interest in the variations observable in differing cultural patterns) became articulate in the decades after 1920. Delinquent children and backward pupils were studied in relation to their home, their school and their street; and it began to be recognised that part of their difficulty arose from the failure of their groups to satisfy certain of their fundamental psychological needs.

The conception of "need" is essentially more social in its implications than is a description of human behaviour in terms of instincts—inherited from hypothetical animal ancestors and conceived of as innate, unmodifiable and common to all members of the species. An instinct is by definition an attribute of an individual. A need implies the co-operation of the group for its satisfaction. It directs attention from the individual to his society and to the means by which, if necessary, the group may modify its methods with the expectation of resultant changes in his reactions.

Various lists have been compiled of the basic psychological needs. One of the earliest was that of Thomas,[2] who threw light on the delinquency of unadjusted girls by an interpretation of their misdemeanours in terms of the needs which their society had failed to satisfy. They longed for new experience, security, response and recognition; and in place of these their homes had given them monotony, insecurity and rejection. Their delinquency was describable as a misguided attempt to find satisfaction for their fundamental wishes.

Out of many such lists[3] perhaps the most useful is that which emphasises as primary the need of the human being for acceptance by his group—for love in the intimate circle of the home, for admiration among his contemporaries and for appreciation from employers or teachers. This takes different forms at different stages and in relationship to different people; but it appears to spring from man's essential nature as a social being—a member of a group. Experience of this acceptance in the years of infancy and childhood leads to the sense of security which later forms an important ingredient in mental health—the morale of the civilian or the soldier who, strengthened by it, is able to face difficulties and disappointments without undue dismay. Deprivation is followed by the distress which lies behind much delinquency and mental disharmony.[4] Children who were rejected or unwanted in infancy preponderate among those who present most difficulty to teachers or probation officers.[5] Rebellious and unhappy adolescents can be saved by the conviction that there is someone in whose eyes they are accepted and by whom they are beloved.

Concomitant with this is the human being's need to give as well as to receive—to display tenderness, to feel admiration, to express appreciation. Case-studies serve also to show the detrimental effects of the thwarting of this complement to primary acceptance by the group. Deprivation of this—the taboo on tenderness—leads to an exaggerated emphasis on the value of substitute satisfactions such as the lust for power or for pleasure.[6]

Next to these comes the need to learn new things—to experience fresh adventures. This is closely connected with the impulse of the human organism towards growth and development; but it is not limited merely to physical growth. It appears continuously as an attribute of human beings from birth to death. In the toddling child it is shown as an exploration of the room, the house or the street. It later widens to include the new experiences of the school and the neighbourhood; and, in the adolescent and the adult, it extends potentially to the limits of the knowledge of the tribe, the nation or the race. Its conquests are marked by the experience of success—the recognition given by the group, or by the individual himself, to the fact that a new victory has been achieved.

Comparable to this is the need for understanding—the search for answers to questions as to what is happening, and (in the civilisations about which we are best informed), from the age of four or five onwards, the question as to why things happen as they do. The metaphysical questionings of the little child are directly in line with the religious and philosophic thinking of the adolescent and the adult. They appear to be associated with this ever-present need for insight into the changing experiences and shifting interrelationships of the essentially social human being in the various groups of which he is a member.

Complementary to these needs for adventure and for understanding is the need to exercise responsibility of some sort—to contribute progressively through action of some kind to the welfare of the group. The little child who is fortunate in his home-life is early drawn into active co-operation with his family. He is permitted to share in the occupations of mother or father, of brothers or sisters. He is allowed to do things for the group or to be responsible for the care of some portion of its possessions; and he learns through such experiences the accepted standard of responsible care for those possessions which he is permitted to call his

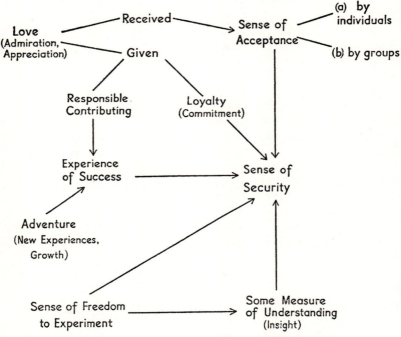

FIG. II. Chart illustrating inter-relationships of certain psychological needs.

own. As an adolescent or an adult the range of his activities widens; but the satisfaction he obtains from mature contributions to the well-being of his family, and from loyalty to his profession, his club, his factory or his trade is quite in line with the satisfactions he won as a little child when he first gave of his skill to the group which permitted his adventures in learning.

Loss of morale in times of adult stress, in unemployment, disablement, bereavement or war, has been shown to be greatest among those who have had least experience of such contributory functioning. Those with a responsible home-life, a successful career, a skilled trade or definite commitments and loyalties to church or club behind them are more able to face unruffled the vicissitudes of adult life.[7]

These basic psychological needs of acceptance, of opportunities to show tenderness, of adventure, of making a contribution to the group and of some understanding of the nature of the universe, are satisfied in different fashions at different ages and in differing social groups; and many of the changes in wishes and in attitudes which puzzle young people and their parents are comprehensible only in the light of a knowledge of such variations.

The social circle within which babies can satisfy their need for acceptance is at first very small. Their love interest reaches out first to the mother or the mother-substitute. From her they receive affection and to her they show tenderness. Father (if he is fortunate or wise) may soon share in this love; and at a later date the social behaviour of the infant develops into the sociability of the child of nursery-school age.[8] Small groups of two or three children then begin to form fleeting associations; and friendly relationships are established with uncles, aunts and adult visitors in the home. With increasing age this circle widens—within the limits of what is permitted by the home. In the free playgrounds of New Guinea[9] or the relatively homogeneous social circles of many villages and towns in North America or Europe, the size of the group fluctuates freely, and it contains both boys and girls. In the more artificial grouping of Samoa[10] or in the segregation of a private fee-paying school there may be separation of boys and girls and, in the latter, there may also be taboos on companionship with those of supposedly inferior speech, manners or customs.

When children mature into adolescence closer bonds may be formed between contemporaries of the same sex, and this may be followed by a love-interest of a more passionate kind in adults of the same or the opposite sex. This sequence is often continued by short-lived attachments to a variety of contemporaries of the opposite sex—leading in turn to the selection of a mate and the narrowing of the love-interest to the circle of a new home and its preoccupations. The date at which these shifts in social relationships occur varies from individual to individual in a fashion as marked as the variations in physical development which were described in Chapter II. To the unprepared adolescent the change of emphasis they imply is often as surprising as the alterations in bodily functioning which are consequent on the onset of puberty.

To the parents the inevitable reaching out beyond the home may seem to denote a lessening of the love which they themselves continue to require. They may try to place obstacles in its way and they may thus frustrate the emotional development of their children.

In similar fashion the child's need for adventure carries with it the demand for a continuous enlargement of experience; and the same sort of change may be noted in the gradual extension of the boundaries of the quest for knowledge and the search for an understanding of the meaning of life. Wishes and attitudes alter with this developing; and, while there is no discontinuity in growth and no sudden emergence of new powers at a specified age, there come times when the adolescents' conceptions of the contributions they can make, the interpretations they can accept and the responsibilities they can undertake have matured so much that types of behaviour which at an earlier age were sufficient for their needs can satisfy them no more.

A sympathetic understanding of the nature of such changes and a serene recognition of their desirability are among the major contributions which can be made by a wise parent to the personal maturing of the adolescent in the home.

REFERENCES

[1] Fleming, C. M., *The Social Psychology of Education*. London: Kegan Paul, Trench, Trubner, 1944, 1959 and 1961.

Fleming, C. M., *Soziale Psychologie und Erziehung*. Bonn: Verlag der Durrschen Buchhandlung, 1950.

Fleming, C. M., *Psicologia Sociale dell'Educazione*. Firenze: La Nuova Italia, 1953.

Fleming, C. M., *Psicologia Social da Eduçacão*. São Paulo: Companhia Editora Nacional, 1955.

Fleming, C. M., *The Social Psychology of Education*. Japanese Translation. Tokyo: Sogensha, 1958.

Fleming, C. M., Participation as a Therapeutic Agent, *Internat. J. Soc. Psychiat.*, IV, 3, 214–20, 1958.

[2] Thomas, W. I., *The Unadjusted Girl*. Boston: Little, Brown, 1920.

This may be compared with the discussion of "wants" in:

Small, A. W., The Category "Human Process"—A Methodological Note, *Amer. J. Sociol.*, 28, 205–207, 1922.

and with that of "desires" in:

Dunlap, Knight, *Civilized Life. The Principles and Applications of Social Psychology. A Revision and Enlargement of Social Psychology, 1925*. London: Allen & Unwin, 1934.

[3] A summary of several such lists is given in:

Wickert, F., Test for Personal Goal Values, *J. Soc. Psychol.*, 11, 259–274, 1940.

[4] Brill, J. G., and Payne, E. G., *The Adolescent Court and Crime Prevention*. New York: Pitman Publishing, 1938.

Rogers, C. R., *The Clinical Treatment of the Problem Child*. Boston: Houghton Mifflin, 1939.

Moodie, W., *The Doctor and the Difficult Child*. New York: The Commonwealth Fund, 1940.

See also:

Finesinger, J. E., The Needs of Youth. The Physiological and Psychological Factors in Adolescent Behavior, *Psychiatry*, 7, 1, 45–57, 1944.

Strang, R., *et al.*, Juvenile Delinquency and the Schools, *Forty-seventh Yearbook Nat. Soc. Study Educ.*, Part I, 1948.

Eissler, K. R., *Searchlights on Delinquency*. London: Imago, 1949.

Powers, E., and Witmer, H., *An Experiment in the Prevention of Delinquency*. New York: Columbia Univ. Press, 1951.

Stott, D. H., *Saving Children from Delinquency*. London: Univ. of London Press, 1952.

Paterson T. T., *Morale in War and Work*. London: Max Parrish, 1955.

[5] Goldfarb, W., The Effects of Early Institutional Care on Adolescent Personality, *Child Dev.*, 14, 4, 213–223, 1943.

Chesters, G. E., *The Mothering of Young Children*. London: Faber and Faber, 1943.

Edelston, H., Separation Anxiety in Young Children. A Study of Hospital Cases, *Genet. Psychol. Monogr.*, 28, 3–95, 1943.

Burlingham, D., and Freud, Anna. *Infants without Families. The Case for and against Residential Nurseries*. London: Allen & Unwin, 1944.

Goldfarb, W., Infant Rearing as a Factor in Foster Home Replacement, *Amer. J. Orthopsychiat.*, XIV, 1, 162–166, 1944.

Goldfarb, W., Psychological Privation in Infancy and Subsequent Adjustment, *Amer. J. Orthopsychiat.*, XV, 2, 247–255, 1945.

Goldfarb, W., Effects of Psychological Deprivation in Infancy and Subsequent Stimulation, *Amer. J. Psychiat.*, 102, 1, 18–33, 1945.

Bowlby, J., *Forty-four Juvenile Thieves*. London: Baillière, Tindall & Cox, 1946.

Bowlby, J., *Maternal Care and Mental Health*. Geneva: W. H. O. Monogr., 1951.

Bowlby, J., edited and abridged by M. Fry, *Child Care and the Growth of Love*. London: Penguin Books, 1953.

See also:

Bowlby, J., *et al.*, The Effects of Mother-Child Separation: a follow-up study, *B. J. Med. Psychol.*, XXIX, 3 and 4, 211–247, 1956.

Fleming, C. M., *Teaching: A Psychological Analysis*. London: Methuen 1958 and 1959: New York: John Wiley, 1958.

Herbert, W. L., and Jarvis, F. V., *Dealing with Delinquents*. London: Methuen, 1961.

[6] Suttie, I. D., *The Origins of Love and Hate*. London: Kegan Paul, Trench, Trubner, 1935.

[7] Angell, R. C., *The Family Encounters the Depression*. New York: Charles Scribner's, 1936.

Rundquist, E. A., and Sletto, R. F., *Personality in the Depression*. Minneapolis: Univ. of Minnesota Press, 1936.

Watson, G., Morale during Unemployment, in Watson, G. (Ed.), *Civilian Morale*. Boston: Houghton Mifflin, 1942.

See also:

Rees, J. R., *The Shaping of Psychiatry by War*. New York: W. W. Norton, 1945.

Stouffer, S. A., *et al.*, *The American Soldier. Combat and its Aftermath*. Princeton: Princeton Univ. Press, 1949.

[8] Murphy, L. B., *et al.*, *Personality in Young Children*. New York: Basic Books, 1956.

[9] Mead, M., *Growing Up in New Guinea*. London: Penguin Books, 1942. (First published New York: William Morrow, 1930).

[10] Mead, M., *Coming of Age in Samoa*. London: Penguin Books, 1943. (First published New York: William Morrow, 1928.)

CHAPTER VI

A GROUP OF PARENTS AND CHILDREN

Homes and what they mean to boys and girls vary as markedly as do the children themselves. It may be useful, therefore, at this point to consider in more detail the experiences and characteristics of a group of actual boys and girls.[1]

MARION AND EVELYN

Marion's father had been intermittently out of work for as long as she could remember. He was a somewhat ineffective tradesman with a surly temper and his services were readily dispensed with by both foremen and employers.* At home he made few helpful contributions to family life. He lay long in bed and spent many hours in languid debate at the street corner or in the nearest public house. Marion's mother was fiercely anxious and thrifty. In times of unemployment she went out to work—scrubbing floors and cleaning in the county hospital. She was determined that her girl would have an easier life than she had had, and while she could not provide a very satisfactory level of physical nutrition, she allowed nothing to interfere with the hours when Marion was supposed to do her lessons and she urged upon her perpetually the necessity for hard work and for success at school.

Marion at thirteen was among the tallest of her group. Puberty had occurred before the age of twelve and she gazed out at the school world from a face characterised by the clear pallor of the somewhat undernourished and unprivileged. She was a quiet pupil, unobtrusive and docile but undistinguished. Little share was taken by her in the social activities of the group. She was not unfriendly nor excessively shy, but she regarded as childish the conversation of the other girls and she had a scarcely tolerant contempt for the activities of all boys and men. Like her mother, she was aware of the seriousness of life and she set herself to fulfil its requirements of hard work and unrelaxing tension of endeavour.

In Evelyn's home also unemployment was not unknown. Her

---

* It may be remarked here that illustrative references throughout are to actual cases whose identity is suitably concealed.

father had been a salesman in a series of small shops which for one reason or another had each in turn become bankrupt. Between each experience there had been long weeks of idleness and for one tragic period his unemployment had extended to two years. It had been ended only by his securing a permanent position at a lower wage as storekeeper in a large factory. In his home, however, morale remained high. He and his wife were active members of a local church. They accepted responsibility and received honour in that group. They were friendly with one another, courteous and co-operative in their home life, and while unemployment meant a lowering of their level of nutrition it did not lead to quarrelling or despair. Both mother and father were interested in the subjects which Evelyn was studying at the county secondary school. They had been pupils there themselves. They did not, however, consider that all would be lost if Evelyn failed to distinguish herself. They gave her encouragement but exerted no undue pressure; and Evelyn at thirteen was beginning to mature into a sweet-faced rather gracious adolescent with a small circle of somewhat similar girl friends. While as yet this group as a whole was only mildly interested in boys, they had no fierce antipathies, no scorn and little apparent anxiety in their attitude to life.

The social and the economic level of the homes of Marion and Evelyn was not dissimilar. Family life as lived in them and the consequent reactions of these two girls both at home and in school were markedly divergent.

ALEC AND GEORGE

Alec and George were friends. They had been born in the same month, had arrived at school on the same day and, as far as either of them could remember, they had been close associates ever since.

Alec at thirteen had still the appearance of a young boy. His father was a doctor—a smallish man of slender build—and Alec's physical development had been slow. His home life was superficially pleasant but somewhat uninteresting. His father's hours of work extended far into the night. He had the successful professional man's absorption in his profession and had little attention to spare for wife or children. His wife considered herself ill-used by his failure to arrange for hours of leisure in which she might go with him to dances, concerts or theatres; but she had found solace in membership of a bridge club and she left Alec and his younger brother largely to their own devices. Their home was comfortably capacious. The library was well stocked. Toys were plentiful in the nursery, and golf clubs, tennis rackets and sports equipment of various kinds were available when the boys grew older. Alec's interests early turned towards books and somewhat solitary employments. His younger brother gave promise of greater prowess in games. Neither was made to feel that he must distinguish himself at school; but both were active-minded and both reacted well to the stimulating teaching they happened to receive. They were friendly with their parents and a similar easy friendliness characterised their relationship to teachers and pupils at school. They took part in most of the schools' activities—the younger boy because he gloried in them, the older one because he was quite willing to play the games which his friends played.

George was the only child of his father, who was a widower. His mother had died at his birth and his father had performed for him most of the functions of both a mother and a father. He had refused to part with the child to his mother-in-law and he had reared him according to his own ideas, with the aid of a housekeeper nurse. As soon as George could walk he had followed his father into the shop, and his earliest memories were of the entrancing rows of bottles in the back premises where his father—a chemist—dispensed according to mysterious prescriptions which George soon learned to respect. George had a box of toys below the counter and he played quietly there until his father was ready to return to the greater freedom of home and garden.

His father was fiercely protective. All his anxieties and his affections were centred upon the child—the living reminder of his brief married life. He organised fully the entire programme of George's days, and it was with great unwillingness that he parted with him when the time came for the child to spend some hours every day at the local school. George was submissive and dependent. His only friend was Alec, and at the age of thirteen he was still quite content to leave even Alec outside his home life and to take no part in any school activities save the organised games and the lessons which interrupted the hours which he could spend in the companionship of his father. He was a tall and somewhat serious-looking boy. Signs of puberty had appeared a few months after the age of eleven, and his interests, his topics of conversation and his outlook resembled those of an adult. He was somewhat impatient of school pursuits, but he was intelligent and there seemed little doubt that he would easily fulfil his ambition of becoming a chemist in partnership with his father.

The homes of the two boys were again similar in material equipment; but the attitudes of the parents differed widely, and their effect upon the adolescents was markedly different.

George had practically no tie with the outer world except his school friendship with Alec. He was afraid of other boys and girls, but he could talk with adults of a type similar to his father. Alec was more socially mature and could make easy contacts with all whom he met. George had quite clear-cut views as to his chosen vocation. Alec had as yet come to no definite decision as to a pre-ferred career, but he thought of himself as quite independent of his parents alike in his choice of a future occupation and in his plans for the conduct of each day.

JOHN AND BILL

John was an orphan. He had no known relatives and was boarded out with foster-parents who attended quite well to his physical needs but gave him little apparent affection and no de-liberate companionship. Mr. Jones was fiercely determined that John would prove a credit to his training. When John was younger he had whipped him freely for the slightest misdemean-our; but John at thirteen was becoming too big for physical punishment. He was a strongly developed, thick-set, sturdy young person with ruddy cheeks and a determined will. He intended to become a sailor like the father he could barely remember; and he had little real regard for the men whom he met in his foster-home or his school. In most classrooms he was obstructive. He was de-fiant of authority and he sought to win by noisiness the attention which he did not secure by brilliance. He was ambitious to do well, but he regarded with scarcely veiled contempt the routine of school learning. Women were beginning to interest him. He watched them as he passed along the streets, and in school he was either especially annoying or surprisingly co-operative in the classes of women teachers. He had long ceased to expect anything from Mrs. Jones, his foster-mother. She was both timid and frigid; and while she washed his clothes and cooked his meals, she did not succeed in conveying any impression of genuine friendliness or concern.

The school behaviour of Bill was not dissimilar to John's except that he showed in no classroom the somewhat wistful co-operation which John offered to the few teachers who had, perhaps unwittingly, conveyed to him the impression of personal interest and appreciation of his sturdy wholesomeness. Bill was the only child of a highly competent woman and a singularly unenterprising man. He had received every indulgence from his earliest years. In her relations with him his mother was both self-sacrificing and protective. She shielded him from all unpleasantnesses and she submitted to his every whim. Her husband (who was himself the child of an autocratic and equally protective mother) connived in the subordination of the home to the supposed interests of the boy; and Bill early learned the social uses of temper-tantrums and the efficacy of displays of violence as a means of satisfying his immediate wishes. In school he had found that it was necessary to employ more subtle means; but as far as he dared he continued to show aggression and self-assertiveness.

He had, as yet, the appearance of a child; but he could, on occasion, show the surliness and obstinacy of an elderly man. He saw no reason for concentrating his attention on work and he fully expected that he would be preserved from the unpleasant consequences of any failure which might occur. Great enthusiasm was on several occasions shown for new subjects; but after a few weeks in a new class he was again to be found in the small group whose obstructiveness and lack of co-operation led to perpetual conflicts with the staff.

INA

Ina might be described as the only child of her grandparents. She was the second of a large family. Her father was poor and her grandmother was prosperous but delicate. After the birth of the third child the grandmother and an unmarried aunt offered to take Ina with the secret hope that she would soon become a useful assistant in their home. The aunt had herself an interesting and absorbing career as a teacher, and the little girl lived in solitary fashion under the careful protection of her grandmother and grandfather. She was permitted no free intercourse with other children. Neither grandparent could tolerate the noise of children in their house or garden; and Ina heard many fragments of adult conversation from which she judged that her own parents were glad to be rid of her and that she would never be much use anywhere.

E

Her own home was at a distance too great for her mother to succeed in paying many visits, and the birth of four younger children led to ever-greater apparent forgetfulness. Ina grew up both timid and suspicious. She showed little initiative and at school she made only languid attempts to share in the activities of the other boys and girls.

LISBETH AND BETH

Lisbeth also took little part in the life of the school. She was the youngest of three daughters of a medical practitioner who had attained only slight success in his profession. He had at an early age begun to compensate for his anxieties by taking drugs, and when she was about ten years of age his addiction had become so confirmed that he had had to give up his practice and undergo prolonged treatment in another part of the country. This breaking of the home had been preceded by long years of discord. The mother was an efficient worker and she had not hesitated to express her views on the laziness and self-indulgence which accompanied her husband's failures. On many nights Lisbeth wept herself to sleep—torn between her love for her mother and her pitying anxiety for her father. She was several years younger than her two sisters. They slept together and comforted one another. They were older and had fuller memories of happier days. Lisbeth seemed to remember nothing but the nightmare of her father's disintegration. After he left home the peace which fell upon the household seemed to her one of stagnation. Her mother went back to her original occupation as a dentist, and Lisbeth gently brooded as she helped the others with household tasks each morning and evening. No one noticed her silence and no one took time to talk to her. In school she was gentle, silent and docile. She gave no trouble. Her work was competent, but she was set apart by a dreamy dignity which seemed to shut her off from the group. Again no one was particularly concerned and no one perceived that days might pass without any effort at self-expression on her part.

Lisbeth's constant attendant in school was Beth. The relationship between them was hardly one of friendship, since Lisbeth seemed to show no signs of reciprocating regard. The two, however, were rarely seen apart. Beth was a well-developed, cheerful, present-minded girl who looked like her thirteen years of age. She was tall and strong. Her body gave promise of the rounded curves of womanhood. Her hands were red. Her movements were rapid. She had something of the forgetfulness and physical prowess of a tomboy, but she was not rebellious or untidy.

Lisbeth lived near her. The two had come to school about the same time and it had become an established custom that they would walk together to school and home again. In school Beth was quite pleased to work with Lisbeth. No one disputed the privilege. And Lisbeth in her dreamy fashion took her physical presence into the activities in which Beth engaged. She did what she was told to do, even when that involved taking a subsidiary part in the school play.

Beth's home could be described as entirely normal in the sense that both parents were healthy, happy, co-operative and full of interest in living. The father was a successful teacher who found in his work abundant opportunities for fascinating experiments. He was active-minded and had savoured the pleasures of continued study and educational research. The mother had been a teacher before marriage. She shared her husband's interests, and he co-operated with her in the drudgery of the evening's household tasks. Both were good-humoured, hopeful and full of amused interest in the wholesome development of Beth and her two brothers. The children were not unduly scolded or repressed, and their progress was not impatiently hastened in any way. The parents shared with them many of the activities of house and garden. Theirs was a home in which there was no boredom; and many childish problems were freely and apparently casually discussed with the mother or the father as the children shared in the tasks of daily living. At the same time the parents had outside interests; and the life of the city impinged upon the children through the adult friends whose companionship the children enjoyed.

ROBERT AND MARY

A comparable home life was that of Robert. Like Beth he stood straight and strong. His father was a prosperous miller and his mother a woman of considerable mental power. Both were leaders in the city community and their son was rapidly maturing to the social ease of an adult.

Very different had been the experiences of Mary. Her father was a tram conductor who found life exhausting. He was several years older than his wife. Neither had many social contacts. They were members of no church and they concerned themselves with no political issues. In the evening he sat at home or he took his wife to the pictures once a week. On Sundays he stayed in bed. Mary had no recollection of ever having been played with by her parents. She had not gone for walks with them. Her father seemed to her indifferent or hostile and her mother had no real part in her life. It did not occur to her that children could be friendly with their parents. Her entire social life centred in her school-companions. She was antagonistic to adults. She did as little work as possible, and since she was somewhat dull, she was perpetually in disgrace in the classroom, and she compensated fiercely in the developing gang-life of a small circle of her school fellows. She was as yet undeveloped physically, and she and her friends were at thirteen still concerned with games rather than with explorations into adult life.

JIM

Jim was the youngest of a large family of boys and girls. His mother, like George's, had died at his birth, but his oldest sister, who was then sixteen, had held the home together with the help of an aunt, and Jim had been accustomed to many companions from his earliest days. His father had been an engineer in the merchant navy, but he had secured work on shore after his wife's death. The family had learned thrift in early poverty, and Jim fitted into the family pattern of diligent and earnest execution of the tasks which seemed to need to be done. His childhood had been somewhat lacking in joy; but his days had been filled with varied activities. He had learned to sew and to knit with his sisters. He had painted with one brother and practised carpentry with another. His ambitions were divided between that of becoming a cook in a transatlantic liner or a tailor in a marvellous ware-house of a kind glimpsed on an occasional visit to the far end of the city. In the meantime he was at thirteen very tall and thin, eager to learn, willing to co-operate in the school activities but more interested in learning to dance than in developing skill in team games with the other boys.

THE GROUP AS A WHOLE

Twelve boys and girls with a background of as many types of homes! What generalisations can be drawn? All were about thirteen years of age. They belonged therefore to the group which can in general terms be described as adolescent. All of them were leaving childhood behind and all were consciously pressing forward to new experiences. The nature of their development and the stages they had reached were, however, quite distinct. Mary, Bill and Alec were still small and childish both in appearance and in outlook. Pre-pubertal growth with them was just beginning. Lisbeth, Marion, George and John were already almost fully mature in physique. The differences between them were associated less with chronological age or physiological development than with differences in their family history and in the attitude towards them of parents, brothers and sisters.

Marion, John, Mary and Evelyn came from homes of relatively low socio-economic level. Differences between them were marked both in apparent intelligence in school performance and in social maturity and co-operativeness.[2]

Alec, Lisbeth, Ina, George and Robert came from prosperous homes where books and other household possessions were plentiful. They also showed differing reactions to adults as well as to their contemporaries; and these differences again seemed related less to variations in socio-economic level than to differences in the treatment the children had received at the hands of both parents and relatives.[3]

Marion, Mary and George had no brothers or sisters. The others occupied various places in the family constellation. Differences between them could be related less to the somewhat extrinsic circumstances of their order of birth than to the differing treatment they had received at the hands of their parents.[4] The reactions they made to society in their adolescence appeared to vary very directly with the treatment they had received and the habits of response they had formed in the years of infancy and childhood.

REFERENCES

[1] Discussion of somewhat comparable cases may be found in:
Abramson, J., *L'Enfant et l'Adolescent Instables*. Paris: Presses Universitaires de France, 1940.
Blos, P., *The Adolescent Personality*. New York: D. Appleton Century, 1941.
Levy, D. M., *Maternal Overprotection*. New York: Columbia Univ. Press, 1943.
See also:
Barker, R. G., and Wright, H. F., *One Boy's Day*. New York: Harper, 1951.
Sarason, S. B., *Anxiety in Elementary School Children*. New York: John Wiley, 1960.

[2] See:
Stoddard, G. D., *et al.*, Intelligence: Its Nature and Nurture (*passim*), *Thirty-ninth Yearbook Nat. Soc. Study of Education*. Bloomington: Public School Publishing Company, 1940.
Fleming, C. M., Socio-Economic Level and Test Performance. *Brit. J. Educ. Psychol.*, XIII, II, 74–82, 1943.
Floud, J. E., *et al.*, *Social Class and Educational Opportunity*. London: Heinemann, 1957.

[3] For fuller discussion of this see:
Fleming, C. M., *The Social Psychology of Education*. London: Kegan Paul, Trench, Trubner, 1944, 1959 and 1961.
For summaries and discussion on birth order, see:

[4] Jones, H. E., Order of Birth, in Murchison, C. (Ed.), *A Handbook of Child Psychology*. Worcester: Clark Univ, Press, 1933.
Murphy, G., *et al.*, *Experimental Social Psychology*. New York: Harper, 1937.
Krout, M. H., Typical Behavior Patterns in Twenty-six Ordinal Positions, *J. Genet. Psychol.*, 55, 3–30, 1938.
Schneiders, A. A., *Personality Development and Adjustment in Adolescence*. Milwaukee: Bruce Publishing Company, 1960.

CHAPTER VII

EMOTIONAL MATURING: PARENTS AS PERSONS

What of the parents in these homes? They also have a point of view and a history. Too often in discussions of adolescent development this appears to be forgotten, and it seems too readily to be assumed that adult society can be wholly remodelled in the service of youth.

Both the reasonable requirements of adults and the probable means by which their behaviour can be modified can best be understood in the light of a consideration of their basic needs. These are fundamentally the same as those of children or adolescents, but after the physical requirements of food, warmth and rest have been met the means by which these basic needs are satisfied may be observed to differ considerably at different stages of development.

The security resulting from the receiving of affection and acceptance by an admired group, the chance to do and to learn new things, and an opportunity to exercise responsibility and contribute to the welfare of others—all of these seem necessary to the healthy mental development of human beings.

In the homes in which children bloom into wholesome maturity these needs are being in large measure satisfied in the lives of the parents.

Happy people make happy marriages.[1] The children of equable parents are most balanced, least aggressive and most sociably developed. Emotionally mature parents are most able to permit and encourage healthy development in their children.[2] Evidence on such matters has accumulated since the 1920's through study of the home circumstances of children referred to educational clinics,[3] and confirmatory findings come from the many surveys of the social background of delinquency which have also in more recent years revealed the importance of family relationships and of the group influences to which children are subjected.[4] Emotionally unstable parents or foster-parents tend to have emotionally unstable children. Delinquent behaviour is associated less directly with the inheritance of anti-social attitudes than with

63

their cultivation through the treatment which children have received.

What, then, is meant by emotional maturity and the stability conducive to wise handling of children?

Emotional maturity may be said to reveal itself not so much in what used to be called the control of the emotions as in a modification in the nature of their stimuli, and in the type and the immediacy of the response made to such stimulating circumstances.[5] What appears to be anger in the infant or the little child is evoked by personal constraint or interference with its immediate intentions. Responses are swift and take the obvious physical forms of flushing, kicking, hitting and the like. Anger in the adolescent is evoked by what appears to be social slighting. The adolescent is as yet unsure of his status; he is thriving to achieve a position in the adult world, and what seems to him a frustration in this endeavour provokes him to wrath. He is now strong enough to deal in an effortless fashion with ordinary physical constraints. He cannot yet cope with social interferences. The response of anger, however, shows itself in less immediate and obviously physical forms than it did in the case of the infant. In so far as his behaviour is recognisable as typically adolescent, he reacts by words rather than by physical violence. Response in the form of kicking, hitting, biting or temper-tantrums is by common consent a form of childish rather than adolescent behaviour.

In the case of the mature adult, anger is, for the most part, of a type different from either of these. He is sufficiently sure of himself to be provoked neither by physical contacts nor by social slights, and his experiences of what may be described as anger are most usually aroused by the sight or the report of injustice. With increasing frequency, if he continues to mature, this indignation relates itself to wrongs done to others rather than to himself; and with increasing frequency his response to it is delayed and takes the form of deliberately planned deeds rather than of physical violence or fiery words. This is the stage which has been reached by those parents who may be classed as emotionally mature in relation to the emotion of anger.

Similar stages are discernible in the case of the other emotions. What may be described as love in an infant is at first experienced in sensuous contact with the mother alone. The baby is conditioned to dependent infancy and finds satisfaction in manifesting and receiving such tenderness.[6] The little child extends its love circle to include father and brothers and sisters. At a later date adults outside the family and an increasing number of school fellows come within the range of its love-objects. Relationship with these is less physical, and the experience becomes one of warmth of feeling rather than of intimacy of contact. In adolescence there begins for many children a narrowing of the circle. Strong feelings are evoked by one particular friend—perhaps an older man or woman, perhaps a contemporary of the same sex. At a later date, for most, there comes an awakening of sexual awareness and a more or less deliberate search for and attachment to some beloved member of the opposite sex. This again is more physical in its nature and more passionate in its accompanying responses. In adult life, after the establishment of a home and a career, the range of love-interest again widens. The happily married couple who continue to develop tend to look out beyond their own homes to the concerns of a wider humanity; and the range of their love-objects is enlarged to include, in more intellectualised fashion, other human beings in their street, their town, their country or the world. The mature parent of the adolescent is to be found among those in whom this widening of the love circle is occurring.

In the case of the emotion of fear similar modifications are observable. The infant may show immediate responses of a type describable as fear when he experiences an unexpected change of support or is awakened from sleep by sudden loud noises. The little child suffers from what can be called irrational fears in the sense that they are related to objects whose existence for the most part is imaginary. Like the baby, he reacts by terror-stricken immobility or by crying for help. Characteristic adolescent fears have as their stimuli unfamiliar social situations. The adolescent dreads failure. His responses are less obviously physical than those of the little child; but he may be tongue-tied or paralysed with terror or he may resort to elaborate planning to escape from social commitments and relationships which to him are unaccustomed and therefore terrifying.

The adult has, for the most part, escaped both from irrational fears and from the dread of social misadventures. He no longer thinks there is a snake behind the curtain or an ogre in the darkness. He knows that he is strong enough to lift the curtain; and he is a master of methods by which the darkness may be lightened and its perils may be conquered. He has already met most of the social situations which are likely to come his way; and he is aware that other human beings are less critical and less sophisticated than he once supposed. There remains, however, the fear of certain real dangers whose nature varies with the district and the circumstances in which he lives. He may dread swift traffic, unemployment, illness, sudden storms, the failure of a harvest and the like. Responses to his fears are, however, less immediate and more intellectualised. They take the form of deliberate planning rather than of cries for help or swift movements of escape. This is the stage which has been reached by those parents who may be described as emotionally mature in relation to the emotion of fear.

Fortunate are the adolescents whose parents have matured to such adult status. They will not be subjected to bursts of irrational anger over unintentional awkwardnesses, physical upsets or social inadequacies. They do not continue to be the sole recipients of a jealously possessive parental love. They are being assisted to escape from the tyrannies of irrational fears and a too-sensitive social timidity. Not all parents, however, are able to reach the stabilities of complete mental healthiness. Few can maintain them continuously without occasional backslidings.

Parenthood in its relation to adolescents in the twentieth century is not without its difficulties. Thirteen or fourteen years have passed since the parents of an adolescent embarked on the adventure of establishing their home. They have become accustomed to the fact that they have family responsibilities. The admired first baby has grown through the conquest of speech and the excitements of his first exploratory footsteps into a child at school whose comings and goings form part of the routine of every day. His mother and father have insensibly come to take his presence for granted. His growth admittedly continues, but its rate is slow, and one year seems very like another year.

Meanwhile, in most homes, other complicating circumstances have arisen which have conspired to distract the parents' attention from the sympathetic devotion they gave their baby when he was passing through the difficulties of infantile weaning or teething. Other children may have been born in rapid succession. The energy to spare for each may have become progressively less.[7] The calls of trade or profession may have become heavier. Household furnishings may have worn out. There may have been periods of ill-health and disappointment. Affection and love within the family in most cases continues; but the adventures of the parents—

the new things they try and the fresh ideas they entertain—tend to be related to their relationships outside the home, to the development of younger children or to the care of their aged parents, who make obvious demands upon their physical assistance and their sympathy.

They have fallen into a routine of expectation as to the child in his teens. They wish him to continue as he has been, and they unwittingly resent any change in his attitudes or his achievements. They still care for him. They include him in their planning; but they may not be prepared to admit that the time will soon come when he would normally be independent and establish a life-nest of his own.

It is a commonplace to remark that parents who appear to have some success with little children do not always mature into parents who can deal wisely with boys and girls in their teens. It may be doubted, however, whether these apparently differing degrees of success are not attributable to the fact that the unwise acts of parents of little children fail to reveal their full consequences until adolescence is reached.

Among the group of parents and children described above, Bill's mother loved him with what appeared to be complete devotion. She did everything for him. She read books on the rearing of children and the psychology of the pre-school child, and from them she extracted items of advice which fitted in with her wish to sacrifice all else to the cherishing of her son. She paid meticulous attention to cleanliness. She fed and exercised him with scrupulous regularity. She allowed no one but herself to serve him, and she gloried in his developing strength and his increasing assertiveness. To the superficial observer she was an excellent and successful mother; but in his earliest months were sown the seeds of the emotional immaturity which characterised him as an adolescent. His mother was herself prone to fierce fits of temper and periods of depression; but she built up her life within a strong façade of respectability and revealed to her neighbours only an extremely tidy front room and a decorous family life in which father, son and mother went walking together—accompanied by a somewhat timid family dog. They formed a picture the like of which is often seen in small towns and cities.

George's father in the early years also presented the appearance of an exemplary parent. He gave up all outside interests and devoted himself to waiting upon his son and organising all his

activities. His attitude, however, was autocratic rather than indulgent, and George's reactions differed in type from those of Bill.
In early childhood he rebelled at paternal interferences which were
unknown to his school companions; but his efforts after independence were met with such sorrowing indignation that they were
soon abandoned and he modelled himself to the pattern of the
docile shadow desired by his father. The beginnings of his personal
and social immaturity were to be discerned early in the history of
his infancy. His father to outside observers appeared an unsatisfactory parent for an adolescent who was supposed to be developing adult strength of character. He was already, in fact, an unsuccessful parent for the toddler whose hand he held so closely in
the first years of his bereavement.

George's father and Bill's mother treated their sons as personal
possessions and satisfied upon them their lust for loving as well as
their passion for organising. John's foster-father regarded his as
an animal which had to be tamed, and he vented upon John his
own immature rage at the interferences with comfort which
followed from the mere presence of an energetic and noisy young
child in his home. John suffered from the emotional immaturity
of Mr. Jones as expressed in the emotion of anger rather than in
that of love. Mr. Jones was an ineffectual parent for his son at the
adolescent stage. He was also an unsuccessful father in the years
when he apparently succeeded in maintaining some authority over
his child.

Marion's mother used her child as a channel for the fulfilment
of ambitions which had been unrealised in her own life. She dis-
trusted her neighbours and dreaded their comments upon her
household arrangements on the frequent occasions when her husband was out of work. She feared social slights for herself and she
was determined that through thrift and hard work her daughter
would win a more secure social position than she herself had ever
held. She had been superficially a model mother in the first few
years of the baby's life. Her child had been fed and exercised with
regularity, dressed with care and talked to with concentrated
attention. Even then, however, she had been over-anxious, unhappy and continually on the defensive; and Marion had early
known that life was a struggle—both serious and full of hazards.

Mary's parents were also not obviously unsuccessful in the first
years of her life. She was their first child, and they provided for
her the conventional equipment of clothes and food. They failed,

however, to love her and she missed the security which results from genuine acceptance into a family circle. They did not enjoy her adventurous first steps in living. They did not admire her, talk to her or play with her. She was never really a part of the partnership of the home. Their own social development was retarded. Their love did not widen to embrace other objects than themselves. It remained at the level of physical passion, and with the passing of years even that glow faded. Mary grew up dully attached to an unexciting home in which she had experienced no adventures and for which she had no sense of responsibility. Parental failure to satisfy her basic needs had its beginnings many years before the onset of puberty sharpened her awareness of her own demands from life.

Very different had been the life-history of Beth. Her parents had rejoiced over the development of each of their three children. They had played with them, laughed with them, loved them. The children were conscious of this love. They were aware that their adventurous living was approved, and they gladly took a share in responsibility for the welfare of their home. They were friends of their parents; and they could not conceive of a home in which parents and children were not co-operating partners. There was little hint of rebellion or rivalry. They wished to grow up, but they knew that their parents did not resent that ambition; and the parents had matured to so many other interests that they did not require either to try to retain the subservience of their children or to seek to purchase their continued attachment by over-indulgence. Their success as parents of adolescents had its roots in their wise relationships to the little children of many years before.

Even in such a home as that of Beth there are, however, contributory circumstances out of which conflict may arise. There are times when parents feel their status threatened by the developing strength of their offspring. There is the temptation to suspect social slighting and to experience anger thereat. There are fears of failure on the part of the parents when unexpected social situations arise. Adolescents may unwittingly cause alarm as they step forward from the expectation of independence in their choice of clothes to initiative in the selection of their friends or from satisfaction in the possession of a tricycle to demands for a latch-key and a time-table of their own. To the parent such strides towards independence may seem more disturbing and more full of potential peril than the adolescent can ever guess. To the degree, however, to which the parents achieve and retain emotional maturity and an adequate life-philosophy of their own, they are enabled to recover from a temporary forgetfulness of the basic needs of their child and they succeed in according to him the necessary freedom of growth.

The years of adolescence are a time of fruition for the fuller exercise of that growing independence which most parents have, to a greater or lesser extent, set themselves to develop through all the preparatory years of childhood. Its beginnings were to be found in the almost imperceptible steps by which the infant learned to crawl, to stand, to walk and to run alone. It was exercised in the adventures of the little child who stepped alone into the garden or the street. It developed in the experiences of the girl or the boy who went out into Sunday school or day school; and it found fuller expression in the life of the child who travelled unattended by parents in buses or trains or slept for even a few nights in the home of a friend. Such loosening of parental ties is, for most children, an accompaniment of the years prior to adolescence; and its culmination comes gradually rather than abruptly. It is a constant accompaniment of a slow process of maturing rather than a special influence peculiar to the period of adolescence. The stages of such growth are of necessity contemporaneous with those sometimes described as "freeing oneself from the parents". Like the gradual acceptance of oneself as a grown-up person, they are, however, in many respects an insensible accompaniment of a widening experience in living. A realisation that a change in attitude or status has occurred may come suddenly. The changes themselves are gradual rather than saltatory in character.

Where friendliness has characterised the family relationships of the little child, that friendliness continues in a deeper and more permanent form alongside the increasing independence of the maturing youth. Its mode of expression varies from district to district and from home to home in accordance with traditional behaviour in the groups of which the families form a part, but, whatever the cultural pattern, there is reason to believe that the years of adolescence merely bring into greater prominence the quality of a relationship which was in its essentials established many years before.

REFERENCES

[1] Terman, L. M., *et al.*, *Psychological Factors in Marital Happiness*. New York: McGraw-Hill, 1938.

[2] See also:
Taylor, K. W., *Do Adolescents Need Parents?* London: D. Appleton-Century, 1938.

[3] Sayles, M. B., *The Problem Child at Home*. New York: The Commonwealth Fund, 1938.
White, M. A., and Harris, M. W., *The School Psychologist*. New York: Harper, 1961.

[4] Van Waters, M., *Youth in Conflict*. New York: Republic Publishing, 1925.
Glueck, S., and Glueck, E. T., *One Thousand Juvenile Delinquents. Their Treatment by Court and Clinic*. Cambridge: Harvard Univ. Press, 1934.
Healy, W., and Bronner, A. F., *New Light on Delinquency and its Treatment*. New Havan: Yale Univ. Press, 1936.
Blumenfeld, W., *Jugend als Konfliktsituation*. Berlin: Philo Verlag G.m.b.H., 1936.
Neumeyer, M. H., *Juvenile Delinquency in Modern Society*. New York: D. van Nostrand, 1949, 1955 and 1961.
Glueck, S. & E., *Unraveling Juvenile Delinquency*. New York: Commonwealth Fund, 1950.
See also:
Cunningham, R., *et al.*, *Understanding Group Behavior of Boys and Girls*. New York: Teachers College, Columbia Univ., 1951.
Coleman, J. S., *et al.*, *Social Climates in High Schools*. Washington: Co-operative Res. Monogr. 4, 1961.

[5] For a more detailed discussion of emotional maturing see:
Fleming, C. M., *The Social Psychology of Education*. London: Kegan Paul, Trench, Trubner, 1944, 1959 and 1961.
Cronbach, L. J., *Educational Psychology*. New York: Harcourt, Brace, 1954.
Hunt, J. T., Emotional Development in Childhood and Adolescence, *Rev. Educ. Res.*, XXVIII, 5, 401–409, 1958.

[6] Suttie, I. D., *The Origins of Love and Hate*. London: Kegan Paul, Trench, Trubner, 1935.

[7] For an accessible description see:
Spring Rice, M., *Working Class Wives. Their Health and Conditions*. London: Penguin Books, 1939.
See also:
Stern, H. H., *Parent Education and Parental Learning*. Ph.D. Thesis, Univ. of London, 1956.
Stern, H. H., Recherche sur la Formation des parents à leur rôle éducatif en Grande-Bretagne, *Le Group Familial*, 2, 3–15, 1959.
Stern, H. H., *Parent Education: An International Survey*. Univ. of Hull: Studies in Educ., 1960.

CHAPTER VIII

PARENT–CHILD RELATIONSHIPS

From the point of view of the children also the period of adolescence in the homes of twentieth-century Europe or America is not without its difficulties. These are related partly to the emotional immaturities and the unsatisfied personal needs of the parents; but they are also associated with social traditions in accordance with which many young people must serve an ever-lengthening apprenticeship before they find themselves permitted to exercise the privileges and enjoy the responsibilities of adult life.

The years of adolescence are spent in the border-land between the state of childhood and that of adult life. Adolescents are still children in many respects, but they may at the same time be adult in others. Some among them have grown into complete physical and mental maturity. Others are quite definitely children both in performance and in wishes. They suffer both as individuals and as a group from this developmental imbalance; and they experience the additional difficulty that the adult world fluctuates in its attitude towards them, while the children whom they are leaving behind view them more definitely as outsiders with each step that they take towards adult behaviour or adult attitudes. Under contemporary conditions in social circles where there is long postponement of economic independence, and consequent lengthening of the period of adolescence and youth, the problems attributable to the delayed recognition of maturity have become more serious and the chances of misunderstanding within the home have inevitably increased.[1]

Some echo of this is found in the answer given to the question as to the qualities which young people desire to find in their parents and the comparable query as to what in actual fact they find most annoying in their parents' present behaviour.

In one study seven hundred adolescents were questioned as to the qualities they most wished in their parents. From their mothers they asked chiefly that they be good cooks and house-keepers and also find time to read, talk, go on picnics and play with them. From their fathers they asked that they spend time with them and respect their opinions.[2]

In another investigation of the attitudes of three hundred and forty-eight boys and three hundred and eighty-two girls, major disagreements with parents were said to be related to the hour at which the adolescent returned at night, the number of times the adolescent went out on school nights, the content of school reports, the spending of money and the choice of friends.[3]

A comparable American study of the relationships of adolescents with their mothers resulted in the finding that among five hundred and twenty-eight boys and girls serious conflicts leading to much unhappiness could be related to about fifty frequently recurring issues.[4] Representative of most acute disturbance among girls were:

(1) objections to their going motoring at night with boys;
(2) scolding if school marks were not as high as other people's;
(3) insistence on the eating of certain foods;
(4) insistence on the taking of a brother or a sister wherever they went;
(5) insistence on exact accounts as to spending of money;
(6) the absence of the mother from home and the spending of much of her time at bridge parties;
(7) the holding up of a brother or a sister as a model;
(8) refusal of permission to use the car;
(9) criticism of personal manners and habits;
(10) interference in the choice of friends.

For boys the comparable list was:

(1) refusal of permission to use the car;
(2) insistence on the eating of certain foods;
(3) scolding if school marks were not as high as other people's;
(4) insistence on exact accounts as to spending of money;
(5) criticism of table manners;
(6) criticism of personal manners and habits;
(7) the holding up of a brother or a sister as a model;
(8) objections to their going motoring at night with girls;
(9) refusal to permit to follow own choice of vocation;
(10) complaints about dirtiness of hands or neck or finger-nails.

Other frequent difficulties occurred in connection with worrying about health, refusal to give permission to take preferred subjects

F

at school, teasing about friends and interference with choice of clothes.

In another enquiry[5] four hundred and fifty twelve-year-old children were asked to write a list of items of their parents' behaviour which they found annoying. Some complained of ill-temper, nagging, moodiness and irritability. Others objected to being treated as infants and prevented from joining in games and activities with other boys and girls. Some longed for greater consideration at home—a chance to study and some degree of silence, orderliness and calm. Others protested against patronage in the presence of outsiders and personal comments before visitors. Others wished that the standards of their home were higher—that father did not break promises and that mother showed better taste in her choice of speech or dress.

All the comments were in some fashion symptomatic of a longing on the part of the adolescents for the satisfaction of the basic human needs combined with a willingness to mature and a desire to be accepted as grown-up persons. They wished to be recognised as responsible and valued members of the family group. They wished companionship with their parents; and they were striving after greater insight into the adult world from which they felt themselves partially excluded.

Their attitudes varied widely, and no easy generalisation is possible as to their relationships with their parents; but the evidence recorded serves to direct further attention to the variety of the family patterns observable among adolescents in communities such as those of Europe or the United States of America.

Under modern industrial conditions[6] the father from the city may, for example, return home weary in the late evening after his children are in bed. His week-end contacts with his family may be fleeting, and his relationships with his children may therefore be very different from those of the heavy-handed dictator of another type of social situation. Both boys and girls in such homes may be brought up under the influence of the mother alone; and brothers and sisters are rivals for her approval—an approval which may be won by achievement, and by rate of growth in physical, intellectual or social acceptability.

In such families the father and the son are not rivals. The mother does not make comparisons between them to the disadvantage of the latter. She, on the contrary, may often be heard to admonish the son to be smarter, more aggressive and more competently successful than his father.

A contrasting picture may, however, be seen not many scores of miles away in the homes attached to farms in the depths of the country. There, something like the patriarchal family structure may still survive.[7] The father may return to the house for every meal. He may then be the dominant figure in the home; or he may be the submissive and silent husband of a wife whose opportunities for domination are increased by the social isolation of the family.

Midway between these may be the home in a small town where there is close contact with neighbours and friends and where life is lived in a publicity undreamt of by the dweller in suburbia or the adolescent whose family life has had the background of a farm.

Still another picture may be seen in the homes in either town or country where the lives of the adults and those of the children are so much separated that they show the characteristics of differing cultures. In some of these the children are reared in nurseries under the supervision of paid attendants and at the age of eight or nine are sent to residential institutions of a single-sex type. Contacts between parents and children are relatively slight. There are many things which the children cannot discuss with their parents; and they are more or less bored during the weeks or the months which they spend at home. They have little knowledge of the interests or the activities of either mother or father; and they have correspondingly little sense of responsibility for the welfare of the family or of the community in which the home is placed. The parents in such homes may, in turn, often be heard to exclaim that they are glad when the holidays are over.[8] Something similar to this is to be found in the segregated adolescent society of those large day schools where prestige in the eyes of fellow-pupils counts for more than the wishes of teachers or parents, and where homes are thought of as dormitories shared with adults whose personal preoccupations are alien or unknown.[9]

Very different again is family life as it is lived in the crowded tenements of city slums, where privacy of any kind is impossible and where all the processes of living are laid bare to the gaze of adults and little children alike.[10]

Such differences render generalisations as to parent–child relationships extremely dangerous; and an awareness of the extent of such differences (like knowledge of the existence of different cultural patterns in the wider sense) has served to render suspect many of the findings of the psychology of the 1910s.

Interpretations and descriptions of the family and its relationships have (like descriptions of adolescents) passed through the stages of philosophic fiction, of reliance on tests, questionnaires and calculations of averages, to a recent recognition of the extent of the differences between one home and another and of an appreciation of the complexity of inter-personal relationships within each home.

Family situations can be classified in various fashions.[11] There are the homes in which there is an excess of affection—with over-possessive, over-solicitous or over-indulgent parents. There are homes in which affection is lacking, where there is nagging, frigidity or neglect. There are family settings in which certain children are discriminated against and others in which some members are frankly rejected. There are homes in which the social climate is one of constant bickering; and homes in which there is genuine friendliness and companionship.

There are democratic homes in which variety is tolerated; and family circles which are unduly mother-controlled or father-dominated. There are homes with too many adult bosses and homes in which the children are the dictators.

There are family patterns of different sizes and differing types of organisation. In some there is co-operation; in others independence, fierce competition or solitariness. There are homes which are broken by death or by separation. There are family goals of differing quality. In some the emphasis is on social success; in others it is on worldly possessions. Some homes are predominantly religious in atmosphere. Others may pride themselves on artistic, scientific or literary ability.

There are differences also in external conditions. In some homes there is perpetual scarcity of money. In others there is an excess of wealth. In some homes both mother and father go out to work. Other families are supported by mother only or by father alone. In some homes there is an unwholesome degree of publicity. In others there is too little contact with any other social group. Some families conform completely to the social pattern of the district in which they live. Others are in continuous rebellion. Some homes are dominated by the whims of an invalid. Others are shadowed by the distresses of mentally defective or insane relatives.

Parent–child relationships within these homes vary in corresponding fashions, and the observable effect of such homes on their adolescent members differs as widely. Neither attitude towards parents nor attitudes towards brothers and sisters can therefore now be interpreted in the relatively simple fashion which was formerly acceptable. It is no longer supposed that the eldest adolescent must necessarily be characterised by confidence, dominance or complacency and the second or third by a sense of inferiority leading to over-assertiveness or undue timidity. The pattern is now believed to be characterised by something like the complexity outlined above;[12] and this variety is recognised as existing within the frame-work of each country to an extent comparable to that which is observable as between one cultural pattern and another. It can readily be seen, for example, that the disabilities attached to order of birth in the typical small family of modern patriarchal systems do not affect children reared in a family system such as that of Samoa.[13] Each child is there accorded the responsibility of caring in turn for the one younger than himself; and deep personal attachment to mother or father, sisters or brothers is prevented by the casualness of the parent–child relationship and by the early taboo on friendly contact with contemporary relatives of the opposite sex. In such homes both the privileges and the disappointments of the first born or the later born are less acutely felt and less fiercely resented.

In similar fashion the variations of social climate, even within one country—of dominance, of affection, of ambitions, interests and shared activities—render suspect any easy interpretation of adolescent behaviour in terms of either sexually motivated rivalry or ordinally determined inferiority. The reactions of adolescents appear on closer study to be social in origin and to be related to frustrations or satisfactions of basic psychological needs rather than inevitable concomitants of the relationships of parents to girls and to boys or of brothers and sisters to one another.

In homes where the mother is aggressive and dominant there is resentment and hostility against her. Where the father is overbearing, the pattern is reversed. The reactions of the adolescent are to the behaviour rather than to the sex of the aggressor; and the resulting pattern of behaviour varies also with the motivation of the adult.[14]

Typical of thoroughness of study of such inter-relationships is a lengthy analysis of twenty cases of maternal over-protection selected from more than two thousand in the files of the New York

Institute for Child Guidance.[15] Examples of compensatory over-protection of rejected or disliked children were excluded along with instances of over-protection by fathers, grandparents or other relatives. Such cases formed the background against which the selected cases of excessive maternal care for "wanted" children were studied. All the cases were observed for periods of approximately two years, and many were followed for five or ten years. Complexities of patterning within the group were reported in detail, and the effect of differing types of protection within differing family situations was recorded along with particulars of differing intra-familial relationships. Over-protection of the dominating type ("This is my child. He must do whatever I wish"), appeared to lead consistently to submissiveness and dependency, while over-protection of the indulgent type ("I am his mother. I will do whatever he wishes") seemed to result in rebelliousness, aggressiveness and cruelty. The over-protective mothers were on the whole women who as a result of their own childish experiences had had to assume responsibility very early. They were competent, stable and aggressive. In many homes also the fathers were men who for one reason or another had failed to co-operate fully in the rearing of their children. They were in turn the submissive sons of dominating fathers or mothers.

A comparable investigation is reported from Teachers College, Columbia University.[16] In this sixty-two children, of whom half had been rejected by either mother or father and half had been accepted, were studied in relation to the history and the attitudes of their parents. The children from homes which were friendly, cheerful and orderly appeared to have matured into parents who in turn were able to accept their children. Those from homes where the parents were irritable, quarrelsome and inconsistent tended to mature into adults who later rejected their own children. Rejected children tended to be less friendly, to be more rebellious, to face the future less confidently and to indulge in more self-pity than accepted children. The latter showed more admirable social characteristics. They were, on the whole, loyal, co-operative and cheerful. They cared for their own property and the property of others; and they tended to succeed both in school and in games. They did not suffer from a sense of injustice or an expectation of persecution.

Another set of twenty-eight pairs of children with dominating as contrasted with submissive or neglectful parents showed similar differences of reaction. The dominated children tended to be submissive, retiring and sensitive. Their personal habits were describable as orderliness, cleanliness and reliability while the children of neglectful or submissive parents were disobedient and irresponsible. The latter lacked interest in school work and showed little capacity for sustained attention, but they tended to be independent and resourceful. Dominated children, on the contrary, were apt to feel humble, inferior, somewhat confused and often bewildered. They had had fewer opportunities to experiment and to make decisions for themselves; and while they were willing to follow tradition, they were somewhat lacking in initiative and enterprise.

Similarly suggestive studies of family situations in their relationship to the behaviour of children and of adolescents are reported from University Education Departments and Child Guidance Clinics in many parts of America and Europe. All provide contributory elements to present awareness of the variety and complexity both of adolescent personality and of the family patterns of the homes in which adolescents find themselves.[17]

All also furnish confirmatory evidence that the personal development and social adjustment of the adolescent within the home are related less to socio-economic level, the size of the family, the neatness and orderliness of the residence, or the carefulness of the parents, than to the satisfactions provided within the home for the basic human needs of recognition, adventure and opportunities for growth.[18]

The good home is one in which the adolescent is not only reassured and encouraged through his awareness of being beloved but also trained towards adult maturity by participation in family activities and family councils. In it there is an attitude of welcome towards the friends chosen by the children. The members of the family know how to have good times together and how to share their happiness with others. There is infrequent punishment, much encouragement and neither undue anxiety nor fussing on the part of the parents. There is no taboo on the visible expression of tenderness; and courtesy and consideration are shown by the members of the family to one another. In such homes adolescents can be observed to mature imperceptibly into adult status without experiencing either catastrophic emotional turmoil or serious mental distress.

It is important that it be realised that conflict and distress are potential rather than inevitable accompaniments of the parent–child relationship. In very many instances their occurrence may be more apparent than real. They may be exaggerated by the complainings overheard occasionally by friends. They are often a mere ripple on the deep waters of the essential harmony of the home.

Distress and conflict when they do appear in the life-history of adolescents are related, not to the fact that the young people are passing through a certain period of their growth or to their inevitable and impelling urge to free themselves from their parents, but rather to the nature of their past history and to the character of the homes in which they have been reared.[19] Difficulties of this kind are social rather than biological or developmental in origin; and the exact degree and type of their manifestation cannot be predicted from a mere knowledge of the distance which human beings have travelled through the border-land between childhood and adulthood.

Recognition of the difficulties which may occur in such years of transition is desirable as a stimulus towards greater sympathy and wisdom on the part of parents and adult observers; but there is no reason to suppose that such difficulties in any distressing form are an inescapable accompaniment of adolescence.

The mere fact that an individual is experiencing the physical disturbance of puberty does not justify the expectation that his behaviour will necessarily be "unstable" or "anti-social". Parents cannot now find support for former beliefs in either the abruptness of the transition or the inevitability of conflict on the part of their adolescent children.

When distressing symptoms appear it is not now sufficient to say, "It's adolescence. Nothing can be done about it." "She must sow her wild oats." The emergence of unhappiness, moodiness, rebellion or aggressiveness is now believed to be a challenge to enquiry and an invitation to the adult to investigate more fully both the physical conditions and the social pressures of the adolescent's life. Modifications in diet may be desirable. Greater wisdom in the routine of rest, exercise, sleep and elimination may be necessary. A fuller satisfaction of the basic human needs may be required. Many such modifications are possible in the homes of most adolescents. Their importance for the personal development of the individual can hardly be over-emphasised.

Their significance for the future well-being of the group is also great. Anti-social conduct is a symptom of distress. It is related to the reactions of an individual with certain potentialities to the social and physical conditions under which he has been reared. Individual differences remain a reality; but the social and physical consequences of differing types of nurture share this reality. If the distress shown by an adolescent is unrelieved through improvement in the social relationships of the inner circle of the home and the outer circles of the school and the community it will result in unnecessary lowering of the mental health of the adult and lessened ability on his part to contribute in turn to the satisfaction of the basic needs of other human beings.

REFERENCES

[1] For a discussion of this frustration and boredom within prosperous homes in England see:

Mannin, E., *Commonsense and the Adolescent*. London: Jarrolds, Revised Edition, 1944.

For evidence on adolescent experiences within the three settings of city, town and rural societies, see:

Landis, P. H., *Adolescence and Youth. The Process of Maturing*. New York: McGraw-Hill, 1945 and 1952.

[2] Taylor, K. W., *Do Adolescents Need Parents?* New York: D. Appleton-Century, 1937.

[3] Lynd, R. S., and Lynd, H. M., *Middletown*. New York: Harcourt Brace, 1929.

[4] Cited Landis, P. H., loc. cit. [1].

[5] Zeligs, R., *Glimpses into Child Life*. New York: William Morrow, 1942.

[6] For discussion of differing social settings see:

Bateson, Gregory, Morale and National Character, in Watson, G. (ed.), *Civilian Morale*. Boston: Houghton Mifflin, 1942.

Mead, Margaret, *The American Character*. London: Penguin Books, 1944.

Kluckholn, C., and Murray, H. A. (ed.), *Personality in Nature, Society and Culture*. New York: Knopf, 1949.

An intimate and sympathetic description of the home-life of suburbia is given in:

Richards, J. M., *The Castles on the Ground*. London: Architectural Press, 1946.

[7] On parent–child relationships see:

Landis, P. H., loc. cit. [1].

See also:

Lynd, R. S., and Lynd, H. M., loc. cit. [3].

Lynd, R. S., and Lynd, H. M., *Middletown in Transition*. New York: Harcourt, Brace, 1937.

Hollingshead, A. B., *Elmtown's Youth*. New York: John Wiley, 1949.

Havighurst, R. J., and Taba, H., *Adolescent Character and Personality*. New York: John Wiley, 1949.

Havighurst, R. J., *Human Development and Education*. New York: Longmans, Green, 1953.

Peck, R. F., and Havighurst, R. J., *The Psychology of Character Development*. New York: John Wiley, 1960.

See also:

Barker, R. G., and Wright, H. F., *Midwest and its Children*. Evanston: Row Peterson, 1955.

Kaplan, B. (ed.), *Studying Personality Cross-Culturally*. Evanston: Row Peterson, 1961.

For an English study see:

Semple, S., *A Comparative Study of the Influences which affect the Education of Children in Urban and Rural Schools*. Ph.D. Thesis, Univ. of London, 1954.

Oeser, O. A., and Emery, F. E., *Social Structure and Personality in a Rural Community*. London: Routledge, 1954.

[8] Such parent-child relationships are described in lively fashion in: Mannin, E., loc. cit. [1].

[9] For a detailed study of adolescent culture in ten schools in communities of varying sizes and types see:
Coleman, J. S., Johnstone, J. W. C., and Jonassohn, K., *The Adolescent Society*. Glencoe: Free Press, 1961.

[10] For a good discussion on the observable effect of over-crowding upon personality and behaviour see:
Plant, J. S., *Personality and the Cultural Pattern*. New York: Commonwealth Fund, 1937.
Vereker, C., *et al.*, *Urban Development and Social Change: A Study of Social Conditions in Central Liverpool*. Liverpool: Univ. Press, 1961.

[11] Useful discussions of varying types of family structure may be found in:
Stern, W., *The Family Past and Present*. New York: D. Appleton-Century, 1938.
Buhler, C., *The Child and his Family*. London: Kegan Paul, Trench, Trubner, 1940.
Tomlinson, C. G., *Families in Trouble*. Luton: Gibbs, Bamforth, 1946.
Radke, M. J., *The Relation of Parental Authority to Children's Behavior and Attitudes*. Minneapolis: Univ. of Minnesota Press, 1946.
Cunningham, R., *et al.*, *Understanding Group Behavior of Boys and Girls*. New York: Teachers College, Columbia Univ., 1951.
Bossard, J. H. S., *Parent and Child. Studies in Family Behavior*. Philadelphia: Univ. of Pennsylvania Press, 1953.

[12] For some discussion of the family constellation see:
Adler, A., *Social Interest. A Challenge to Mankind*. London: Faber and Faber. 1938.
See also:
Jones, H. E., Order of Birth, in Murchison, C. (ed.), *A Handbook of Child Psychology*. Worcester: Clark Univ. Press, 1933.
Fleming, C. M., *The Social Psychology of Education*. London: Kegan Paul, Trench, Trubner, 1944, 1959 and 1961.
Schneiders, A. A., *Personality Development and Adjustment in Adolescence*. Milwaukee: Bruce Publishing Company, 1960.

[13] Mead, M., *Coming of Age in Samoa:* London: Penguin Books, 1943. (First published New York: William Morrow, 1928.)

[14] Stagner, R., and Drought, N., Measuring Children's Attitudes towards their Parents, *J. Educ. Psychol.*, XXVI, 169–176, 1935.
Meltzer, H., Sex Differences in Parental Preference Patterns, *Character and Personality*, X, 114–118, 1941.
Stott, L. H., Parent–Adolescent Adjustment, *Character and Personality*, X, 140–150, 1941.
Helfant, K., Parents' Attitudes *vs.* Adolescent Hostility in the Determination of Adolescent Sociopolitical Attitudes, *Psychol. Monogr. General and Applied*, 66, 13, 1952.
Phillips, D. J., *A Study of the Concepts of Family Life Held by a Group of Adolescent Girls*. Leeds: Researches and Studies, 10, 1954.
See also:
Edwards, N., (Chairman). The Social Framework of Education, *Rev. Educ. Res.*, XIX, I, 1949.
Gage, N. L., (Chairman). The Social Framework of Education, *Rev. Educ. Res.*, XXII, I, 1952.

[15] Levy, D. M., *Maternal Overprotection*. New York: Columbia Univ. Press, 1943.

[16] Symonds, P. M., *The Psychology of Parent–Child Relationships*. New York: D. Appleton-Century, 1939.

[17] For an illuminating series of case-studies see:
Blos, P., *The Adolescent Personality*. New York: D. Appleton-Century, 1941.
See also:
Schneiders, A. A., loc. cit. [12].

[18] For fuller discussion of such family influences see:
Fleming, C. M., loc. cit. [12].

[19] See Adler, A., loc. cit. [12] and Ganz, M., *The Psychology of Alfred Adler and the Development of the Child*. Translated by P. Mairet. London: Routledge and Kegan Paul, 1953.
Way, L., *Alfred Adler*. Pelican Books, 1956.
For a comparison of the uncertainties and insecurities of adolescents with those of "marginal man", see:
Lewin, K., Field Theory and Experiment in Social Psychology. Concepts and Methods, *Amer. J. Sociol.*, 44, 868–896, 1939.
This may usefully be compared with the discussion of the attributes of "marginal man" in:
Stonequist, E. V., *The Marginal Man. A Study in Personality and Culture Conflicts*. New York: Charles Scribner's, 1937.
See also:
Andry, R. G., *Delinquency and Parental Pathology*. London: Methuen, 1960.

PART II
THE ADOLESCENT AT SCHOOL

CHAPTER IX

VARIETY AND VARIABILITY

"I'm sick of being at school."
"I wish school could go on for ever."
"I don't want to grow up."
"I'm bored with it all."
"I want a good time while I can get it."
"I'll be sorry to leave school."
"Nobody at home understands me."
"Why should I have to grow up?"
"I'm all for adventure. I want to see things."
"I'd leave school to-morrow if I could."
"My family is queer. I can't stand them."
"It's only at home that I'm happy."
"I am at my best at school."

Such remarks are not uncommon in any classroom. They are overheard occasionally by slightly startled adults who may have been tempted to forget the infinite variety of youth. Not only do adolescents differ in bodily outline, glandular balance, physical power and home-life but they show no uniformity in attitudes towards schooling and they exhibit little sameness in the response they make to the instruction or the social life of a school.

The recognition of individual differences in educability is not new in theory. It may be traced in educational discussion through many centuries. Aristotle, Isocrates, Quintilian, Da Feltre, Rousseau may all be quoted in support of the belief that "each has his own cast of mind" (Rousseau); that "not every one is called to be a lawyer, a physician, a philosopher to live in the public eye; nor has every one outstanding gifts of natural capacity" (Da Feltre); that "orators can be made only of those who excel by virtue of talent and of training" (Isocrates); that "everyone's natural Genius should be carry'd as far as it could; but to attempt the putting another upon him, will be but Labour in vain" (Locke).[1]

In schools, however, for many decades after the establishment of

87

popular education, very little importance was attached to such opinions. Teachers behaved as if they were faced by a homogeneous group. They talked of "impressing", of "influencing" and, in more recent days, of "leading" their pupils as if the response to instruction might be expected to be uniform and the effect of teaching would be the same in the case of each of the children entrusted to their care. This belief was shared by many psychologists, who described in great detail the characteristics of "the child", "the adolescent" or "the adult", with the implication that such stages were clearly definable and quite distinct and that considerable uniformity characterised each group. In similar fashion the psychologists discussed the "laziness" and the unwillingness of unsuccessful pupils; and when, in the second decade of the twentieth century, the results of group testing began to reveal a wide range of differences they recorded their distress at the "inefficiency" of the teachers who (through lack of effort) had permitted so many children of potentially equal ability to remain weak in spelling, arithmetic or reading.[2] Comparable assumptions on the part of reformers of the nineteenth century had been that all men were born equal, and that such inequalities as existed were traceable to deprivation of education or to reprehensible failure to profit by it when it was offered.

Towards the end of the nineteenth century there was a reaction against these assumptions; against the first on the part of those teachers who rebelled at the system of payment by results; and against the second by scientists such as Galton, Pearson and Woods, who collected evidence on the incidence and apparently hereditary character of intellectual brilliance or mediocrity. Payment by results was a logical sequel to the belief that, since all minds were alike, any differences in performance were traceable to mere lack of effort on someone's part. The protests of teachers against its injustice led, in the 1890s, to what was probably the first recorded modification of administrative procedure in the light of experimental evidence. (Its significance as such does not seem to have been recognised at the time.) Ten to fifteen years later the use of objective testing in school surveys resulted in the astonished admission in learned journals that the phenomenon of individual differences was too widespread to be accounted for in terms of local inefficiency or mere laziness.[3]

This demonstration of individual differences was received in differing fashion by different groups of workers. To the teacher its most important consequence was the evidence that in one class-room there might be representatives of six or seven "ages" in scholastic ability. There was also wide overlapping as between one age-group and another and one class and another. The best pupils of Class I (if that was the title given to the youngest class) might be found to be similar in performance to the worst pupils of Class V, while a substantial minority in Class I might do as well as the majority of Class II or Class III.

A few years later similar findings were reported after the analysis of the results of group tests of intelligence. There was a wide range of differences within each class and each age-group; and much overlapping from one age-group or class to the next. The pattern presented by an entire school is indicated by Table I, which shows objective test results expressed in terms of ages obtained from a test of Silent Reading and a test of Intelligence.*

These findings led to widespread interest among teachers in the study of their concomitant conditions; and this resulted in proposals for the modification of traditional methods of teaching and in the acceptance of a fresh interpretation of the nature of learning.[4] It became customary to agree that teaching should be adapted to the differing requirements of different pupils—that it should some-how be individualised—and that learning was an active process in which the interested co-operation of pupils was as necessary as the diligent enthusiasm of teachers.[5] Such claims had been made prior to the third decade of the twentieth century; but they had lacked the support of evidence and had shown in consequence only the relative ineffectiveness of mere opinion. From the third decade onwards an awareness of individual differences became more and more widespread; and its influence on school organisa-tion and methods showed itself in extensive experimentation with schemes such as the Dalton Plan or the Winnetka Technique. These invited the active co-operation of pupils (a) by giving them responsibility for the organising of their work on assignments to be completed by a prescribed date, or (b) by presenting each topic in a series of clearly worded descriptions so that independent pro-gress and work at a pupil's own optimum rate were less impossible than they had been under the class method of mass instruction.[6]

A slightly different analysis of the same findings was favoured by psychologists who were pre-occupied with discussions of the

* See: Fleming, C. M., *A Survey of Reading Ability*. Ph.D. Thesis, University of Glas-gow, 1930.

G

DISTRIBUTION OF READING AND INTELLIGENCE IN AN ENTIRE SCHOOL

Year		6	7	8	9	10	11	12	13	14
Jun. V	Chron. Age	1	32	10	1	1				
	Reading Age	26	13	2	3	1				
	Mental Age	10	19	13	3	–				
Jun. IVB	Chron. Age	–	7	29	4	–	2			
	Reading Age	18	14	3	5	–	2			
	Mental Age	15	17	9	–	1	–			
Jun. IVA	Chron. Age		5	35	2	2				
	Reading Age	12	14	8	10					
	Mental Age	3	11	16	12	2				
Jun. III	Chron. Age			21	15	1	1	1		
	Reading Age	9	9	1	8	4	8			
	Mental Age	2	6	11	11	3	4	2		
Jun. II	Chron. Age			21	20	2	2			
	Reading Age	1	2	–	16	11	10	3	2	
	Mental Age			9	14	16	5	1		
Jun. I	Chron. Age			3	29	14	2			
	Reading Age		5	4	13	13	8	1	4	
	Mental Age		3	8	14	11	8	4		
Sen. V	Chron. Age				8	24	1	1		
	Reading Age		1	2	5	5	12	1	8	
	Mental Age			2	1	9	14	8		
Sen. IVB	Chron. Age		4			13	12	10	1	
	Reading Age		4	2	11	10	6	1	2	
	Mental Age		3	8	8	10	4	3		
Sen. IVA	Chron. Age				4	21	9	5	1	
	Reading Age		1	1	1	4	8	1	24	
	Mental Age	1	–	2	4	7	7	10	9	
Sen. III	Chron. Age					7	27	6		1
	Reading Age					4	15	7	15	
	Mental Age				2	13	10	10	6	–
Sen. II	Chron. Age						33	14	3	
	Reading Age				2	5	15	9	19	
	Mental Age				4	6	9	16	15	
Sen. IB	Chron. Age					1	14	23	4	
	Reading Age					1	6	2	33	
	Mental Age					1	2	3	36	
Sen. IA	Chron. Age					1	2	10	17	4
	Reading Age				3	3	8	4	16	
	Mental Age			1	1	8	4	5	15	

growth of intelligence at the successive "stages" in child development. These psychologists were concerned with the discovery of observable differences between one age-group and another; and they reported such differences in terms of averages in a fashion similar to their contemporary analyses of averages for height or for weight (see Chapter II above). No mention was made of the extent of the variations masked by curves of growth based upon such averages, and exaggerated emphasis was laid on their regularity and uniformity. Standard deviations were not reported; and attention was not drawn to the wide divergencies at each age between the most fully developed child and the least mature.

In many reports on adolescence, for example, statements were made as to the growth of intelligence which indicated that curves of growth formed "practically ascending straight lines from the age of three to that of twelve", that they then showed a "sharp bend" and became "practically horizontal from the age of sixteen onwards".[7] Annual increments were reported as being about equal from the age of five to that of twelve; and it was implied that growth might be expected to be fairly similar for all pupils, and that with puberty the maturation of intelligence as such came rapidly to an end. By some investigators the cessation of intellectual growth was represented as occurring as early as fifteen. Others postponed it to sixteen. Emphasis was not laid upon the fact that these figures represented merely central tendencies and that the range of individual differences discussed in other connections applied with equal relevance to this issue of intellectual growth.

Estimation of the nature and growth of intelligence is of necessity more difficult than is a comparable judgment as to the amount and the rate of growth in physical development. This is partly the consequence of the means and the materials used for its assessment. Intelligence is measured by comparing the performance of an individual in selected tasks with that of the majority of his contemporaries. (A question is, for example, said to be suitable for ten-year-old pupils if sixty to seventy per cent of a representative sample of ten-year-old children can answer it.) The intellectual yardstick used is therefore less independent of the standardisation of the test, and is also more empirical than are the comparable units of linear measure or avoirdupois. All that is observable can be described as the direction and extent of changes in performance; but it is assumed that these changes are the products of growth, and from them records can be made of relative mental status at successive ages.

It is for this reason not surprising that according to the findings of earlier tests intelligence appeared to cease to grow at about the age at which compulsory schooling ended. After the age of twelve to fourteen, unselected samples of the population became harder to secure, and tests standardised on children in attendance at school proved somewhat difficult for their contemporaries who had left school and had become less accustomed to responding to standardised questions, whether oral or written. An extension of effective measurement to older age-groups has since become possible—through the postponement of the school-leaving age and as a result of increasing emphasis on the importance of an adequate sampling of groups of older adolescents and adults.

Meanwhile, the administrative consequences of contemporary psychological interpretations were becoming established. Pupils differ. Teaching commonly takes the form of class instruction. Perhaps it would be well if pupils were classified in such a way that all those in a group were sufficiently alike to learn at the same rate and in the same fashion. In this simple fashion the notion of grouping by similarity was born; and many administrators—by elaborate schemes of selection, rejection and classification—sought to evade the sequelae of an acceptance of the notion of classroom adaptation to individual differences. Classes were to be so arranged as to be homogeneous in content. Bright pupils were not to be handicapped by being taught alongside dull pupils. Boys were not to be put at a disadvantage by being educated in the company of girls. Children from homes of differing socio-economic level or race were not to be confused by being brought together. So the arguments ran, and further support was lent to the position by a revival of emphasis on the hereditary origins of behaviour—good or bad. Official encouragement was in consequence given in many countries to the continuance of schools with different levels of tuition and different types of curricula. Terminology varied; but the essential distinctions remained. Pupils were thought of as divisible into types, and the classifications made were accepted both as inevitable and as fixed by heredity.

In this setting the publication in the 1940s of the results of long-term studies had a special significance which merits a somewhat detailed survey of the findings they offered as to the nature of growth, as to the variety of human performing and as to the variability of individual development.

Many of the earlier assumptions as to the nature of growth had been illustrated by extrapolations of curves obtained from the testing of groups of different pupils within Junior Schools with a narrow age range, such as, for example, the years between seven and eleven. The results of annual testing of pupils over a greater number of years have produced data which contradict former pronouncements as to the early ending of the growth of intelligence.

In the Harvard Study already mentioned in Chapter II more than 3,500 children who entered the first grade of all schools in three cities in the autumn of 1922 were tested annually each year that they remained in school.[8] Careful records were kept not only of elaborate physical measurements but also of scores in tests of intelligence and scholastic attainment and of details of home and school environment and personal and family history. The results of this testing appeared to show that mental growth continues to about thirty years of age and that approximately two per cent of average mental growth may take place after twenty-one or twenty-two. These findings were obtained by extrapolation from results of unselected samples between the ages of seven and sixteen; but these years were estimated to cover growth from about the twelfth to the eighty-sixth percentile. Similar indications of the reality of continuous mental development are available in Thorndike's study of adult learning;[9] and pointers in the same direction are given by the published results of many other tests used in recent years. The level of approximately fifty per cent of adult status seems reached at about the age of eleven; and growth appears to be still continuing at eighteen to twenty years.[10]

It is not, of course, assumed in the discussion of such test results that intelligence at one age manifests itself in a fashion exactly comparable to intelligence at another age. Intelligence is not a simple variable. It has proved measurable only through the use of many assessments of its somewhat differing manifestations. In similar fashion, however, physical attributes such as weight may also be described as complex variables in the sense that at different ages they correspond to differing proportions of length, width and girth. The contribution of these to total weight varies from age to age and from individual to individual to a degree quite comparable with the changing composition of intelligence test scores. In spite of this, profitable use can still be made of records of weight at different ages. Comparison of data so obtained is, however, less hazardous if raw scores are transformed into percentiles* or into "standardised scores" (multiples of a standard deviation of a predetermined size).†

These precautions were taken in the studies described above. The same tests were used for several consecutive years and with each group of pupils. It may therefore be claimed that their findings represent a genuine tendency of growth rather than variations consequent on the nature of the testing material employed.

A valuable confirmation of this is reported from Chicago as a result of repeated retests of more than 400 children.[12] By the age of sixteen there was in their case also no evidence of approaching cessation of growth. The bottom ten per cent showed, if anything, rather greater gains in the last year of the period than did the group as a whole. All, however, appeared to be still developing. Similar findings from students at College level seem to indicate a

---

* The word percentile may be understood in terms of the division of a group of pupils arranged in order of merit into one hundred numerically equal sets. Each such set of pupils can then be said to have a "percentile" rank. Thus a "percentile score" of 75 is the average score of the set of pupils holding the 75th "percentile" rank.

† A "standard score" takes account of the dispersion or spread of results in a slightly different fashion. It is calculated by finding the ratio of the amount by which a score deviates from the mean to the standard deviation of the distribution. That is to say, it records a pupil's position relative to his group in terms of the number of standard deviations which his score is above or below the mean. If test results have been adjusted so that the standard deviation of their distribution is 15 and if their mean is called 100, the following approximate relationship holds in a normal distribution between percentile ranks, standard scores and such standardised scores:[11]

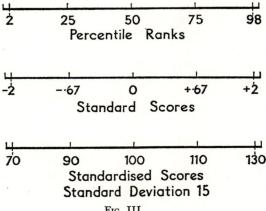

FIG. III.

comparable ability for continued improvement in that composite which is commonly described as intelligence. The curves for the brightest and the dullest groups do not intersect, but both continue to show measurable progress; and the extent of the annual gains at the upper limit is such that it seems justifiable to assume that growth has not quite ceased.

The social consequences of these findings are important. If manifestations of what is commonly called intelligence are of such a nature that growth continues into and after the late teens and if it is true that dull children have at least as long a period of development as clever children, there seems reason to believe that an extension of educational opportunities for all children is fully justified. The slowly developing child would appear likely to profit as much as, if not more than, his brighter contemporary, by continuation of schooling and by the protection from industrial exploitation which that secures. There appears to be in these findings no statistical support for administrative schemes which reduced the intellectual stimulation of duller children at an early age and allocated them to activities (in school or in workshop) which are commonly described as of greater "practical" appeal.

These more recent enquiries into the results of long-term studies of large groups seem to indicate also that mental development increases more steadily with chronological age than does physical growth. They seem also to reveal less relationship between mental growth and the onset of puberty than is observable in the case of physical maturing.[13] There is some reason to suppose that earlier sexual maturity is associated with slightly higher mental scores, in the case of both boys and girls, and that a higher percentage of gifted children attain puberty early. On the other hand, an abnormally early incidence of puberty has been reported to have no effect on intellectual development;[14] and extensive statistical studies have failed to establish sizeable correlations between mental development and pubescence. The relationship of physical and mental development does not, however, appear to be negative. There are group differences in height and weight, such as those between brilliant children, mediocre children and the dull or feeble-minded, but correlations with the results of tests of intelligence and of scholastic achievement are so low and the amount of overlapping is so great that for the purpose of predicting the development of an individual they are valueless.[15]

Various theories have been held as to the relationship of

physical to mental development. It used to be supposed that the two were compensatory rather than concomitant. Bright children were expected to be physically immature—with large heads, thin limbs and inadequate muscular development. Great scholastic success was not anticipated from a school's leaders in physical prowess. Rapidity of physical growth was often offered as an excuse for poor school work—especially during adolescence, when physical changes in status were most marked.

In recent years an attempt to obtain evidence on this has been made by deliberate analysis of the figures obtained from various large-scale studies. Certain of these appear to indicate a certain degree of concomitance. Results of testing intellectually gifted children have shown that for the most part their superiority extends to physique as well as to school performance and that it is associated with a wide range of other interests and abilities.[16] At the other end of the scale there are indications that the greater the degree of mental defect, the greater the physical inadequacy which accompanies it. It has for this reason been suggested that an estimate of readiness for learning school subjects might be got by calculating an "organismic" age from available measurements of general physiological development.[17] It is to be noted, however, that these findings as to brilliant children and dull children relate merely to average scores. The scatter of performance in both groups is considerable. When correlations of intelligence quotients* with height and weight are calculated these approximate to + 0·13 to + 0·14 for those below 100 I.Q., + 0·04 to 0·06 for those above 100 I.Q., and + 0·15 ± 0·03 for an unselected sample.[18] These figures have been confirmed by many investigations showing correlations usually below + 0·30 and commonly between + 0·10 and + 0·20.[19] (The use of more elaborate combinations of anthropometric indices have not succeeded in producing evidence of an appreciably higher relationship.)

Such correlations can hardly be claimed to be large enough to establish a significantly concomitant relationship, and very careful analysis of long-term records does not support the belief that, for example, failure to learn to read can be accounted for in terms of organismic age.[20] It is thus coming to be accepted that there is a

---

* The intelligence quotient, like a percentile rank or a standardised score, provides a record of a child's performance in an intelligence test as compared with that of his contemporaries. It is obtained by dividing his mental age by his chronological age and multiplying the quotient by 100. Thus a child of mental age 7 and chronological age 10 is said to have an intelligence quotient of 70.

third possibility. Physical and mental development may be neither directly associated as concomitant nor negatively related as compensatory. It may be that they are independent—separate in hereditary origin and influenced by differing stimuli.

Important evidence on this issue was supplied by the Harvard growth study.[21] In this an analysis was made of a series of consecutive records from an unselected sample of more than a thousand children. Correlations were calculated between gains in arithmetic and reading and increases in height and weight at the periods of average greatest growth—between the ages of twelve and fourteen for boys and eleven and thirteen for girls. These correlations approximated to + o·03, and none was large enough to be significant. There seemed to be merely a chance relationship between increase in physical size and the scholastic progress of either boys or girls. Similar conclusions were reached by an analysis of individual case studies and after a combination of more elaborate anthropometric measures of physical status.

These findings relating to scholarship and intelligence have been confirmed by many other less-extensive surveys. Little relation has been found between periods of acceleration in mental and in physical growth; and intellectual growth on the average has been shown both to proceed more steadily than physical growth and to continue after physical growth has ceased. There seems, therefore, no justification for the older theories that intellectual retardation can be explained or excused on the ground of rapid physical growth or that observable intellectual development may be expected to occur at the expense of physical maturing. One social consequence of this is that it provides a challenge to parents and to teachers to reject any facile interpretation of scholastic or physical retardation on the ground of its inevitability during adolescence. It thus makes possible the more accurate determination of the treatment required by any child who is showing marked deceleration in rate of growth—either physical or intellectual.

Physical growth spurts do not appear to be accompanied by a decrease in the rate of mental development. They are not paralleled by marked increments in mental ability; but they appear to take place more or less independently of changes in performance either in school subjects or in tests of what is commonly called intelligence.

Perhaps for this reason it is difficult to establish clear-cut differences in intellectual growth between early and late maturers; and it is also not easy to discover clearly defined differences between the sexes.

Mental growth curves for boys and girls are closely similar; and at each stage in early adolescence evidence as to sex differences is quite unlike that commonly reported in the case of comparable physical measurements.* This is the more remarkable, since the two sets of curves have in many cases been obtained from the same groups of pupils; and indications of mental achievement might have been expected to have been equally influenced by any selective sampling due to cessation of attendance at school by differing numbers of boys and girls. Taking this into account, it is noteworthy that in most studies there is no evidence of significant differences† between the average mental status of boys and of girls; and that differences in dispersion also fail to reveal consistently significant sex differences.[22] In one competent sampling for groups ranging from age ten to age sixty there was some evidence for a generalised superiority of girls in early adolescence; but this was not large enough to be of practical significance, and the impressive fact was reported to be not the degree of sex difference but rather the similarity of the developmental curves for the two sexes, throughout the whole age-range.[23] Certain earlier studies seemed to indicate a real difference in the scatter of results for boys and girls—boys tending to produce more brilliant and more imbecile reactions;[24] but more adequate statistical treatment of results appear to show that differences between girls and boys in either central tendency or range of performance are not significant.

In fifty-six comparisons of means or medians (to which tests of significance could be applied) it was found, for example, that only nineteen yielded critical ratios of two or more and only eight gave critical ratios of three or more. (In eight of the nineteen the girls' average was higher than that of the boys'.) In the remaining reports there was no evidence of significant differences, and the trends which did appear were as inconsistent as the indices of significance. In similar fashion, out of forty-eight recorded differences in dispersion, only ten (seven in favour of boys and three for

* See Chapter II above.
    † For discussions of methods of estimating the degrees of significance of the difference between two means see Dawson, S., etc., loc. cit. [11].
    An "index of significance" or "critical ratio" of 1.96 may indicate a probability of twenty to one that the differences between the two means are great enough to be significant in the sense that they are not attributable to chance. An index of three or more is commonly associated with a difference which is practically certainly not due to chance.

girls) gave critical ratios of two or more, and only one of three or more (in favour of a group of boys).[25]

Comparable findings are reported from the Scottish Mental Survey, in which a group test was given to a total age-group of over 87,000. In this the difference between the means for girls and boys was not significant; but the boys showed a significantly greater variability.[26] Neither standard deviation nor mean, however, proved significantly different on the results of an individual intelligence test administered later to every surviving child (with the exception of one who changed residence and could not be traced) born in Scotland on one of four specified days in 1926;[27] and in an enquiry in Bath in 1934 the difference between the means was shown to be statistically unreliable, while that for the standard deviations was barely significant at the lower ratio of 2.[28] Similar lack of consistency in sex differences was shown in later follow-up studies of pupils born in Scotland in 1936 and tested individually and by group tests of general mental ability in 1947.[29] On the whole, therefore, differences within one sex are now considered to be more pronounced than differences either in average or in standard deviation between sexes.

This finding is probably less surprising in the light of the evidence described above as to the relatively specific and independent character of physical and mental development. There are structural differences between the sexes; but these do not seem to be related directly to differences in the sorts of behaviour which are commonly accepted as manifestations of intelligence.

A similar absence of convincing evidence of significant differences between the sexes characterises the type of imagery which they experience, their interests and their performance in objective measurements of scholastic status.[30] Many of the reports which claim, for example, greater success for boys in mathematics or in knowledge of history, geography or current events, and a higher average for girls in tests involving linguistic skill or perceptual discrimination prove, upon closer analysis, to have been derived from selected samples influenced by differences in the school history of boys and girls. Many also are taken from results obtained in single-sex schools, where the emphasis placed upon certain subjects and the time given to them are observably different and the personality and the methods of the teachers differ completely.

Of this type, for example, are those of an analysis of results of School Certificate examinations taken after four or five years in

English secondary schools.[31] In this analysis of the successes of nearly 60,000 pupils in each of five years the average number of credits obtained by boys and by girls was not significantly different; and there was no significant difference in the percentage of boys and of girls to whom a certificate was awarded. Such differences as were observed in the averages and standard deviations of marks for different subjects were also much less significant at the stage of the Higher School Certificate. This decrease in differences with what amounts to greater equalisation of specialised training may be compared with Scottish findings as to the lack of significant differences between men and women at the level of Honours Degrees in a University.[32] It may also be compared with the findings secured from large-scale testing of boys and girls prior to segregation. Study of marks obtained in Special Place examinations in Britain has shown that, although the boys' scores in certain sub-tests of Arithmetic, English or General Mental Ability in the 1940s were lower than those of the girls, differences between them in age-groups of 20,000 pupils fell within the limits of the normal; and by the 1950s the observable differences were much reduced.[33]

Analysis of results taken from one such examination shows, for example, no significant differences either in the total score for the whole test or in the totals for English, for Arithmetic or for Intelligence.[34] Out of seventeen sub-tests[35] used in another examination the girls' average was higher than that of the boys' with a critical ratio of 2 or more in two sets of computation in Arithmetic, in a test of Spelling, a test of Word Usage and an Analogies test. On the other twelve tests (as in the total scores mentioned above) there was not a significant difference of this amount, and in no case did the critical ratio rise above 2·53.* The scatter in four sub-tests—English Comprehension, Vocabulary, Intelligence–Reasoning and Non-verbal Classification—was significantly greater for boys (with a critical ratio of 2 or more), but in the other thirteen tests and in the total score the standard deviation for girls was not significantly different from that for boys (and in no instance was the critical ratio greater than 2·44).†

Comparable evidence as to the absence of significant and consistent differences between the performance of groups of boys and girls was obtained by studying the interrelations between the results of the same seventeen sub-tests. Calculation of the degree of

* Critical ratios were 2·33, 2·20, 2·53, 2·14 and 2·37.
† Critical ratios were 2·1, 2·44, 2·25 and 2·06.

correspondence or correlation between the scores showed such variations in the degree of apparent relationship that it seemed justifiable to think that different "factors" might be at work and that the test results might be classified in terms of these factors. When the results were submitted to factor analysis by a variety of methods it was found that such classifying of the data showed that the ability defining the first factor was not significantly different in the scores of boys and girls.

The whole topic of relative variability and its assessment is, of course, a highly technical one. There is, however, reason to believe, as has been indicated above, that there is some decrease in the range of mental differences under comparable educational stimulation with growth into and through the teens—followed by an extension of relative variability among adults as their experiences become more and more diversified. (For a summary of findings reference may be made to an article by R. S. Ellis in the *Psychological Bulletin* of January 1947.) Sex differences in variability must therefore, on this account also, be considered in relation to differences in expectations, exposure and experience.

Similar findings are recorded in analyses of samplings reported from American sources.[36] There seems some tendency for girls to receive higher ratings than boys in a variety of school subjects at all stages, but this may be balanced by their lower marks in achievement tests. (It may also be related to the tendency for bright boys to leave school at an earlier age.) In some subjects boys appear to be assessed by teachers less highly than they merit. In others, there seems a tendency for them to receive a "halo" from custom and expectation. The differences between girls and boys prove, however, on the whole, inconsistent in direction in those comparatively few reports in which the data are sufficiently complete to permit a calculation of the statistical significance of the figures given.

Where opportunities for tuition have been comparable and where social pressure has been even approximately equal, the variations traceable to sex appear to have proved for the most part insignificant or conflicting; and extended testing has served chiefly to emphasise the futility of attempting to classify performances into the two types of male and female.

In the light of this evidence it becomes progressively more easy to account for the wide differences of custom at different social levels, in different countries and in different centuries in relation to the activities in which success is expected from boys and girls. It also becomes less hard to account for the changes in preferred occupations which can occur within the compass of a very few years in times of social change.[37]

Boys and girls do differ in certain respects—in average physical development and bodily functions. These differences in physique are, however, accompanied by a large measure of overlapping in physical measurements, and they cannot be proved to be accompanied by corresponding differences in mental capacity or educability. Individual variations within sex groups are much more impressive than average differences between the sexes; and success in the differing activities of adolescence and adult life are related much more closely to variations in training, in social expectations and in wishes than to what can fairly be described as biologically determined differences between the sexes.

The social consequences of these findings are important. The suggestion has sometimes been made that co-education is undesirable because of the earlier physical maturing of girls. The first assumption behind this appears to have been that pronouncements on average measurements of boys and girls could usefully be taken as representative of each total group—the second that greater physical growth was necessarily accompanied by greater intellectual maturity. These interpretations received emphatic presentation in the pioneer writings of Stanley Hall. Their echoes are still heard occasionally, and it therefore seems necessary to remark again that the discovery of an earlier average appearance of the physical growth spurt of adolescence among girls does not imply that all girls are taller and heavier than their male contemporaries between the ages of eleven and fourteen or twelve and fifteen. Consideration of the standard deviation for each sex makes it clear that differences between the most advanced and the most retarded of each group are much greater than is the difference between the average girl and the average boy. Separation into single-sex classes or single-sex schools does not therefore result in the production of more genuinely homogeneous groups.

Still less does greater homogeneity result from a comparable proposal that pupils should be classified according to their physical growth by associating older boys with younger girls. There is reason to believe that this would merely create new problems of intellectual inequality. There appears to be little more than a chance relationship between physical growth and mental development; and any classes so organised would prove much more heterogeneous in respect of intelligence or of scholastic level than would classes arranged roughly on the basis of chronological age.

Similar complexity has to be recorded when comparisons are made between pupils who come from homes of differing socio-economic level or race. Enquiries into their test performance and educational history have shown the amount of overlapping from one level to another, the variations of scholastic competence among pupils from homes of similar status and the importance of the part played by something other than prosperity and material possessions. In this field also prediction of success or failure in terms of a simple classification is now admittedly hazardous. While good homes contribute much to good schooling, discovery of good homes cannot be made through a mere knowledge of their externals of wealth, poverty or ethnic origin.[38]

Most of these proposals for segregation—whether according to sex, to physical maturity, to mental level or to social status—are, as has been noted above, based upon attempts to avoid the consequences of the infinite variety of youth, the range of individual differences and the complexity of the combinations of personal attributes which characterise all human beings. Segregation into so-called homogeneous groups is attractive to administrators and looks as if it might conduce to economy of effort on the part of teachers who wish to teach on class lines. Accumulating evidence both from schools and from research laboratories serves to show that it provides no escape from the fact of human variability expressed in simple form by the standard deviation which accompanies each average.

Further reminders of this variability are provided in the case of mental as of physical growth by the increasingly wide divergencies of groups of both boys and girls when educated under dissimilar educational conditions. The standard deviation of the distribution of mental scores is a function not merely of the test employed but also of the total experience and attributes of the testees. Probably for this reason it tends to increase steadily from ages seven to seventeen in unselected samples subjected to diversified types of training.

Comparison of the performance of an individual with the average scores made by his contemporaries is therefore even more uninformative during the period of adolescence than a comparable comparison would have been in childhood or infancy. Many quite normal adolescents mature intellectually much later or earlier than their contemporaries; and the attainments of many of them differ considerably from those of the average of their group. For this reason no tables of average scores representing mental development are reproduced here. Attempts to determine the educational fate of adolescents by predictions based upon comparisons between any one measurement and an average score are as hazardous as would be attempts to predict later physical status from one such earlier comparison. Efforts to secure uniformity of performance by exerting social pressure upon dissimilar boys and girls

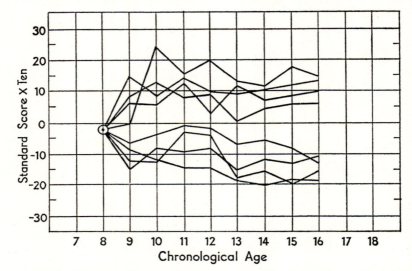

Fig. IV. Variability in mental growth in terms of standard scores of eight girls who reached the position of 9·2 sigma below the mean of 256 girl subjects of the Harvard Growth Study at age eight (from Dearborn and Rothney).

are also as unwise and as unlikely to achieve success as comparable attempts to promote conformity to "average" norms of height or weight by drastic exercises or by deliberate overfeeding.

Not only are there these wide variations within age-groups and much overlapping in performance from one age-group to another but there is also considerable variability in the life history of any one individual.[39] This is particularly obvious during adolescence. Each pupil seems to follow his own pattern of growth relative to the average of his contemporaries.

If, for example, an attempt is made to follow the relative performance over ten years of a group of pupils who at age seven made a score of a specified number of deviations above the mean in an intelligence test it will be found that a graph representing their annual status assumes a fan-like shape and that the progress of no pupil is quite steady. Some pupils are higher in each year and others are lower; but it is not always the same pupil who excels each year, nor does a pupil who changes his position in one year necessarily show the same increment of growth in each year which follows. The position of the pupil relative to his contemporaries changes according to an individual pattern.

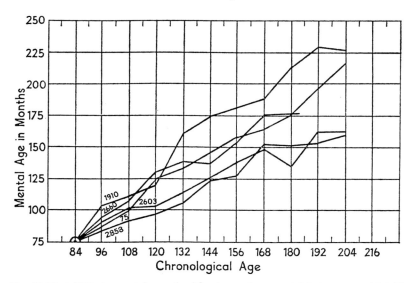

FIG. V. Variability in mental growth of five boys whose mental test scores and intelligence quotients were equivalent at age seven (from Dearborn and Rothney).

A tracing backward of the performance of pupils of equal final status at age seventeen results in a comparably fan-like series of graphs. Pupils who are equal at seventeen did not make equal scores at seven. Some did relatively better. Others were comparatively less successful. On the whole, however, the average of the group remains stable, and if the total range of scores is divided into five or six categories pupils tend to remain within the same category for the period over which they have been tested.

Similar variations have been revealed in other studies by a comparison of standardised scores for individuals who were selected at

H

random from extensive annual testing of large numbers. Changes occur which appear to be related to individual idiosyncracies in the pattern of growth rather than to any discrepancies attributable to the nature of the tests employed.[40] These changes when considered in relation to one another have considerable relevance to educational guidance. Their existence provides a justification for the insistence of many teachers upon the value of cumulative records as a reminder of the fact that there is a wide range of differences of rate of growth among quite normal individuals, just

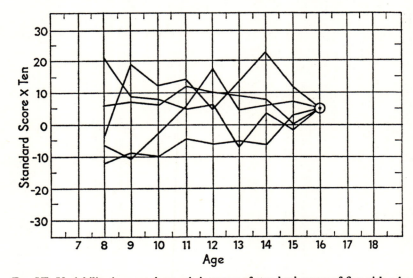

FIG. VI. Variability in mental growth in terms of standard scores of five girls who reached the position of 0·5 sigma above the mean of 256 girl subjects of the Harvard Growth Study at the age sixteen (from Dearborn and Rothney).

as there is a great variety in the resulting combinations of personal attributes at maturity.[41]

These differences in rate of growth are also very relevant to the admininistrative assumption still made in certain countries that the relative status of pupils will remain fixed—with its corollary that advanced schooling need be provided only for those who do well at an early age.[42] It is hardly necessary to remark that this opinion is a survival from the 1920s when attention was given only to the stability of averages, and when evidence had not been obtained as to the individual variations which they concealed. Terman, for example, reporting on the results of a limited number of retests of individuals, remarked in 1921 that "speaking roughly, fifty per cent of the I.Q.'s found at a later test may be expected to fall within the range between six points up and four points down. . . . It is evident, therefore, that the I.Q. is sufficiently constant to make it a practical and serviceable basis for mental classification."[43]

These comments and those of other psychologists were repeated without the qualifying clauses of their original formulation, and many investigations were undertaken to demonstrate the general constancy of the I.Q.[44]

Such studies passed through certain definite stages. The earliest, as has been indicated above, were concerned with test–retest, and comments were made upon differences in average scores—with or without references to standard deviations and the degree of significance of the differences recorded. These differences were for the most part much larger than those which Terman reported in the early investigation referred to above. Standard deviations were also distinctly greater.

At a slightly later date there was a series of studies in which attempts were made to estimate by correlation techniques not merely the direction but the degree of the relationship between earlier and later performance. Analysis of a large number of these showed that the size of the correlation appeared to vary with the interval between test and retest—dropping from about $+ 0.81$ for an interval of less than two years to approximately $+ 0.61$ where the interval was between five and twelve years.

Such direct comparisons of averages and their more indirect comparison through correlations involved two testings of many groups of different children. When the same children were later (in long-term studies) followed over a number of years the degree of their "constancy" of performance was even less than this[45] and annual correlations with initial status fell steadily from $+ 0.7$ to $+ 0.5$.[46]

The retesting of sub-normal children in a residential school in another careful investigation[47] showed in similar fashion that the rate of mental growth of many pupils over a period of nine years did not correspond to that suggested by their initial intelligence quotients. There was a tendency for a substantial decline in rate with age, and this decline was progressive and increased with the length of the interval between testing. Educational prognosis was especially misleading in the case of children showing emotional abnormality, and it was still more precarious with those who showed a low intelligence quotient at an early age. The change from an inferior environment to the relatively superior conditions of the school appeared to lead to retardation in the rate of decrease; but there seemed to be no significant relationship with the physical condition of the pupils, or with mental abnormality in their immediate ancestry.

This variability is revealed in slightly different fashions in many enquiries into the predictive value of examinations for selective entry into secondary schools in England.[48] Correlations of subsequent performance with entrance tests are of the order of $+ 0.4$ to $+ 0.5$ for pupils both in Grammar Schools and in Technical Schools. The relative lowness of this figure appears to be related not merely to the selective nature of the groups and not so much to the nature of the measurement of performance at age eleven or age thirteen as to the complexity of the factors which determine subsequent performance. Very slight initial differences in ability may act as directive agencies in the building up of a complicated structure of preferences, interests, habits and consequent educational choices. The variability of individual development thus limits the possibility of prediction.

This finding seems supported also by recent studies of the shifts of relative position revealed by teachers' gradings when these are analysed quite simply as variations in ratings.[49]

It has been estimated that about thirty per cent of pupils in each year of a secondary school course interchange relative positions—moving upwards to the top twenty-five per cent or downwards to the bottom twenty-five per cent. When the original scores of these pupils prior to entry are analysed it has been found that there is no significant difference in the initial average scores of these groups in English, in Arithmetic or in a test of general mental ability. There is no evidence of a level of mental ability higher than that of attainment at the entrance examination stage, which might account for the variations in later achievement. There is also no indication of greater average strength in English or in Arithmetic, such as might have been caused by special coaching at the primary school level. On the basis of the average score in three initial objective tests it also seems impossible to differentiate between the group which will move up from the bottom quartile and the group whose relative position will remain unchanged.

The initial average score of the ten to twelve per cent who remain in the lower position does not differ significantly from that of their companions who move up. The attempt at exact prognosis of the later success of those admitted on the results of a selective examination thus seems as hazardous as the attempt to predict the approximate figure of an intelligence quotient after the lapse of a few years. On the whole those within the top two-fifths of the population retain their position in that wide grouping; but the relative progress of each pupil follows a personal pattern from year to year, and the exact character of that pattern cannot be fully estimated from his test performance a few years earlier.

The whole question is bound up with the wider one of environmental influences upon performance, whether in intelligence tests or in tests of attainment. Upon this the emphasis of twentieth-century workers was at first in the direction of a belief in the overriding importance of the hereditary differences to which Galton and other nineteenth-century pioneers had drawn attention. The lack of present support for such beliefs has been indicated above.

In challenge to this the findings from long-term studies carried within them the justification for a much greater emphasis upon the effects of environment; and they serve in some measure to account for the greater hopefulness of outlook and the greater belief in educability which has characterised educational thinking since the opening of the fifth decade of this century.

This emphasis on the possibility of changes resulting from environmental influence has been supported by a series of investigations[50] of the performance of children:

(a) in unstimulating environments;
(b) transferred to more stimulating environments.

There seems reason to believe that the longer children remain in unstimulating environments, the lower becomes their performance in tests of what is commonly called intelligence, and that the earlier they are transferred to intellectually stimulating situations, the brighter is their subsequent measurable response.

Treatment of the whole topic has in recent years become both more competent, more carefully controlled and more technical. Its interpretation is associated with current assumptions implicit in test construction and with the statistical devices adopted to ensure the reliability and validity of the tests employed. The volume of evidence now available is, however, so great that it seems justifiable to claim that it has been established that fluctuations in relative status do occur in the development of individuals from infancy through adolescence, and that these changes are related to observable changes in family life, school life or the social expectations of the group in which they find themselves.

From the point of view of parents or teachers, acceleration or deceleration of rate of growth provides a challenge to enquiry—whether it occurs in relation to physique or to mental development. In the light of present knowledge adults no longer expect that children will conform to a "normal" pattern of growth. Adults no longer believe that the progress of any child will be quite regular—that size (of any kind) at any one age is necessarily a prediction of size at a later stage. They do not claim that the exact conditions (hereditary or environmental) which determine increments of growth are fully understood. They do not attempt to separate nature from nurture. Nor do they attribute a certain percentage of a child's performance to inheritance and a certain percentage to environment. Teachers are concerned rather with the much humbler enquiry into intelligence or educational performance—their nature and the conditions contributing to their nurture from year to year. Parents are similarly concerned with acceptable behaviour in general—its nature and its nurture from childhood through adolescence. The approach of both is, however, in the light of recent investigations much more optimistic than it would have been in the 1920s. Awareness of the extent of individual differences and of the variability of growth is a stimulus to greater willingness to experiment, and it results in greater expectations of the probable success of methods of treatment more exactly suited to the requirements of boys and girls as they grow.

REFERENCES

[1] For statements on individual differences see:
Boyd, W., *The History of Western Education*. London: Black, 1921.
[2] Courtis, S. A., Standards in Rates of Reading, *Fourteenth Yearbook Nat. Soc. Study of Educ.* Chicago: Univ. of Chicago Press, 44–58, 1915.
[3] For early findings see:
Starch, D., *Educational Measurements*. New York: Macmillan, 1916.
Burt, C., *The Distribution and Relations of Educational Abilities*. London: King, 1917.
Burt, C., *Mental and Scholastic Tests*. London: King, 1921.
[4] An accessible account of experimentation is given in:
Fleming, C. M., *Teaching: A Psychological Analysis*. London: Methuen, 1958 and 1959; New York: John Wiley, 1958.
[5] McConnell, T. R., *et al.*, The Psychology of Learning, *Forty-first Yearbook Nat. Soc. Study of Educ.* Part II. Bloomington: Public School Publishing Company, 1942.
Fleming, C. M., ibid. [4].
[6] Representative discussions may be found in:
Parkhurst, H., *Education on the Dalton Plan*. London: Bell, 1922.
Dewey, E., *The Dalton Laboratory Plan*. London: Dent, 1924.
Kilpatrick, W. H., *Foundations of Method*. New York: Macmillan, 1925.
Washburne, C., *et al.*, *Results of Fitting Schools to Individuals*. Bloomington: Public School Publishing Company, 1926.
See also:
Rowe, A. W., *The Education of the Ordinary Child*. London: Harrap, 1959.
[7] Burt, C., *Memorandum on the Mental Characteristics of Children between the ages of Seven and Eleven*. Appendix III, Report Consult. Committee on the Primary School. London: H.M.S.O., 1931.
See also:
Terman, L. M., and Merrill, M. A., *Measuring Intelligence*. Boston: Houghton Mifflin, 1937.
Thurstone, L. L., and Ackerson, L., The Mental Growth Curve for the Binet Tests, *J. Educ. Psychol.*, XX, 569–583, 1929.
Richardson, C. A., and Stokes, C. W., The Growth and Variability of Intelligence, *Brit. J. Psychol. Monogr.*, XVIII, 1933.
Freeman, F. S., *Individual Differences*. London: Harrap, 1934.
[8] Dearborn, W. F., Rothney, J. W., *et al.*, *Predicting the Child's Development*. Cambridge, Massachusetts: Sci-Art Publishers, 1941.
Jones, H. E., and Conrad, H. S., Mental Development in Adolescence, in Jones, H. E., *et al.*, Adolescence, *Forty-third Yearbook Nat. Soc. Study of Educ.* Chicago, Illinois: Univ. of Chicago, 1944.
[9] Thorndike, E. L., *et al.*, *Adult Learning*. New York: Macmillan, 1928.
Vernon, P. E., *The Training and Teaching of Adult Workers*. London: Univ. of London Press. (n.d.)
[10] Brooks, F. D., Mental Development in Adolescence, *Rev. Educ. Res.*, VI, 1, 85–101, 1936.
See also:
Jones, H. E., and Conrad, H. S., loc. cit. [8].

Essert, P. L. (Chairman), Adult Education, *Rev. Educ. Res.*, XXIII, 3, 194–283, 1953.

Clift, D. H. (Chairman), Adult Reading, *Fifty-fifth Yearbook Nat. Soc. Study Educ.* Part II. 1956.

McClusky, H. V., and Jensen, G., The Psychology of Adults, *Rev. Educ. Res.*, XXIX, 3, 246–255, 1959.

[11] For discussions of the meaning of elementary statistics see: Dawson, S., *An Introduction to the Computation of Statistics.* London: Univ. of London Press, 1935.

Vernon, P. E., *The Measurement of Abilities.* London: Univ. of London Press, 1940 and 1946.

Lindquist, E. F. (ed.), *Educational Measurement.* Washington D.C.: Amer. Council on Educ., 1951.

Thomas, R. M., *Judging Student Progress.* New York: Longmans, 1954.

[12] See:

Brooks, F. D., loc. cit. [10].

Jones, H. E., and Conrad, H. S., loc. cit. [8].

See also:

Nisbet, J. D., Intelligence and Age, *Brit. J. Educ. Psychol.*, XXVII, III, 1957.

Terman, L. M., The Discovery and Encouragement of Exceptional Talent, *Amer. Psychologist*, 9, 6, 221–230, 1954.

[13] A competent summary is given in:

Conrad, H. S., Freeman, F. N., and Jones, H. E., Differential Mental Growth, in Jones, H. E., *et al.*, Adolescence, *Forty-third Yearbook*, loc. cit. [8].

[14] Gesell, A., Precocious Puberty and Mental Maturation, in Terman, L. M., *et al.*, *Twenty-seventh Yearbook Nat. Soc. Study of Educ.* Bloomington: Public School Publishing Company, 1928.

Stone, C. P., and Doe-Kuhlmann, L., Notes on the Mental Development of Children Exhibiting the Somatic Signs of Puberty Praecox, in Terman, L. M., *et al.*, ibid.

Keene, C. M., and Stone, C. P., Mental Status as Related to Puberty Praecox. *Psychol. Bull.*, 34, 3, 123–133, 1937.

Benton, A. L., and Hagmann, F. A., Psychometric Test Results in Two Cases of Precocious Puberty, *Ped. Sem. J. Genet. Psychol.*, 54, 455–456, 1939.

See also:

Dennis, W., The Adolescent, in Carmichael, L. (ed.), *Manual of Child Psychology.* New York: John Wiley, 1946.

[15] Dearborn, W. F., *et al.*, loc. cit. [8].

[16] Terman, L. M., *et al.*, *Genetic Studies of Genius. Mental and Physical Traits of a Thousand Gifted Children.* Stanford: Standford Univ. Press, 1925.

Burks, B. S., *et al.*, *The Promise of Youth: Follow-up Studies of a Thousand Gifted Children.* Stanford: Stanford Univ. Press, 1930.

Terman, L. M., and Oden, M. H., *The Gifted Child Grows Up. Twenty-five Year's Follow-up of the Superior Child.* Stanford: Stanford Univ. Press, 1947.

Terman, L. M., and Oden, M. H., *The Gifted Group at Mid-Life. Thirty-five Year's Follow-up of the Superior Child.* Stanford: Stanford Univ. Press, 1959.

Parkyn, G. W., *Children of High Intelligence. New Zealand C. Educ. Res.*, 30, 1948.

MacPherson, J. S., *Eleven-Year-Olds Grow Up.* London: Univ. of London Press, 1958.

[17] Olson, W. C., and Hughes, B. O., The Concept of Organismic Age, *J. Educ. Res.*, 35, 525–527, 1942.
Olson, W. C., *Child Development*. Boston: Heath, 1949.
With this may be compared:
Boyne, A. W., Secular Changes in the Stature of Adults and the Growth of Children, with Special Reference to Changes in Intelligence of 11 year-olds in Tanner, J. M. (ed.), *Human Growth*. Oxford: Pergamon Press, 1960.

[18] For an accessible summary of such evidence see:
Dearborn, W. F., *et al.*, loc. cit. [8].

[19] Jones, H. E., Relationships in Physical and Mental Development, *Rev. Educ. Res.*, VI, 1, 102–123, 1936.
See also:
Froehlich, G. J., Mental Development during the Pre-adolescent and Adolescent Periods, *Rev. Educ. Res.*, XIV, 5, 401–412, 1944.

[20] Tyler, F. T., Organismic Growth: Sexual Maturity and Progress in Reading, *J. Educ. Psychol.*, 46, 2, 85–93, 1955.
Blommers, P., Knief, L. M., and Stroud, J. B., The Organismic Age Concept, *J. Educ. Psychol.*, 46, 142–150, 1955.
Blommers, P., and Stroud, J. B., Note on the Organismic Age Concept, *J. Educ. Psychol.*, 49, 106–7, 1958.
See also evidence as to the independence of growth curves:
Tanner, J. M., *Growth at Adolescence*. Oxford: Blackwell, 1955.

[21] Dearborn, W. F., *et al.*, loc. cit. [8].

[22] Wellman, B. L., Sex Differences, in Murchison, C. (ed.), *A Handbook of Child Psychology*. Worcester: Clark Univ. Press, 1933.
See also:
Kuznets, G. M., and McNemar, O., Sex Differences in Intelligence Test Scores, in Stoddard, G. D., *et al.*, Intelligence: Its Nature and Nurture, *Thirty-ninth Yearbook Nat. Soc. Study Educ. Part I*. Bloomington: Public School Publishing Company, 1940.

[23] Conrad, H. S., Freeman, F. N., and Jones, H. E., loc. cit. [13].
See also:
Conrad, H. S., Jones, H. E., and Hsiao, H. H., Sex Differences in Mental Growth and Decline, *J. Educ. Psychol.*, XXIV, 3, 161–169, 1933.

[24] For useful summaries on sex differences see:
Wellman, B. L., loc. cit. [22].
Freeman, F. S., loc. cit. [7].
Terman, L. M., *et al.*, Psychological Sex Differences, in Carmichael, L., (ed.), *Manual of Child Psychology*. New York: Wiley, 1954.
Anastasi, A., *Differential Psychology*. New York: Macmillan, 1958.

[25] Kuznets, G. M., and McMemar, O., loc. cit. [22].

[26] Scottish C., Res. Educ. V. *The Intelligence of Scottish Children*. London: Univ. of London Press, 1933.

[27] Scottish C. Res. Educ. XV. MacMeeken, A. M., *The Intelligence of a Representative Group of Scottish Children*. London: Univ. of London Press, 1939.

[28] For detailed references see:
Kuznets, G. M., and McNemar, O., loc. cit. [22].

[29] See: Scottish C. Res. Educ.
XXX. *The Trend of Scottish Intelligence.*
XXXV. *Social Implications of the 1947 Scottish Mental Survey.*
XLI. *Educational and Other Aspects of the 1947 Scottish Mental Survey.*
London: Univ. of London Press, 1949, 1953 and 1957.
and XLII. MacPherson, J. S., loc. cit. [16].

[30] Wellman, B. L., Sex Differences, loc. cit. [22].

Coutts, D. V., *Studies of the Mental Imagery Experienced by Young Adolescents during the Silent Reading of Descriptive Passages*. Ph.D. Thesis, Univ. of London, 1946.

Fleming, C. M., Preferences and Values among Adolescent Boys and Girls, *Educ. Res.*, II, 3, 221–224, 1960.

[31] Crofts, J. M., and Jones, D. C., *Secondary School Examination Statistics*. London: Longmans, Green, 1928.

[32] Scottish C. Res. Educ. IX. *The Prognostic Value of University Entrance Examinations in Scotland*. London: Univ. of London Press, 1934.

[33] Vernon, P. E., *Intelligence and Attainment Tests*. London: Univ. of London Press, 1960.

[34] Scottish C. Res. Educ. XIX. McClelland, W., *Selection for Secondary Education*. London: Univ. of London Press, 1942.

[35] King, W. H., *A Comparative Study of the Factors Entering into the Boys' and Girls' Results in a Special Place Examination*. London: Univ. of London, M.A. Thesis, 1945.

The tests used were later published as:

Fleming, C. M., and Jenkins, J. W., *Cotswold Ability Tests, Series I*. Glasgow: Gibson, 1946.

[36] Wellman, B. L., loc. cit. [22].

[37] Williams, G., *Women and Work*. London: Nicholson & Watson, 1945.

Luetkens, C., *Women and a New Society*. London: Nicholson & Watson, 1946.

Mead, M., *Male and Female*. New York: William Morrow, 1949.

Mueller, K. H., *Educating Women for a Changing World*. Minneapolis: Univ. of Minnesota Press, 1954.

[38] Klineberg, O., *Race and Psychology*. UNESCO, 1951.

See also: Ashley-Montagu, M. F., *Man's Most Dangerous Myth: The Fallacy of Race*. New York: Harper, 1942, 1945 and 1952.

[39] Dearborn, W. F., Rothney, J. W., *et al.*, loc. cit. [8].

Honzik, M. P., Macfarlane, J. W., and Allen, L., The Stability of Mental Test Performance between Two and Eighteen Years, *J. Exper. Educ.*, XVII, 2, 309–324, 1948.

Sontag, L. W., *et al.*, Mental Growth and Personality Development, *Child Dev. Publications*, XXIII, 68, 2, 1958.

[40] Jones, H. E., (unpublished), cited in: Jones, H. E., and Conrad, H. S., Mental Development in Adolescence, in Jones, H. E., *et al.*, Adolescence, *The Forty-third Yearbook*, loc. cit. [8].

[41] For a discussion of cumulative records see:

Fleming, C. M., *Cumulative Records*. London: Univ. of London Press, 1945.

Strang, R., *Every Teacher's Records*. New York: Teachers College, 1936 and 1947.

Rothney, J. W. M., and Roens, B. A., *Guidance of American Youth*. Cambridge: Harvard Univ. Press, 1950.

Walker, A. S., *Pupils' School Records*. London: Nat. Found. Educ. Res. in England and Wales, 1955.

[42] Typical of this point of view was a report such as:

Burt, C., Experimental Tests of General Intelligence, *Brit. J. Psychol.*, III, 94–177, 1909.

See also:

Terman, L. M., *et al.*, Nature and Nurture: Their Influence upon Intelligence; and Nature and Nurture: Their Influence upon Achievement, *Twenty-seventh Yearbook Nat. Soc. Study Educ.* Parts I and II. Bloomington: Public School Publishing Company, 1928 (*passim*).

Burt, C., *The Subnormal Mind*. London: Oxford Univ. Press, 1937.

With these may be compared the discussion of deferred maturing in:
Burt, C., *Mental and Scholastic Tests*. London: King, 1921.
[43] Terman, L. M., *The Intelligence of School Children*. London: Harrap, 1921.
[44] A compact summary of research on the constancy of the I.Q. is given in:
Neff, W. S., Socio-Economic Status and Intelligence. A Critical Survey, *Psychol. Bull.*, 35, 10, 727–757, 1938.
See also:
Stoddard, G. D., *et al.*, Intelligence: Its Nature and Nurture, *Thirty-ninth Yearbook Nat. Soc. Study Educ.* Bloomington: Public School Publishing Company. Parts I and II. 1940 (*passim*).
Fleming, C. M., *The Social Psychology of Education*. London: Kegan Paul, Trench, Trubner, 1944, 1959 and 1961.
McRae, H., The Inconstancy of Group Test I.Q.'s, *Brit. J. Educ. Psychol.*, XII, 1, 59–70, 1942.
Ferguson, G. A., *The Reliability of Mental Tests*. London: Univ. of London Press, 1941.
Honzik, M. P., Macfarlane, J. W., and Allen, L., loc. cit. 1948. [39].
Sontag, L. W., *et al.*, loc. cit. [39].
Clarke, A. M., and Clarke, A. D. B., *Mental Deficiency*. London: Methuen, 1959.
[45] For relevant discussions of the nature of mental growth see:
Goodenough, F. L., *Mental Testing: Its History, Principles and Applications*. New York: Staples, 1949.
Anastasi, A., *Psychological Testing*. New York: Macmillan, 1954.
Heim, A. W., *The Appraisal of Intelligence*. London: Methuen, 1954.
Vernon, P. E., 1960. loc. cit. [33].
[46] Dearborn, W. F., *et al.*, loc. cit. [8].
See also:
Anderson, J. E., The prediction of Terminal Intelligence from Infant and Pre-School Tests, in Stoddard, G. D., *et al.*, loc. cit. [44].
[47] Phillips, G. E., *The Constancy of the Intelligence Quotient in Subnormal Children*. Austral. C. Educ. Res., 1940.
[48] For reports relevant to a discussion of English Special Place Examinations, see:
Jeffrey, G. B., (Chairman) *Transfer from Primary to Secondary Schools*. Report Consult. Committee Nat. Union of Teachers. London: Evans, 1949. and publications of the Nat. Found. Educ. Res. in England and Wales, such as:
Yates, A., and Pidgeon, D. A., *Admission to Grammar Schools*. London, 1957.
Husén, T., *Educational Structure and the Development of Ability*. Paris: O.S.T.P. 1961.
[49] Published findings illustrative of this may be found in:
Coombes, D. M., A Study of the Careers of Pupils who Enter a Secondary School after a Second Attempt in the Admission Examinations, *Brit. J. Educ. Psychol.*, IX, II, 145–163, 1939.
Evans, H. A., The Secondary School Careers of Children not Recommended by Heads of their Elementary Schools, *Brit. J. Educ. Psychol.*, X, II, 154–170, 1940.
[50] Stoddard, G. D., *et al.*, loc. cit. [44].
Fleming, C. M., The Social Psychology of Education, loc. cit. [44].
Jones, H. E., Environmental Influences upon Mental Development, in Carmichael, L. (ed.), *A Manual of Child Psychology*. New York: Wiley, 1954.

See also:

Vernon, P. E., and Parry, J. B., *Personnel Selection in the British Forces*. London: Univ. of London Press, 1949.

Husén, T., *Testresultatens Prognosvärde*. Stockholm: Hugo Gebers Vörlag, 1950.

Watts, A. F., Pidgeon, D. A., and Yates, A., *Secondary School Entrance Examinations*. London: Nat. Found. Educ. Res. in Eng. and Wales, 1952.

Screiber, D., A School's Work with Urban Disadvantaged Pupils In *The Search for Talent*, 57–66. New York: College Entrance Examination Board, 1960.

Riessman, F., *The Culturally Deprived Child*. New York: Harper, 1962.

CHAPTER X

ABILITIES

Much of the educational research of the first half of the twentieth century was planned in the attempt to answer two questions:

(*a*) What are the differences in the abilities and personal attributes of children at different stages of growth?

(*b*) By what means, if any, can the later success of pupils in differing sorts of activities be predicted from a study of their present performance?

It was expected that research workers would discover clearly distinguishable abilities and highly differentiated aptitudes,* and in many countries it was believed that it would be useful if any such differences could be clearly formulated with a view to allocating pupils at different stages of mental and physical growth to the distinct types of training which were available.[1] It was also thought that it would be both convenient and economical if an early classification could be made in order that no time should be wasted in the provision of unnecessary or ineffective educational stimulation.

Definite changes in viewpoint on both these issues have resulted from the findings of long-term studies; and these are therefore very relevant to a consideration of adolescents at school.

In the early years of the twentieth century emphasis had been laid upon the abrupt changes to be expected at the transition from childhood to adolescence. Alterations in physical structure are very obvious during adolescence; and it was tempting to assume

---

* It may be relevant to note here that in these discussions the words capacity, ability and aptitude were often rather loosely used. The first serves to direct attention backwards to original innate attributes. The "capacity" of a child (that which he is potentially capable of doing) may be inferred from his present performance or "ability" (that which he is able to do). It cannot be assessed apart from such ability. The word "aptitude", on the contrary, directs attention forward to an achievement which has not yet been reached. It refers to future learning (that to which the child's powers will prove to be adapted) and to the readiness with which success will be achieved. It carries with it inevitably a reference not merely to potentialities but to probabilities in their relation to methods of working, to interests and to motives. In many discussions it has, however, been associated with a claim for exact prediction which has brought it into disrepute.

that similar dramatic modifications occurred in connection with memory, reasoning, imagination and the emergence of specific "aptitudes" for the chief types of adult vocational activities.[2]

The theories of earlier centuries (outlined above in Chapter IV) were still accepted in many important respects. The ability to memorise, for example, was supposed to reach its peak during childhood and to suffer a decline soon after puberty. Abstract reasoning ability was thought of as maturing suddenly in early adolescence, and imagination was conceived of as changing about the same age from a pre-occupation with the fantasies of childhood to the more constructive activities of adult life. Mechanical, artistic and commercial abilities were discussed as if they, too, were a function of age and manifested themselves clearly for the first time in the years from eleven to fourteen. It was claimed that an urge towards wage-earning (an economic motive) became strong about the age of thirteen, that "instinctive" antipathy towards parents and teachers showed itself at about the same time and that there was therefore, on all these grounds, psychological justification both for deliberate restrictions in the type of training offered in early adolescence and for a cessation of compulsory schooling for most pupils not later than fourteen.

Even as recently as 1931 it was possible for an English official publication to state that "the period between seven and eleven displays features sufficiently characteristic to render it desirable, on psychological as well as on administrative grounds, to treat these years as marking a distinct stage in education",[3] and to claim that the steady increase in the scatter of test results up to and into adolescence necessitated the provision not merely of separate classes but of separate types of schools for pupils of differing capacity. Such views are still held in many quarters in spite of their repudiation by certain of their early sponsors.[4] It is important to note that their promulgation implies a belief in the predictive value of a relatively early measurement of mental status as well as an acceptance of the desirability of acting upon the nineteenth-century conviction that learning takes place best in a state of comparative passivity under the class tuition of an eloquent pedagogue. Since there is now reason to doubt the early fixity of the intelligence quotient, the abruptness of other changes during adolescence, the clear delimitation of specific abilities and the absolute necessity for class instruction, the foundations of much of the structure of educational organisation in many European countries has been shaken; and a case has been established for rather re-markable modifications both in curriculum and in methods.

Long-term studies in connection with these issues are fewer than comparable enquiries into the growth of intelligence. There have, however, been sufficient short-term investigations and cross-sectional researches to make certain comments seem justifiable.

There is reason to believe that, like the growth of intelligence, the development of ability to memorise and to reason corresponds quite closely to chronological age and is relatively insensitive to the onset of puberty. Tests of reasoning ability have shown, for example, that from the age of about seven years onwards all forms of syllogistic thinking are employed by children[5] and that the chief difference between old and young thinking is found in its content of experience and special interests rather than in the nature of the process employed.

This finding appears to be related to the fact that the type of problem-solving or thought process employed varies with the situation which calls it forth; and its complexity appears related more closely to the experience and general mental development of the thinker than to his physiological age. The solving of problems which are simple to the solver occurs so rapidly at any age as to merit the term "insight". Problems which are difficult result in "trial and error" thinking—blundering, explorations of possible solutions and gradual approximations to success. These types of behaviour may occur at any age; and the transition from one type to another does not appear to be directly related to pubescence.[6]

The same seems to be true of the verbal expression of the processes of thought. Certain continental thinkers, such as Piaget, have distinguished sharply between the egocentric, somewhat concrete and primitively animistic thinking of little children and the more socialised, abstract and logical thinking of adolescents and adults.[7] It is important to note that these conclusions were not reached from long-term studies of development from childhood to adult status, but were the fruit of anecdotal and selective recording of responses to questions and to experiments on the part of a small number of children of differing ages. Piaget's work is directly in line with that of many thinkers of the opening years of this century. Like theirs, it assumes clearly demarcated stages and distinctly discernible types of response in the verbal expression of thinking. The ingenuity of his experimental situations has, however, stimulated many enquiries; and the publication of the work of his students has provided useful illustrations of interpretations of the growth of vocabulary obtained in other countries in other fashions.[8] Fuller experiment seems to show that within the limits of their experience and their interests, young children can generalise as competently as adolescents; and in certain circumstances both adolescents and adults express themselves in egocentric, animistic and illogical fashions.[9]

Careful testing of the activities involved in memorising has also shown a steady progression from, say, ages ten to twenty-five, which is quite comparable to that obtained in similar populations with a test of intelligence. Where motivation is adequate there seems no reason to accept the older supposition that the power to memorise decreases sharply during adolescence. This finding is supported by experimental studies of adult learning[10] and by evidence on the relatively greater speed of learning foreign languages observable in late adolescence as contrasted with that shown in the years prior to puberty.[11]

As has been indicated above, there is considerable complexity in the mental functioning which is commonly called intelligence. Attempts have been made to trace growth curves for success in sub-tests composed of the differing types of questioning most frequently employed in intelligence tests. Evidence seems to show that sub-tests, such as analogies, reasoning, number-series or vocabulary, are relatively specific and that with increasing age their results show different increments in average scores. Their relative importance tends, therefore, to change at different ages. Some non-verbal and performance tests cease to obtain increasing scores at about eleven years. Others show a growth curve with a progression up to seventeen or eighteen quite comparable in type to that obtained by composite verbal tests.[12] Similar data can be obtained by analysis of the inter-correlations of types of test material like that in the Stanford revision of the individual Binet scale. Inter-correlations reveal marked variations in the size of the apparent relationships between one type of material and another; and differing methods have been evolved for classifying test results and describing the classifications in mathematical or statistical terms.[13]

The chief contribution of such "factor-analysis" has been its clear formulation of the specific character of much of the test-material in current use and of the complexity of the mental functioning which is measured by such tests. It is difficult to determine the exact meaning of the variations in differential growth which appear to be involved in these changing patterns. They may mean that certain functions mature earlier than others. They may indicate that some forms of skill are more directly influenced by continued education or training. They may be related merely to variations in the suitability of test items. Whatever their interpretation, the social consequences of the evidence at present available seem to be that the full realisation of an individual's intellectual potentialities cannot be expected to be reached in early or late adolescence, and that there is, in the light of analysis of growth curves for test responses, no justification for an early curtailment of education in the belief that a comparative cessation of growth in one form of intellectual activity will be paralleled by deceleration in all.

A slightly different picture is presented by studies of the development of physical abilities, such as manual strength, shoulder strength, strength of legs and arms and associated athletic development.[14] Strength of grip appears to develop earlier among those whose physiological maturing is early. Maximum gains occur on the average about the age of thirteen for girls and sixteen for boys. Growth curves for boys and girls are similar up to about fourteen; but thereafter girls show little gain, while boys on the average continue to develop.

It is not known how much of this difference is related to differences in the type of activity which is expected from boys and girls; but marked differences in concomitant physical prowess in games —running, jumping, swimming—are known to occur among both girls and boys under different environmental conditions.

Distinct differences are also found in the prestige accorded to success in such activities. Soon after puberty more girls than boys appear to lose interest in competitive sports and to attach more value to skill in socially approved physical activities such as tennis, swimming, skating, dancing or golf. Preferences vary in differing social groups, and it is uncertain whether their prestige in any particular instance depends upon female superiority in strength of shoulder thrust and relative cessation of growth in other directions or whether it is determined by the social expectations of the group. Where popularity and group-prestige are directly related to any specific activity an important service can be rendered by adults who help backward adolescents to gain social confidence by increases in physical or athletic skill.[15]

I

The possibility of producing marked changes in relative status has been demonstrated by evidence that great improvement can be secured by suitable training accompanied by adequate encouragement. It is not always realised, either by adolescents or their teachers, that such skills are specific and that failure in one form of athletic or physical activity cannot be predicted from failure in another. Still less can it be predicted from a knowledge of the general mental level of the pupil. Physical and mental development, in this connection also, appear to be independent. The correlation between intelligence and gross motor functions is in most school populations approximately zero. In the learning of new games or new forms of skill intelligent children have, however, a certain advantage in their greater ability to understand instructions and to anticipate the conditions under which the skill will require to be used.

Intelligent children who wish to succeed may therefore effect outstanding changes if they can be helped to realise how directly differences in these respects depend upon differences in experience —within the limits set by individual potentialities of strength and speed. Lack of confidence and unwillingness to make social contacts can in many cases be much reduced by judicious help from friendly adults. Fuller enjoyment of games can also be secured by training towards more skilful techniques of play. This seems especially true in early adolescence, when participation in unskilled games and in make-believe play can often be observed to decline in favour of co-operation in team games of a more definitely organised type. To what extent this is due to developmental changes rather than to social convention it is difficult to say. That the latter plays a not inconsiderable part may be inferred from the fact that adults play so-called childish games with considerable enthusiasm when suitable social opportunities occur in parties, picnics or camping.

Equally important from the point of view of the social adjustment of an adolescent is the acquisition of an acceptable degree of skill in the finer motor and mechanical abilities demanded from most members of present-day adult society.[16] In some social situations certain types of bodily co-ordination, balance and agility may seem to be lacking, but there is reason to believe that what appears to be clumsiness is social rather than physical in origin. It occurs at a time when the practical or recreational value of such skills is beginning to be understood by adolescents and in circumstances in which the young people concerned are unduly anxious to please. Such temporary difficulties are less frequent in speed of movement of fingers, wrist, elbow or shoulder.

Sex differences in relation to motor abilities—where motivation and practice effects have been equalised—are not consistently large enough to be of any practical significance.[17] In speed of reaction to sound, and in eye–hand co-ordination, a limit of growth appears to be reached by both girls and boys at about fourteen years. Tests of eye–hand co-ordination, of reaction time and of bi-manual co-ordination show no reliable sex differences. In speed of tapping girls tend to fall behind boys after the age of fourteen. In steadiness tests and in tests of response to a series of numbers they tend to excel at all ages. With special practice, however, the differences decrease; and in all tests differences between average scores for boys and girls are considerably less than the range of variation within each group.

The social consequences of this are again important. The differences between the sexes do not support any exclusion of girls from skilled motor training on the grounds of biological unsuitability.

Little is known as to the direct relation of motor abilities to pubescence; but there seems reason to believe that the differences between early and late maturers are less than in the case of strength of grip and other gross physical abilities. There appears to be no uniform age at which growth ceases, and no support from test results can be given to recommendations that training in practical activities involving motor skills should be begun at any specified age. Decisions as to age of commencement must be made in the light of individual circumstances, and with the knowledge that these motor skills are both specific and highly sensitive to training. The variations in the growth curves for different tests also appear to point to the finding that present readiness for any highly complex technical activity cannot be determined from the results of any one such test of motor skill.[18]

In relation to mechanical ability also there is not evidence that boys and men are definitely superior to girls and women. Differential opportunities for practice rather than anything which may be described as innate differences appear to account for most of the differences between the sexes.[19]

Results of studies of sub-tests of mechanical ability from year to year during adolescence appear to show that scores made in them are less related to age and show less steady average improvement than comparable scores in tests of intelligence. Performance in such tests also appears, like that in tests of motor skills, to be very susceptible to the effects of practice. Single scores in such tests may therefore be expected to be peculiarly unreliable as an aid to the diagnosis of general mechanical ability.

This issue has been investigated not only by observation of average increments and average changes of performance in sub-tests but also by the use of factorial analysis.[20] This shows so little inter-correlation between the scores in separate tests of motor skills that it appears to provide no justification for speaking of a general motor factor. Certain groups of tests seem to be qualitatively alike. Tests of reaction time, of tapping, of steadiness, of ability to assemble common gadgets, such as bells or pumps, and tests of ability to perceive spatial relations appear, for example, to be inter-related within these small groups; but the groups show little relationship to one another; and the correlations are throughout so low that the tests seem to be measuring narrowly specific activities.

When attempts are made to use batteries of different types of such tests for the purposes of aptitude testing it is possible by certain statistical devices to decide upon a weighting of the scores obtained in each which shall produce the highest possible correspondence with an independent estimate of success in a complex practical activity such as engineering, dentistry and the like. The nature of such weighting can be illustrated by a regression equation of the type

$$i = + 0.14\,x + 0.22\,y + 0.24\,z + 0.19\,w$$

where x, y, z and w represent standard scores obtained in the tests of the battery.[21]

With such weighted scores multiple or total correlations up to about $+ 0.5$ have been obtained with the criterion of skilled performance. This is not unlike that between the results of special place examinations and recorded success in secondary schools two or three years later.

When such correlations are corrected by recognised statistical devices to the value they would have had if the whole population had been tested their estimated size approximates to $+ 0.8$.[22] This certainly encourages some measure of confidence in the tests as a means of prediction; but it is well to notice that the errors of estimate associated with a correlation of + 0·8 account for sixty per cent of the variance of the achievement scores. This is a large proportion to attribute to error in cases where important vocational decisions are to be made, and it indicates a considerable degree of uncertainty of prediction when the border line is reached.[23]

The practical usefulness of such weighted scores is also much reduced by the difficulty of administering a complicated series of tests, and by the fact that evidence is accumulating from a variety of sources that later skilled performance is related as much to interest, ambition and general competence of methods of working as to anything which can fairly be described as initial mechanical aptitude.[24] Definite reductions in the size of the correlation between the so-called aptitude tests and the criterion score have been reported after further periods of differential training. Improvements in the kind of tuition given and in the attitude of the trainees, as well as increases in the amount of practice, appear to be of greater practical usefulness in determining the final skill of a group of employees than excessive attention to refinements in the techniques of selection.

Assessment by means of such batteries of motor, mechanical or industrial tests is for these reasons being increasingly recognised as a measure of present status in specific skills rather than as a means of making exact predictions as to later proficiency in the much more complex activities of workshop or factory.* There seems, in recent work, no justification for the claim that accurate predictions can be made by the use of any one such test or group of tests. Still less is there support for the belief that human beings are divisible into clearly demarcated types—some suitable only for training in intellectual pursuits, some for technical and some for commercial occupations. Both these claims have, however, been made by enthusiastic manipulators of the results of factorial analysis and aptitude testing. The matter therefore merits further consideration.

It is important that it be realised that the exact nature and arrangement of the factors obtained in any factorial analysis depends in some measure upon the method of analysis employed. This can more readily be understood when it is remembered that there are many different ways of classifying most objects—in terms of their differing attributes. The mathematical techniques involved are highly elaborate; but undue reliance will not be placed

* See also Chapter XIV below.

upon any one finding, and unwarranted psychological interpretations will not be made if it is remembered that factorial analysis represents merely a means of classifying test scores. It does not carry with it the assumption that, if a group of test results such as those relating to speed of reaction times can be classed together because of a certain similarity in the size and direction of their inter-correlations, there will necessarily be found a group of pupils who all excel only in such speed of reaction and who can therefore be described as belonging to a pure "type" of speedy reactors. There might prove to be such individuals; but their existence would have to be proved by other methods as elaborate as any undertaken in the factorial analysis of test scores.

Further grounds for caution are to be found in the fact that it is often by no means easy to interpret the nature of the factors obtained. It may be possible to suggest a psychological meaning as a result of introspection based on one's own experiences while performing the tests, or as a sequel to a study of the observed reactions of other people to the group of tests which appear to be linked by a common factor. There remains, however, an element of subjectivity in such interpretations—even when refuge is taken in alphabetic symbols such as G, S, P or N, instead of the more readily debatable terms, such as a general factor, a spatial factor, a perceptual factor or a numerical factor.

As in the case of discussion of the differing components in human physique (see Chapter II above), it seems less profitable to think of the mind as divided into a small number of unitary factors, or to conceive of people as consisting of two or three discrete types, than to interpret any factors obtainable by statistical analysis as dimensions of axes of reference and to think of tests and persons as being continuously distributed in the space enclosed by these axes of reference.

The diversity of pattern obtained by the use of slightly different groups of subjects as well as by the employment of different types of factorial analysis serves also to emphasise the fact that any such classification is relative not only to the particular battery of tests and to the method employed but also to the sample of the population tested.

For these reasons it is coming to be recognised that the mind is probably both more complex in functioning and more of an integrated whole than a superficial interpretation of any one mathematical analysis might lead one to suppose. "Far from being divided up into unitary factors the mind is a rich, comparatively undifferentiated complex of innumerable influences."[25] "It is capable of expressing itself in the most plastic and Protean way, especially before education, language, the subjects of the school curriculum, the occupation, and the political beliefs of adult life have imposed a habitual structure upon it."[26] Each test samples some fraction of its powers—some "sub-pool" of the whole (to use Thomson's phrase)—and the categories describable by factors appear to be "interlaced and interwoven, like the relationships of men in a community, plumbers and Methodists, blondes, bachelors, smokers, conservatives, illiterates, native-born, criminals, and school teachers, an organisation into classes which cut across one another right and left".[27]

This variety is illustrated in the differing patterns obtained by expressing the results of factor analysis in a form similar to that of a regression equation. Factor profiles can then be constructed by calculating for each person the weighting estimated for the factors which appear to associate each set of tests. (This is done from a series of equations of the type

$$\frac{A}{x_0} = + \ 0 \cdot 4495 \ x_1 + 0 \cdot 2762 \ x_2 + 0 \cdot 1466 \ x_3 + 0 \cdot 1531 \ x_4$$

where $+ \ 0 \cdot 4495$, $+ \ 0 \cdot 2762$, $+ \ 0 \cdot 1466$ and $+ \ 0 \cdot 1531$ are the estimated loadings of one factor in each of four tests, and x_1, x_2, x_3, x_4 are the standard scores obtained by an individual in the tests.)[28]

The resulting complexity is shown in Fig. VII and Fig. VIII.

These particular diagrams were obtained from testing of a group of boys promoted to a secondary grammar school and a group allocated to an adjacent secondary modern school. The boys were examined with twenty tests (both verbal and spatial), and results from four of these tests were used in the estimation of each factor score. Two methods of analysis (with and without rotation of axes) were applied to the data. (The divergencies of the resulting estimations are shown by the sets of factor scores in the diagrams.)

This study is interesting because it was undertaken in a situation in which it was still expected that it was possible to discriminate between pupils at the age of allocation to different secondary courses in terms of a division into the three "types" of those successful with ideas or words, those endowed exclusively with technical skill and those suited for a more indeterminate kind of training. A study of the factor profiles showed that the pupils could not be classified into distinct types corresponding to pre-dominating factor scores. There was a general tendency towards even all-round development in eighty per cent of the grammar school boys and forty-five per cent of those from the modern school.

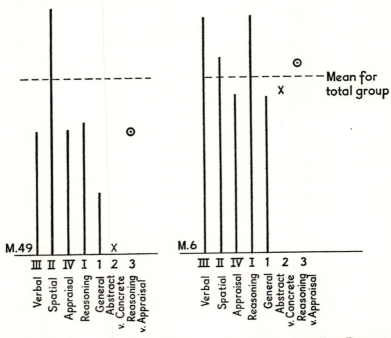

Fig. VII. Factor profiles of two boys from Secondary Modern School (from Dempster). Factor 1 shows the general factor for the battery, 2 that contrasting tests using abstract and concrete data and 3 that contrasting tests needing reasoning and those which may be solved by appraisal. After rotation of axes, factor 1 shows that which is common to the group of reasoning tests, IV that which is common to the tests needing appraisal, II that which is common to the group of spatial tests and III that which is common to the group of verbal tests.

There was not a sufficiently marked difference to indicate a bias in the direction of any one factor score.

While the range of variation was greater in the modern school group, there was within both schools evidence of sub-groupings which could be used to distinguish between boys who had higher scores in the verbal tests and in tests using abstract material and boys who had higher scores in the spatial tests and in tests using concrete material. There was not justification for supposing that the grammar school boys as a whole had a verbal bias and the modern school pupils a bias towards concrete reasoning. The over-lapping of the two groups in estimated factor scores was as striking as the overlapping of the scores in each of the twenty tests used in the investigation.

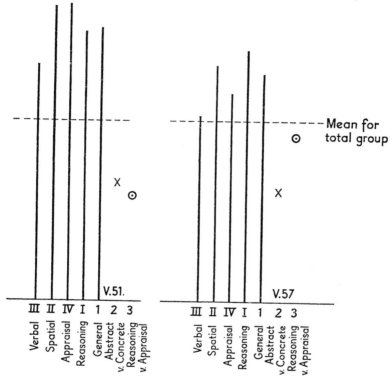

FIG. VIII. Factor profiles of two boys from Secondary Grammar School (from Dempster).

On evidence such as that outlined above it is therefore now considered that there is not support either in the findings of aptitude-testing or of factorial analysis for a belief in the divisibility of human beings into a small number of clearly demarcated mental types.

In similar fashion the search for predictive certainty which motivated extensive experimentation with aptitude-testing a number of years ago has led to much greater caution in the interpretation of present performance as an index of future success than was anticipated by the enthusiasts of the 1930s. "It is comparatively simple to show the presence of independent factors and to trace general tendencies; it is another matter entirely to measure the factor scores for each individual child. It is only possible to estimate these from test scores and the value of these estimates for allocation will naturally depend upon the errors involved. These are very considerable; they cannot simply be neglected."[29]

A protection against unwise interpretations is also afforded by noting that findings reported in terms of the weighted scores of a group of tests do not apply to the use of unweighted scores. Still less do they apply to the use of the raw scores of single tests abstracted from a composite battery. Weighted sets of test results may be shown to be directly related to records of successful performance in skilled occupations. Raw scores of isolated sub-tests of the battery cannot, without further evidence, be assumed to reveal the same relationships. Still less can human beings whose abilities remain complex and whose probable success or aptitude can be shown to be related to their entire development be proved to be adequately described in terms of their performance in any one test so specific in nature as tests of mechanical ability or motor skill have been proved to be.

Consideration of individual scores obtained in other batteries of tests designed to reveal abilities in the interpretation of words or numbers, the recognition of relationships, the ability to order and to classify, competence in memorising, or in speed and dexterity of movement lends support to the evidence outlined above.

A pupil's performance in such sub-tests varies widely, but it rarely falls into specialised patterns of such a kind that it can be fairly claimed that a pupil is achieving only one type of success.

The profiles of results of tests of ability, like those of derived factor scores, are rather of the diversified type shown in Fig. IX.

The period of growth in all such functioning also appears to extend well into adolescence, and all measurable performance in these complex functions appears amenable to later training to a degree which was unrecognised prior to the extensive experimenting of recent years. A person with a low initial score is only temporarily handicapped if his wishes, ambitions and desires point the way towards acceptance of remedial training and if expert assistance is available to guide him towards optimum methods of work or practice.

Similar findings are reported from research in connection with abilities in music or in art, and similar scepticism is now beginning to be shown as to the possibility of assured prediction of later skill from performance at an early age. It used to be supposed that aesthetic abilities, like mechanical abilities, were clearly distinguishable from other human abilities in that they were very

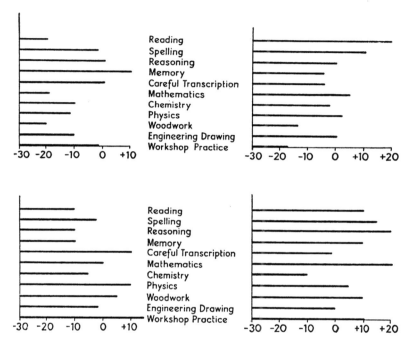

Fig. IX. Ability profiles of four boys expressed in terms of standard scores × 10. Technical school pupils aged 15 years. Fleming, C. M., V.S.3. *Unpublished Selection Test and Examination Results for Mathematics, etc.*

directly limited by hereditary endowment, appeared among fewer members of the population and were relatively little affected by training. Research appears to show that with more highly skilled remedial techniques and more belief in human potentialities, it will not prove true that large numbers of children are of a type that can fairly be described as "quite unable to benefit by" artistic or musical education. Differences between individuals in these respects also are beginning to be recognised as differences in "exposure" or training operating on individuals with many unrealised potentialities rather than as differences in "type".[30]

Little has yet been done in the way of investigation into the annual relative status of individuals in mechanical or artistic performance over a period of years. There is reason to believe, however, that if it should prove possible to speak of a "motor quotient" or an "artistic quotient" in relation to specific tests, it would be found that considerable variability of growth is a characteristic of the years of adolescence in these fields also.

Accumulating evidence from the study of growth curves, from factorial analysis and from aptitude testing thus seems to show that human variety and variability in mental functioning present at least as complex a picture as do recent anthropometric studies in physical measurement and that human beings are no more divisible into two or three mental types than they are adequately described in terms of a small number of physical patterns.

With some regret it must therefore be noted that no success can be reported in the quest for an administratively neat assortment of types of child to correspond to a similarly clearly defined grouping of schools. Neither can it be confidently claimed that final classification and prediction of future relative status can be made in the light of any initial assessment of ability—whether in relation to intellectual, mechanical, motor, artistic or practical activities.

At best, any narrow classification made will be admittedly as rough as that which speaks of three main types of physique—with the knowledge that seventy-six varying combinations of these three components are barely sufficient to describe the infinite variety of human structure and development.

One implication of these findings seems to be that all adolescents are capable of benefiting by continued education of a widely diversified type. Not all will learn at the same rate. Not all will be interested to the same extent; but there is, in the research evidence summarised above, strong justification for believing that "all provision for education at the secondary stage should be made both well-balanced and stimulating". "Opportunities should be offered for intellectual, social and practical activities in all departments—whether these are 'academic or professional', 'technical or practical', 'commercial or social' in their special emphasis; and frequent rearrangement of pupils should be accepted as not impossible."[31]

The obstacles to this generosity of provision and flexibility of programme are much reduced in schools in which it has been agreed that allocation to secondary courses shall be made quite frankly on the basis of choice of future work—rather than of determination of type of child. Educational decisions at the age of eleven or twelve are in effect vocational decisions. If their vocational character is recognised there is little difficulty, both on the part of parents and of teachers, in admitting that an error of judgment has been made. When, however, allocation to a certain sort of course has carried with it the assumption that the pupil is of a specified "type" some loss of prestige is suffered by the adult adviser if it is later discovered that the child is more suited to another kind of educational treatment. If parent and child and teacher have merely agreed that Tom shall begin to train to be a cook (for reasons which seemed adequate at the age of eleven) no one of them is personally implicated if at the age of thirteen it seems wiser that he transfer into a slightly different course which may lead to his becoming a plumber. A similar absence of emotionally toned obstruction is found in the case of other changes, such as those from courses planned for prospective teachers, doctors or chemists, to courses designed for secretaries, salesmen or dental mechanics. Pupils with widely differing points of view may be interested and successful in the study of languages, mathematics or science. In a flexible programme they can have opportunities of access to such knowledge and at the same time direct their attention with increasing definiteness to the courses which are most relevant to the vocation or occupation they seem likely to follow.

Where seating accommodation is limited it will be necessary to give preference to those most immediately ready for promotion to the more difficult studies; but rejection on such grounds does not carry so much sting nor result in so dangerous a psychological trauma as does exclusion on account of unsuitability of "type". There is a certain finality in the conception of type which paralyses effort and leads to educational despair and its sequelae of indifference and apathy.

While there are individual differences among pupils and also levels of ability below which success is unlikely in certain specifiable activities of adult life, it is desirable that all adolescents be given the widest possible opportunities of intellectual stimulation and physical and artistic training. Unnecessary defeatism need no longer be encouraged in the belief that if a pupil shows no present prowess it is necessarily the case that he will not profit by skilful tuition and improve under the stimulation of adult faith in his potentialities. There seems no reason to think that there are groups of pupils who will benefit only by intellectual stimulation, and who must therefore prove quite unsuccessful in mechanical, artistic or motor activities. In similar fashion it is not necessary to suppose that there are groups whose potentialities are so one-sided that they must be left to the quite illiterate repetition of relatively simple mechanical manipulations. Adolescents are both more susceptible to educational influences and more capable of continued all-round development than was supposed by the educational theorists in the early years of the century.

Confirmation of this, if further confirmation is needed, may be found in the recorded experiences of the armies of the world in the opening years of the fifth decade. Ancient myths as to racial or sexual differences in educability were then exploded by the observable power of young adults to react to specialised training of a completely unaccustomed type. New languages were learnt at a rate which challenged former suppositions as to the linguistic adaptability of adolescents and adults. New skills were acquired by shop girls, by women teachers from grammar schools and by men from the jungles or deserts of Africa and Asia, who would not, under normal conditions, have been given any opportunity of developing either competence or interest in the management of anti-aircraft guns, of radar or of the internal intricacies of fighting and bombing aeroplanes. In the search for means of selecting those most ready for such training the predictive usefulness of factor analysis and regression coefficients again proved to be less than that of continued observation of the whole person, and further evidence as to the capacity of quite ordinary people came later in the success of resettlement schemes in many countries. Unsuspected abilities, interests and ambitions were uncovered among discharged members of the Forces; and the contributions since made by these mature students have confirmed a belief in the multi-potentiality of human beings.[32]

In all this is to be found the educational and psychological justification for the establishment of schools which are comprehensive rather than selective and for educational procedures which require neither segregation nor exclusion. Where modifications of traditional methods or organisation have been tried there is now abundant evidence that comprehensive schools of mixed ability, undifferentiated grouping (an absence of streaming) and classroom procedures which reflect a belief in the educability and modifiability of pupils have resulted in success where formerly

there was failure and in wholesome attitudes to schooling where
formerly morale was low and early leaving was endemic.[33]

There are many reasons in all countries for believing that the
pool of ability is both wider and deeper than was formerly
supposed; and these educational reasons for the maintenance of
schools whose flexible organisation shall be truly comprehensive
are as valid for administrators in England as in Sweden—in
America as in Scotland, Wales, Australia or New Zealand.[34]

REFERENCES

[1] For a valuable survey see:
Husén, T., *Problems of Differentiation in Swedish Compulsory Schooling*. Stockholm: Teachers College. (n.d.).
[2] Wheeler, O. A., *The Adventure of Youth*. London: Univ. of London Press, 1945. *The Needs of Youth in These Times*. A Report of the Scottish Youth Advisory Committee. Edinburgh: H.M.S.O., 1945.
[3] Burt, C., *Memorandum on the Mental Characteristics of Children between the Ages of Seven and Eleven*. Report Consult. Comm. Primary School. London: H.M.S.O., 1931. Appendix III.
[4] Burt, C., The Education of the Young Adolescent, *Brit. J. Educ. Psychol.*, XIII, III, 126–140, 1943.
[5] Burt, C., The Development of Reasoning in School Children, *J. Exper. Pedag.*, V, 68–77 and 121–127, 1919.
[6] For discussion see:
Anderson, J. E., Child Development and the Growth Process, in Washburne, C. et al., Child Development and the Curriculum, *Thirty-eighth Yearbook Nat. Soc. Study Educ.* Bloomington: Public School Publishing Company, 1939. Part I.
Brownell, W. A., The Effects of Premature Drill in Third Grade Arithmetic, *J. Educ. Res.*, 29, 19–35, 1932.
Katona, G., *Organising and Memorising*. New York: Columbia Univ. Press, 1940.
Brownell, W. A., *Arithmetic in Grades I and II*. Durham: Duke Univ. Press, 1941.
McConnell, T. R., et al., The Psychology of Learning, *Forty-first Yearbook Nat. Soc. Study Educ.* Bloomington: Public School Publishing Company. 1942. Part II.
Wertheimer, M., *Productive Thinking*. New York: Harper, 1945.
Brownell, W. A., and Moser, H. E., *Meaningful v. Mechanical Learning*, Durham: Duke Univ. Press, 1949.
Hebb, D. O., *The Organization of Behavior. A Neuropsychological Theory*. New York: Wiley, 1949.
Russell, D. H., *Children's Thinking*. Boston: Ginn, 1956.
Fleming, C. M., *Teaching: A Psychological Analysis*. London: Methuen, 1958 and 1959; New York: Wiley, 1958.
Bruner, J. S., *The Process of Education*. Cambridge: Harvard Univ. Press, 1960.
[7] Piaget, J., *Judgment and Reasoning in the Child*. London: Kegan Paul, 1928.
Piaget, J., *The Moral Judgment of the Child*. London: Kegan Paul, 1932.
Piaget, J., *Le Développement des Quantités chez l'Enfant. Conservatisme et Atomisme*. Neuchatel: Delachaux & Niestlé S. A., 1941.
Piaget, J., et al., *La Genèse du Nombre chez l'Enfant*. Neuchatel: Delachaux & Niestlé S. A., 1941.
Piaget, J., *La Formation du Symbole chez l'Enfant. Imitation, Jeu et Rêve, Image et Représentation*. Neuchatel: Delachaux & Niestlé S. A., 1945.
Piaget, J., *The Child's Conception of Number*. London: Routledge, 1952.
Piaget, J., *The Child's Construction of Reality*. London: Routledge, 1955.

[8] Peel, E. A., *The Pupil's Thinking*. London: Oldbourne, 1960.

Lovell, K., *The Growth of Basic Mathematical and Scientific Concepts in Children*. London: Univ. of London Press, 1961.

Lunzer, E. A., *Recent Studies in Britain Based on the Work of Jean Piaget*. Nat. Found. Educ. Res., 1961.

See also:

Hebb, D. O., loc. cit. [6].

Russell, D. H., loc. cit. [6].

[9] Oakes, M. E., *Children's Explanations of Natural Phenomena*. New York: Teachers College, 1947.

Navarro, J. G., *The Development of Scientific Concepts in a Young Child*. New York: Teachers College, 1955.

For criticism of Piaget from another viewpoint see:

Langeveld, M. J., *Verkenning en Verdiepung*. Purmurend: J. Muusses, 1950.

Bunt, L. N. H., *The Development of the Ideas of Number and Quantity According to Piaget*. Groningen: Wolters, 1951.

Langeveld, M. J., *Studien zur Anthropologie des Kindes*. Tubingen: Max Niemeyer, 1956.

Van Hiele, P. M., *Development and Learning Process*. Groningen: Wolters, 1959.

[10] Thorndike, E. L., *et al.*, *Adult Learning*. New York: Macmillan, 1928.

Clift, D. H., (Chairman), Adult Reading, *Fifty-fifth Yearbook Nat. Soc. Study Educ.* Part II. 1956.

McClusky, H. V., The Psychology of Adults in Kreitlow, B. W. (Chairman), *Rev. Educ. Res.*, XXIX, 3, 224–311, 1959.

See also:

Pinneau, S. R., and Jones, H. E., Mental Development in Infancy and Childhood and Mental Abilities in Adult Life, *Rev. Educ. Res.*, XXV, 5, 415–437, 1955.

Pinneau, S. R., and Jones, H. E., Development of Mental Abilities, *Rev. Educ. Res.*, XXVIII, 5, 392–400, 1958.

[11] Brooks, F. D., and Arndt, C. O., Foreign Languages, in Washburne, C., *et al.* loc. cit. [6].

[12] Brooks, F. D., Mental Development in Adolescence, *Rev. Educ. Res.*, VI, 1, 85–101, 1936.

Conrad, H. S., Freeman, F. N., and Jones, H. E., Differential Mental Growth, in Jones, H. E., *et al.*, Adolescence, *Forty-third Yearbook Nat. Soc. Study Educ.* Chicago: Univ. of Chicago. 1944. Part I.

Froehlich, G. J., Mental Development during the Pre-adolescent and Adolescent Periods, *Rev. Educ. Res.*, XIV, 5, 401–412, 1944.

[13] Thurstone, L. L., *The Vectors of Mind*. Chicago: Univ. of Chicago Press, 1935.

Thomson, G. H., *The Factorial Analysis of Human Ability*. London: Univ. of London Press, 1939 and 1946.

Vernon, P. E., *The Measurement of Abilities*. London: Univ. of London Press, 1940 and 1956.

Burt, C., *The Factors of the Mind*. London: Univ. of London Press, 1940.

Holzinger, K. J., and Harman, H. H., *Factor Analysis. A Synthesis of Factorial Methods*. Chicago: Univ. of Chicago Press, 1941.

Burt, C., Mental Abilities and Mental Factors, *Brit. J. Educ. Psychol.*, XIV, II, 85–94, 1944.

Vernon, P. E., *The Structure of Human Abilities*. London: Methuen, 1950.

[14] For accessible summaries of findings see:

Wellman, B. L., Motor Development from Two Years to Maturity, *Rev. of Educ. Res.*, VI, 1, 1936.

Jones, H. E., The Development of Physical Abilities, in Jones, H. E., *et al.*, *Adolescence*, loc. cit. [12].

Bayley, N., and Espenschade, A., Motor Development and Decline, *Rev. Educ. Res.*, XX, 367–374, 1950.

[15] Jersild, A. T., Education in Motor Activities, in Washburne, C., *et al.*, loc. cit. [6].

For a description of development in terms of the story of one boy see:

Jones, H. E., *et al.*, *Development in Adolescence*. New York: D. Appleton-Century, 1943.

Jersild, A. T., *et al.*, *Child Development and the Curriculum*. New York: Teachers College, 1946.

[16] Jones, H. E., and Seashore, R. H., The Development of Fine Motor and Mechanical Abilities, in Jones, H. E., *et al.*, loc. cit. [12].

[17] Wellman, B. L., Sex Differences, in Murchison, C. (ed.), *A Handbook of Child Psychology*. Worcester: Clark Univ. Press, 1933.

Jones, H. E., and Seashore, R. H., loc. cit. [16].

[18] Wellman, B. L., loc. cit. [14].

Jones, H. E., and Seashore, R. H., loc. cit. [16].

Bayley, N., and Espenschade, A., loc. cit. [14].

[19] See:

Paterson, D. G., Elliott, R. M., *et al.*, *Minnesota Mechanical Ability Tests*. Minneapolis: Univ. of Minnesota Press, 1930.

Viteles, M. S., The Influence of Training on Motor Test Performance, *J. Exper. Psychol.*, XVI, 556–564, 1933.

[20] Cox, J. W., *Mechanical Aptitude*. London: Methuen, 1928.

El Koussy, A. A. H., The Visual Perception of Space, *Brit. J. Psychol. Monogr.*, XX, 1935.

Thurstone, L. L., *Primary Mental Abilities*. Chicago: Univ. of Chicago Press, 1938.

Earle, F. M., and Macrae, A., Tests of Mechanical Ability, *Nat. Inst. Ind. Psychol.*, 3, 1929.

Earle, F. M., and Milner, M., The Use of Performance Tests of Intelligence in Vocational Guidance, *Ind. Fat. Res. Board*, 53, 1929.

Allen, E. P., and Smith, P., *Selection of Skilled Apprentices for the Engineering Trade*. City of Birmingham, 1931, 1934, 1939.

Holliday, F., An Investigation into the Selection of Apprentices for the Engineering Industry, *Occup. Psychol.*, XIV, 2, 69–81, 1940.

Earle, F. M., and Kilgour, J., A Vocational Guidance Research in Fife, *Nat. Inst. Ind. Psychol.*, 6, 1935.

Alexander, W. P., Intelligence, Concrete and Abstract, *Brit. J. Psychol. Monogr.*, XIX, 1935.

Price, E. J. J., The Nature of the Practical Factor (F), *Brit. J. Psychol.*, XXX, 4, 341–351, 1940.

Slater, P., Some Group Tests of Spatial Judgment or Practical Ability, *Occup. Psychol.*, XIV, 1, 40–55, 1940.

Slater, P., The Development of Spatial Judgment and its Relation to some Educational Problems, *Occup. Psychol.*, XVII, 3, 140–155, 1943.

Bradford, E. J. G., Selection for Technical Education, *Brit. J. Educ. Psychol.*, XVI, 1, 20–31, 1946, and XVI, 11, 69–81, 1946.

[21] Shuttleworth, C. W., Tests of Technical Aptitude, *Occup. Psychol.*, XVI, 4, 175–182, 1942.

[22] Emmett, W. G., *An Inquiry into the Prediction of Secondary School Success*. London: Univ. of London Press, 1942.

[23] Jenkins, J. W., Allocation at Eleven Plus, *Times Educ. Sup.*, September 2, 1944, and September 9, 1944.

McClelland, W., *Selection for Secondary Education*. London: Univ. of London Press, 1942.

[24] Cox, J. W., *Manual Skill: Its Organisation and Development*. Cambridge: Univ. Press, 1934.

Bennett, G. K., and Cruikshank, R. M., *A Summary of Manual and Mechanical Ability Tests*. New York: Psychol. Corpor., 1942.

Jones, H. E., and Seashore, R. H., loc. cit. [16].

Testing for the Secondary Technical School. London: The Association of Principals of Technical Institutions, 1945.

Crawford, A. B., and Burnham, P. S., *Forecasting College Achievement*. New Haven: Yale Univ. Press, 1946.

Thorndike, R. L., and Hagen, E., *Ten Thousand Careers*. New York: John Wiley, 1959.

[25] Thomson, G. H., *The Factorial Analysis of Human Ability*. London: Univ. of London Press, 1939, p. 267.

[26] Ibid., p. 280.

[27] Ibid., p. 283.

[28] Dempster, J. J. B., *An Investigation into the Use of Estimated Factor Scores in Describing Groups of Secondary and Senior School Boys of Eleven Plus*. M. A. Thesis, Univ. of London, 1944.

[29] Jenkins, J. W., loc. cit. [22].

[30] Peel, E. A., On Identifying Aesthetic Types, *Brit. J. Psychol.*, XXXV, 3, 61–69, 1945.

Peel, E. A., A New Method for Analyzing Aesthetic Preferences: Some Theoretical Considerations, *Psychometrika*, 11, 2, 129–137, 1946.

Jones, H. E., and Seashore, R. H., loc. cit. [16].

Woods, W. A., Language Handicap and Artistic Interest, *J. Consult. Psychol.*, XII, 4, 240–245, 1948.

Barney, W. D., *A Study of Perception and its Relation to the Art Expression of a Group of Adolescents*. Ph.D. Thesis, Univ. of London, 1952.

[31] Fleming, C. M., *Cumulative Records*. London: Univ. of London Press, 1945.

Fleming, C. M., *Teaching: A Psychological Analysis*. London: Methuen, 1958 and 1959; New York: John Wiley, 1958.

[32] Oakley, C. A., *Men at Work*. London: Hodder and Stoughton, 1945.

Garforth, F. I. de la P., War Office Selection Boards (O.C.T.U.), *Occup. Psychol.*, XIX, 2, 97–102, 1945.

Vernon, P. E., and Parry, J. B., *Personnel Selection in the British Forces*. London: Univ. of London Press, 1949.

Landis, P. H., *Adolescence and Youth*. Revised edition. New York: McGraw-Hill, 1952.

See also:

Harris, H., *The Group Approach to Leadership Testing*. London: Routledge & Kegan Paul, 1949.

Higham, M. H., Some Recent Work with Group Selection. Techniques, *Occup. Psychol.*, XXVI, 3, 169–175, 1952.

Powdermaker, F. B., and Frank, J. D., *Group Psychotherapy: Studies in Methodology of Research and Therapy*. Cambridge: Harvard Univ. Press, 1953.

[33] Miller, T. W. G., *A Critical and Empirical Study of the Emergence, Development and Significance of the Comprehensive Secondary School in England with special Reference to Certain Educational and Social Effects*. Ph.D. Thesis, Univ. of Birmingham, 1958.

Rudd, W. G. A., *The Psychological Effects of Streaming by Attainment*. M.A. Thesis, Univ. of London, 1956.

Chetcuti, F., *A Study of the Morale of A Stream and C Stream Pupils in Secondary Schools*. M.A. Thesis, Univ. of London, 1960.

See also: Educ. Res. London: Nat. Found. Educ. Res. in England and Wales. *passim*.

Husén, T., and Svensson, N. E., Pedagogic Milieu and Development of Intellectual Skills. *The School Review*, 36–51, 1960.
Husén, T., *Educational Structure and the Development of Ability*. Paris: O.S.T.P., 1961.
Miller, T. W. G., *Values in the Comprehensive School*. Educ. Monogr. V. Edinburgh: Oliver and Boyd, 1961.
Husén, T., loc. cit. [1]
London Comprehensive Schools. London: London County Council, 1961.
Husén, T., Detection of Ability and Selection for Educational Purposes in Sweden, *Yearbook of Educ.* London, 1962.
34 McIntosh, D. M., *Educational Guidance and the Pool of Ability*. London: Univ. of London Press, 1959.
Fleming, C. M., Can the Pool of Talent be Increased? *Yearbook of Educ.* London, 1962.

CHAPTER XI

PERSONAL AND SOCIAL DEVELOPMENT

The point of view of the teacher in the school, like that of the research worker concerned with the study of abilities, has changed in certain very definite fashions.

At the opening of the twentieth century strong emphasis was laid upon intellectual stimulation. In the second decade there was much questioning as to the suitability of existing curricula and prevalent methods of class instruction;* and in the third decade there was a concern with sociological values which encouraged a study of the relevance of each school subject to the demands of society and the later requirements of adult life. Enquiries were begun as to the social uses of Arithmetic, Spelling, Reading, Modern Languages or Science; and marked improvements were effected by the introduction into the classroom of more individualised methods of work.[1]

In more recent years this has been further developed by a realisation of the social consequences of the experiences which a pupil meets in the classroom. Attention is therefore now being given to the socialising effect both of methods and curricula. Individual work was, many years ago, proved to result in no diminution of the intellectual effects of teaching. It is now being advocated on the grounds of the social benefits which may follow from the greater opportunities it presents for both personal and social development.[2]

This concern with social maturing is contemporary with a shifting in emphasis from the intellectualised psychology of the nineteenth century and the biological approach of the early twentieth to the more recent concern of psychologists as well as teachers with the essentially social nature of human beings. It manifests itself in differing fashions in curriculum-experiments in schools in America and Europe. It reveals itself in methods of group therapy and group analysis, to which attention has been increasingly directed since the opening of the fifth decade;[3] and it justifies the rejection by Army Selection Boards and School

* See Chapter IX above.

141

Authorities of the findings of a single interview or test in favour of cumulative recording of the results of continued study of the whole person in action.*

Adolescents experience something more than mere intellectual or physical development. Account must also be taken of their growth from the social immaturity of childhood to the more balanced behaviour of the adult, who in his relations with his social group has attained in some measure the status of the fully developed and adequately acculturalised human being.

Careful studies of the stages observable in this development formed part of the adolescent growth studies of which mention has already been made. In California, for example,[4] records were kept by the staff of the University Institute of Child Welfare as to the development of a group of about two hundred girls and boys from the last year of the elementary school at six-monthly intervals over a seven-year period. Attention was given to physical and physiological changes, to school achievement, interests and activities, and to social relationships at home and in school. The actual test devices included:

(1) photographs;
(2) anthropometric measurements and observations on muscular and skeletal development;
(3) tests of pulse rate, blood pressure, rate of respiration and temperature;
(4) X-ray examinations;
(5) tests of reactions to exercise;
(6) analyses of urine;
(7) tests of physical abilities—control, accuracy and strength;
(8) tests of motor skill—eye-hand co-ordination, steadiness, speed and bi-manual co-ordination;
(9) measurement of intelligence and of school attainment;
(10) measurement of interests and attitudes;
(11) tests of learning—immediate and delayed recall;
(12) records of recent activities;
(13) teachers' ratings on interest in school-work and achievement in school;
(14) ratings by "Guess Who?"—technique by which pupils are asked to name the one who best fits each one of forty

* See Chapters XII and XIV below.

items such as "Here is someone who is often bad-tempered". "Here is someone who likes to talk very much." "Here is someone who is very unfriendly";

(15) investigations into fears, annoyances, mannerisms, motives;
(16) assessment of social adjustments in school and at home;
(17) records of behaviour in social situations of classroom and playground;
(18) interviews as to habits and daily routine;
(19) collection of data as to socio-economic level and family history;
(20) records of responses to Rorschach series of ink-blots— ("What does this remind you of?" etc.);
(21) photographic records of reactions to films, to standardised questions and to association word-tests.

The thoroughness of such investigations has made possible a series of long-term studies of the social and emotional development of adolescents which is comparable to longitudinal records of the growth of intelligence.

Observation of personal and social development is rendered difficult both by the diversity of individual reactions towards groups and by the complicated effects of personal tensions within these groups. Adolescents differ in rate of development as well as in regularity of growth. They come from homes with differing attitudes towards themselves as individuals and towards the importance of their acceptance as members of specified social groups. They vary also in their ambitions; their expectations and their wishes. All of them, however, are experiencing certain of the physical changes accompanying pubescence; and all of them are engaged upon the problems of adjustment consequent on their emerging status as adults in a world of men and women. There is therefore observable in each one both the actual fact of growth into a maturity of greater or lesser physical perfection and the accompanying impulse towards development into a condition of greater or lesser social competence.

The life history of each adolescent is an individual one. The pattern of growth of each is in some respects unique; but certain sequences of attitudes and demands are discernible in any cultural pattern, and these in turn (as has been indicated in Chapter III above) exert profound influence upon the behaviour both of the adolescent and his group.

The attitudes of adults towards children, for example, not uncommonly pass through various stages describable as:

(1) admiration or adoration;
(2) annoyance at the dirtiness and untidiness of the toddler;
(3) amusement at the adventures of the same toddler;
(4) irritability at the persistent questioning and the restless exploration of the pre-school child;
(5) tolerant entertainment of the infant at school;
(6) admiration of the rapid progress of the young primary school child;
(7) indifference towards the familiar scholastic endeavours of the older child;
(8) indignation at the recklessness of the child on the streets;
(9) ridicule of the awkwardness of the adolescent indoors;
(10) intolerance of the adolescent's wish for independence;
(11) expectation of maturity and trustworthiness in the young adult;
(12) pride in the establishment of vocational success.

And the children are in turn expected to be the centre of attention, to get out of the way, to sit still and keep quiet, to work hard, to accept absolute authority, to develop social skills, to show independence, to do nothing of which the family would not approve and to achieve rapid financial success.[5]

In similar fashion the demands of contemporaries vary in a fashion which is almost as bewildering. In the adolescent growth study of California, for example, it was found, from an evaluation of adolescents by adolescents, that the most admired qualities among boys between eleven and thirteen years were skill in organised games, aggressiveness, boisterousness and unkemptness.[6] Activity of any kind was attractive, and good looks, a sense of humour and pleasantness of manner, while acceptable, were not emulated. The boys who had no special interest in games were shunned or ostracised by the majority of the group and found themselves in one of the sub-pools which with a greater or lesser degree of contentment existed alongside the main stream of class-activities. The boys in these minority groups were in some cases retarded physically and physiologically. In other instances they consisted of those who were markedly more mature. Some of these deviating children were observably distressed at their exclusion.

Others who found support in close friendships appeared to suffer little from lack of status in the group as a whole.

Three years later the same group of boys retained an admiration for physical skills, courage, strength and aggressiveness; but they asked also tidiness, social ease and poise, and they regarded as somewhat childish the boy who was merely boisterous and indiscriminately noisy in classroom or club. Less prestige was attached to the boy whose restlessness and untidiness led him into conflict with adult demands; and more status was accorded to the one who began to be successful in co-educational activities.

Another three years' growth brought with it further emphasis on social skills, good looks, and ability to co-operate with grown-up people. Skill in athletics had still prestige-value; but if a boy was socially mature he could win high status in group activities of various kinds through intellectual ability and academic achievement. Hetero-sexual activities occupied an increasing proportion of their leisure-time, and attractiveness to girls became one of the attributes of the ideal boy.

In similar fashion a sequence of development was traceable among groups of girls. At about twelve years of age the most admired girls were those who were friendly, pretty, tidy, sedate and only mildly interested in organised games. Tomboyish girls who were leaders in the classroom and successful in games were quite acceptable to their contemporaries, but were not imitated. (Many of these were girls whose physiological development was rather retarded but who had had marked success a few months earlier in the group activities of the elementary school playground.)

Three years later there was among the same girls a shifting to an outlook more comparable to that of the boys. Buoyancy and amiability and somewhat aggressive good sportsmanship were much admired. Ability to organise group activities was acceptable; and the girls who received high ratings from their contemporaries were those who were enthusiastic, energetic and obviously happy in the mixed-groups of the co-educational parties. These were not necessarily the same girls who had received admiration three years earlier as conforming to the adult standards of being ladylike and demure.

After another three years it became less important to be a good mixer and popular in large groups. The most admired girls were those who had become discriminating in their social contacts— who were well-groomed, sophisticated and attractive to the right boys. Skill in activities such as tennis, dancing and swimming was an advantage; but athletic prowess carried little prestige unless it was accompanied by personal charm and social ease.

The relative position of boys and girls in these co-educational groups varied from year to year. Dorothy began by being a leader—pleasant, smiling, talkative and outstandingly successful in athletic contests. Six months later she still took control in games, but at other times she retired to a seat and looked on. Her physical blooming seemed delayed. There was "a more masculine air about her in her carriage, her hair and her mannerisms". Another six months showed her as stolid, shy, self-conscious and unhappy. None of her contemporaries took any notice of her; and after another six months her reactions were definitely those of boredom and refusal to co-operate in the activities of the group. Rather different was the development of Ted, who began by being relatively small, unsuccessful in games, teased by other boys, and undesirably neat and tidy, but two years later was observed to be quite popular in club-house parties and able to avoid unfavourable mention by the other boys.

These variations in relative status were, of course, associated not merely with changes in physiological development but also with decreases or increases in contemporary approval of the patterns of behaviour fostered by the home life of each pupil. The opinion of one's contemporaries becomes of increasing import with adolescent development of awareness of the necessity for becoming independent of one's family. Its relative significance depends, however, upon one's attitude to the home and to the values recognised in the home. Acceptance by an admired group is essential for healthy functioning. There are cases in which the prestige of the family circle remains higher than that of the school group. This seems particularly true of the day school as contrasted with the boarding school and of schools whose population is drawn from a wide area as compared with schools in which the homes of the pupils are in closely adjacent streets. In such cases variations in acceptability to the school group may be seen to accompany changes in the standards of the group rather than changes in the physiological developing of the pupil. Beth, for example, in a comparable Scottish group was at eleven years of age socially competent, talkative and at ease. She showed initiative in social affairs partly because of the traditions of a home in which she was accustomed to take the part of the eldest daughter in a socially active family. Her father had a certain public position, and she was accustomed to meet and to talk to a variety of adults of differing outlooks and interests. At that time, however, her contemporaries admired quiet demure little girls and she had no particular standing at school. Her greater social maturity made her an isolate—somewhat suspected by other girls and boys. Three or four years later she had several acknowledged admirers in the school: and at eighteen, on entrance to the University, she found herself favourably regarded by many and elected for positions of trust and prestige. The change was not so much a change in Beth as a shifting in the standards and values of her contemporaries.

Other studies have been made of the qualities admired in boys and girls at different ages, both by their contemporaries and by adult parents, teachers or clinical workers. The special contribution of the California Growth Study is that it provides a consecutive record of the development of the same individuals at six-monthly intervals over the whole period of secondary education: and that the ratings summarised above from "Guess Who" tests and personality inventories were supplemented by extensive observation of the same pupils in classrooms, in playing fields and in an experimental club house. Their findings are, of course, of chief importance as a study of the background of the pupils who made up the California groups. It is not suggested that they may be taken as representative of all eleven-year-old or seventeen-year-old pupils. The picture presented is, however, recognisably akin to that familiar to any teacher who attempts to notice the spontaneous behaviour of classroom or playground. From the rough-and-tumble play of the junior to the sedate playground stalking of the senior there is an observable sequence of growth. From the disregard of appearance of the child to the acute sensitivity of the young adolescent there is an obvious development of social awareness; and at each stage there are the deviating children who find themselves alone because they are either in advance of or behind the pattern accepted by the majority of their contemporaries.[7]

Adolescence is admittedly a period of learning. Too often in the past it has been supposed that this learning was merely intellectual or physical and that its direction and control was solely in the hands of the adult organisers of activities in school or in workshop. One of the main contributions of long-term studies of adolescent development has been their emphasis both upon the variety and variability of the processes of physiological maturing and upon the complexity of the influences of boys and girls upon one another and the subtlety of their inter-relationships with the adult groups of which they form the fringe.

Emotional maturing may be conceived in the fashion described above in Chapter VII as a transition from the narrow love circle of the little child through the widening hetero-sexual interests of the adolescent to the nest-building of the young adult and the wider social sympathy of the mature citizen. It may be thought of as exemplified in the escape from the unnecessary fears of the little child through the adolescents' dread of social slighting to the relative serenity of the adult. It may be typified by the progression from the tempestuous temper-tantrums of the child essaying social control to the measured indignation of the fully grown person whose wrath is aroused more swiftly by wrongs done to others than by any personal frustrations. Social maturing may in similar fashion be described as the development from the stage of intolerant discovery of the extent of individual differences to a state in which such differences and divergencies are accepted with patience or with smiling appreciation.

Social learning in this sense is particularly relevant to the consideration of the personal and social development of adolescents in relation to their contemporaries. The adolescent who matures successfully may be said to be the one who achieves progress in four fields:

(a) the acceptance of one's self—adjustment to one's appearance and one's ability;

(b) the acceptance of one's self in relation to a group—recognition of the variability of one's status and of the specificity of leadership;

(c) the acceptance of others—their differences and the unpredictability of their behaviour;

(d) the acceptance of others in relation to oneself—the relativity of friendship and of the means by which one may make oneself acceptable to others.

Successful adjustments of these kinds are believed by most adolescents to be of primary importance—to a degree of which many adults remain largely unaware. They form the background against which all other activities are judged; and in comparison with them other forms of learning are of relatively little interest.

School subjects must be studied and vocational skills must be acquired. The real importance of this learning is, however, not so much the prestige which it earns in the eyes of the adult instructor as its social value in terms of its contribution towards acceptance by other boys or girls, by the community of girls and boys and, later, by one selected member of the opposite sex.

Learning to accept one's appearance is in many cases not an easy task. Out of one hundred boys studied in the Californian series there were ten who were two or more years retarded in physiological maturity ("in appropriate male structural and functional characteristics").[8] There were also seven who were not only retarded in the development of the expected maleness of physique but who also showed tendencies towards the normal female pattern. All of these boys found themselves unexpectedly different from their companions and experienced greater or lesser difficulties of adjustment—dependent on their earlier experiences in the more intimate circle of their home and on their present opportunities for finding satisfaction in other directions.

It was calculated[9] that at one time or another in the seven-year period about thirty-one per cent of the boys were definitely disturbed over physical characteristics such as shortness, fatness, poor physique, unusual facial features, unusual development of the nipples, lack of muscular strength, acne, bowed legs, unusually small or large genitalia or narrow shoulders.

During the same years forty-one per cent of the girls were known to suffer anxieties from such divergencies from the group pattern as excessive tallness, fatness, unusual facial features, heaviness of build, shortness, thinness, small breasts, the need for eye-glasses, squint, acne, unattractive hair, big legs or facial scars.

Such sexually inappropriate physique in the case of boys and sexually inappropriate face or figure in the case of girls provide obvious reasons for sensitivity as to personal abnormalities. Similar distress may often, however, be noted among adolescents in whom photographic records reveal no obvious peculiarity. Much of the energy of these young people in early adolescence is devoted to efforts to improve upon the realities of their physical endowment: and while a wider range of experimentation is at present permitted to girls than to boys in Europe or America, it seems true to say that most girls and boys tend to pass through a stage in which serious study is given to the effects of such attempted modifications. For some the associated disturbance is so great that normal acceptance of actual attributes is not achieved: and they grow into adults who continue to struggle with their appearance and persist in the attempt to compensate dramatically for real or imaginary defects. For the healthily developing boy or girl the period of acute concern with bodily variations is followed, however, by a stage in which keeping oneself presentable becomes part of the routine of life—one interest and activity among many, and recognisable as only one of the various means by which one becomes an acceptable member of an admired group.

Progression into this more mature state of self-respecting acceptance of oneself is assisted by the patience and serenity of adults (whether parents, teachers or employers) who attach no undue significance either to physical divergencies or to adolescent experimenting with hair oils, cosmetics or startlingly novel costumes. The adolescent may often be comforted by an absence of concern on the part of such an admired adult, or by the assurance that asymmetrical growth is but a passing phase. They may also be assisted by learning techniques of dress which render a physical defect less obvious; and they may find support in the social appreciation of some compensatory skill which permits them to make a useful contribution to the activities of a group.

Similar acceptance of one's actual powers in knowledge or in vocational skills is an accompaniment of wholesome maturing. This is not dissociated from continued enterprise and striving; but there is such a thing as a healthy awareness of one's present position on a scale representing relative degrees of ignorance–knowledge or strength–weakness.

A similar balancing of personal success and failure characterises the acceptance of one's self in one's relationships to a group. The mature individual is aware that leadership is specific—that one is sometimes a leader and sometimes a follower, that one's status varies, that one is sometimes admired and that on other occasions and in other circumstances one may expect to attract very little attention.[10] The adolescent tends to be acutely perturbed by such fluctuations. The adult who is socially mature encounters them with unruffled indifference or amused serenity.

Not all who are physically adult escape, in this sense, from the experiences of adolescence. There are some adults who remain immature to the end of their days and there are many who experience occasional regressions. The fostering of mature flexibility of relationship is now, however, recognised as part of the responsibility of a good school; and to this end use is made both of individualised methods in the classroom and of extended opportunities for social intercourse in clubrooms and playing fields. The successfully maturing adolescent is not now thought of as the dominant or arrogant senior in a hierarchical school structure, nor as the submissive and subservient junior in a patriarchal family. The ideal picture is rather of one who exhibits a blending of domination and submission in varying degrees in response to the changing requirements of differing group activities in a variety of social situations.

A similar development of social tolerance may be seen in relation to the third field—that of the surprising range of individual differences. Awareness of this is often an accompaniment of the adolescent's awakening criticism both of himself and of his relationship to the group. It is a normal sequel to the emergence of the growing child from the family-circle in which similarity rather than dissimilarity prevailed. One of the advantages of the large class over the small one (and the large school over the small one) is that it introduces the pupil to the fact of such differences at a time and in circumstances in which crucial decisions rarely require to be made. The over-protected child from a tiny school may at adolescence, or in the transition from school to work, suffer unnecessary shock through the discovery that there are others who are remarkably different from any human being who has hitherto been encountered.

The first reaction to the strange and the different tends to be one of intolerance. "Tom can't do this. He is stupid." "Mary doesn't know that. She is silly." "Jack can't run as fast as we can. He is a baby." "Ann has a swimming suit of the wrong shape. She is queer." Only at a much later stage in the development of social maturity will it be realised that: "There are nine and twenty ways of composing tribal lays, and every single one of them is right." Some approximation to such adult toleration may be noted in the social relationships of the more mature members of an adolescent group.

The fourth field for such social maturing is that of the acceptance of others in relation to oneself. This is associated with a gradual development of understanding of the relativity of friendship; and it also is more satisfactorily achieved within a group of considerable flexibility and substantial size. The socially experienced adolescent realises that there are degrees in the intimacy of friendships. Not every one is to be desired as a friend. Not all of the community are kindred spirits. The fortunate adolescent is aware that he is an acceptable member of some basic group such as his home or his most intimate circle of friends. He has had satisfaction of his basic needs through the giving and receiving of affection and through adventurous contribution to the welfare of this group. In relation to the majority of his contemporaries he can therefore accept the variability of his position on the gradient of popular–unpopular, friend–acquaintance.

To the degree to which the adolescent learns in some such fashion to accept himself without apology and to accept others without impatience or fear, he will find himself acceptable to others in a fashion related again to the nature of the contribution he can make to the attainment of the ends accepted at the time by the group.

The California Adolescent Growth Study provides an illuminating sampling of these varying forms of developing social maturity. The preferred activities, the relative status and the choice of associates among two hundred young people changed in dramatic fashion from year to year.[11] At one time a boy was an enthusiastic athlete; at another he preferred to sit and dream. For many months he declined to have anything to do with girls; and later he became one of the most accomplished dancers in the co-educational club. Most boys and girls passed through a period of lively interest in occupations such as drawing, painting, modelling, woodwork, sewing or cooking. In many cases these interests continued; but in others they were later somewhat neglected because of the greater prestige attached to academic success and the increasing attractiveness of more socialised activities of the type of discussion groups, dancing, swimming, badminton, golf or tennis.

Adjustments of this kind have to be made by most human beings, not only to a group of their own sex in the fashion preferred by many pubescents, nor to a group of boys and girls indifferently as in the case of little children; but also in relation to members of the opposite sex. The boy or girls requires, in this setting also, to accept physical and mental realities and to be unruffled by fluctuations of status and undisturbed by unexpected similarities or surprising differences of preferences, apparent attributes and performance.

The extent of many such differences and the degree of many such resemblances among groups of boys and girls are now believed to be related as much to the sex role accepted by current tradition as they are to biologically determined differences. They vary admittedly from one place to another and from one period to another:[12] and an awareness of their attitudinally controlled character is of assistance to the adult who wishes to help an adolescent to serene acceptance of the part which he is permitted to play in any given circumstances.

In some respects the conventional character of accepted masculine or feminine roles and attributes makes adjustment to present reality hard to achieve—especially in the case of girls. In Europe and in North America in relatively recent years there have been marked changes in the character of the occupations, interests and activities considered to be appropriate to women.[13] Girls are therefore somewhat more confused in their attitude than their brothers or their fathers. The standards and expectations of their homes may be in conflict with those of their schools or their workshops; and they may suffer from uncertainty as to whether their main contribution to the life-work of the community will be made through the running of a house or the undertaking of activities in office, school, factory or warehouse. The present tendency towards greater equivalence of expectation as between girls and boys is, however, an encouragement to the belief that with the removal of sex-restrictions more boys and more girls will ultimately be permitted to play a role which is suited to their individual preferences and their present abilities. The social distresses of deviating individuals will then become less acute and their path to social maturity will become more similar to that of the majority of their contemporaries.[14]

This does not mean that individual differences may be expected to disappear with modifications in social expectations and in the roles allotted to differing members of social groups. While much behaviour is attitudinally controlled and many human beings either accept their assigned roles or experience distress in rebellion against them, there seems reason to believe that there are inborn differences in potentialities and also that there is an observable relationship between certain types of behaviour and certain forms of glandular balance.[15] Changes in the strength of the tendency to dominate and modifications of manner as well as of appearance have been reported to result from alterations in gonadal balance through injections of testosterone and similar hormonal preparations. Such changes, however, may occur in women as well as in

L

men, and there is some doubt as to whether any observable increase in confidence or assertiveness is to be attributed merely to alterations in physiological functioning or partly to the satisfaction which follows from a knowledge of such changes. Certain correspondences have also been traced between personal attributes and relative degrees of "masculinity" or "femininity" of body build among male students.[16] In this connection it has, however, again to be remarked that these feminine or masculine patterns of endocrine balance or physical structure are not divisible into two clearly demarcated types of male and female. The overlapping between girls and boys and men and women is considerable: and the consequent virtual independence of dominant sex pattern and personal preferences or observable abilities is quite in line with the corresponding absence of correlation between mental development and other anatomical or physiological indices. The behaviour which is possible for any maturing adolescent is related not only to the fact that he functions predominantly as a male but also to his other potentialities as a human being. He has to make certain adjustments as he develops towards social maturity; and release from the tyranny of a predetermined social or occupational role is now serving in many cases to reduce the difficulties experienced in this period of transition to adult status.

Evidence is, in recent years, accumulating to the effect that learning of the type required in all these fields of adjustment—to the realities of one's own endowment as well as one's relationship to others—can take place best within a heterosexual group; and in this fact (coupled with the acknowledged importance of such learning) lies one of the main justifications for a co-education which extends—in normal family fashion—from the cradle to the grave.

There is nothing in the known facts as to differences of average height and weight or rate of intellectual learning to justify the belief that segregation of the sexes will result in homogeneity of groups. The standard deviations of test scores for both sexes are large. The differences within a group of boys (or of girls) are greater than any observable average differences between the sexes; and in similar fashion average differences in rate of social maturing do not justify monastic or conventual segregation. All girls do not attain social maturity at the same age and all do not follow quite the same sequence. There is also no reason to believe that the observable changes are anything but gradual; and there is no evidence of a high correspondence between such social development and either skeletal age or mental age (Research figures give correlations of + 0·19 and + 0·12 with age held constant.)[17] In similar fashion long-term studies in co-educational clubs and schools have shown that development is equally gradual in the case of groups of boys, that it is accompanied by comparable individual variations and that on the average the difference in age of social-sex maturing between groups of girls and groups of boys approximates to half a year (rather than the eighteen months or two years postulated in early discussions).

A careful following up of large groups of pupils from the ages of five to sixteen in the co-educational recreational clubs attached to the Merrill-Palmer School in Detroit resulted,[18] for example, in a confirmation of the belief that there appeared to be what can be described as three stages in the free choice of companionship among school-mates. The timing of these stages was, however, in that district very different from that used as a basis for comments upon co-education by Stanley Hall and his followers.[19] The three levels which were detected by exact recording are described as follows:

(a) one involving little sex discrimination in attitudes, contacts or choice of associates during the years of five to eight for girls and five to eight and a half for boys;

(b) one characterised by preferences for playmates of one's own sex from the ages of eight and a half to thirteen and a half in the case of girls and nine to fourteen in the case of boys; and

(c) one accompanied by attraction towards and companionship with members of the opposite sex from fourteen to sixteen for girls and from fourteen and a half to seventeen for boys.

Within these groupings, however, there were again marked fluctuations, recombinations and retentions of older attachments along with the formation of new friendlinesses. (The average differences were again accompanied by standard deviations descriptive of the scattering of test results.)

Educational or recreational segregation of the sexes could only be supported on the grounds of differences in the rate of social-sex development if it could be shown that all boys (or all girls) matured at once and to quite the same extent, and that the ages of maturing of the two groups were clearly separated. The fact that neither assumption can be shown to be valid is, however, now less surprising than it was in the years prior to the discoveries of endocrinologists as to the bisexuality of human hormonal balance. Such findings are further supported by comparable evidence as to the overlapping of the ages as between girls and boys for physical growth-spurts in height or weight, for individual development in various human abilities and for the onset of puberty as indicated by the appearance of menstruation or the discovery of spermatozoa in the morning urine.

It will be remembered (see Chapter II above) that the average differences in age between the appearance of menstruation and of seminal emissions have been estimated to approximate to not more than about six months,[20] and that when other criteria of maturity are used such as the appearance of pigmented and curly pubic hair in the case of boys there seems reason to believe that girls and boys reach comparable stages of sexual development at approximately the same ages.

Popular opinion to the effect that the maturing of girls occurs eighteen months to two years earlier than that of boys appears to be traceable partly to the repetition of Stanley Hall's eloquent pronouncements on co-education and partly to the assumption that all forms of maturation occur simultaneously and are concomitants of growth in height or weight. This assumption is not supported by any evidence from long-term studies of adolescent development.

The social significance of all statements as to "maturity" is nevertheless as yet largely conjectural. It is not yet known, for example, whether mature ova appear in the female at an earlier average age than that at which mature spermatozoa appear in the male; and even if it were known, the fact by itself would mean little.[21] The social-sex development of boys and girls from the co-educational schools and clubs of Detroit or Chicago is not necessarily quite the same as that of adolescents in other types of home or school situations. (It approximates, for example, more closely to that observable in the co-educational public schools of Scotland than it does to that in the single-sex Public Schools of England.) What can, however, be said is that, while girls as a group may be known to "mature" in some details earlier than boys and boys may prove to "mature" in some respects earlier than girls, it is not possible to make predictions as to suitable companionship from a knowledge of age alone; and only within the flexibility of a genuine co-educational grouping can provision be made for informal opportunities for social learning for each boy or girl at the time which is most propitious.

Experimentation of various sorts has been undertaken in the attempt to discover the optimum conditions for such learning. A useful analogy may be drawn from observation of the social contacts of little children. There it can be seen very clearly that there are what may be described[22] as three stages in the approach of a newcomer to a group:

(*a*) observation from a distance—more or less wistful and appreciative;

(*b*) superficially casual and non-participating engaging in a parallel activity—more or less near to the group;

(*c*) direct contact and open offers of participation—with physical entrance to the activities of the group.

In the case of little children the desired activities are those of the playground, street or nursery. They are relatively simple, and fluidity of inter-relationship is accepted by most adult spectators.

In the case of similar experimentation in social participation among adolescents the group barriers are usually more difficult to pass. Adult spectators are more critical: and the fear of rejection is correspondingly greater. For these reasons it seems important that adolescents should have a place in which their tentative approaches to participation can be made without undue publicity or distress.

In schools in which corporate living is genuine co-educational such beginnings are frequently made in casual contacts in class-rooms or corridors—in school games, debating societies, art rooms, workshops, cookery departments—where freedom of movement and shared activities encourage casual personal contacts. More deliberate provision of such opportunities is now known to be desirable both in schools and in factories.

Adolescents require chances of watching one another from a distance, of approaching without awkwardness and of joining new groups in an unobtrusive fashion. Experimentation in Californian schools[23] showed that a club-house with an entrance and an exit, a floor space large enough for dancing or ping-pong and side rooms for a variety of activities was more useful than a single room of smaller size with only one entrance and a more limited equipment of apparatus and books. Similar findings are reported from enterprising youth clubs, camps and educational institutions in many parts of the world.[24] Adolescents wish to acquire social skills. Their social maturing can be aided by the provision of such informal opportunities for learning both to accept themselves in relation to others and to accept others in relation to themselves.

The effect of this realisation of the importance of such learning may be seen partly in an increased provision of informal opportunities for social contacts and partly in widespread classroom experimentation and discussion of curriculum reform. The challenge to traditional practice has been particularly active and fruitful at the secondary level.[25] Modifications of educational procedure are not easily achieved at any stage. They are especially difficult to secure for pupils in the years immediately prior to entrance upon University, College or business when the competitive pressure of the need to excel is reinforced by the attitudes of parents, teachers and prospective employers. Even at this stage, however, there have been successful assaults upon the accepted practices of secondary schools.[26]

In America, for example, in the years from 1933–41 there was an eight-year experiment in which thirty schools and school systems co-operated in an endeavour to discover what would be the consequences of the removal of the external pressure of traditional college-entrance examinations.[27] About three hundred colleges and Universities agreed to accept candidates from these schools on the evidence of the school's record of development— without reference to the usual standards of entry. The schools were very varied in type. The modifications introduced were in many respects diverse; but all the staffs concurred in a belief in the benefits of the freedom they had won. The pupils matured into greater confidence, competence and independence; and at the same time they retained a resilience of mind which enabled them at the later stages of University or College to hold their own with graduates of similar age, sex, race and social background who had experienced the full rigours of traditional training in a control group of secondary schools. (More than fourteen hundred pairs of students were compared in respect of success in College examinations and participation in extra-curricular activities. Those from the schools where curriculum experimentation had been permitted came out a little ahead of the others according to academic standards. They were also more often reported as showing a high degree of intellectual curiosity and drive, of interest in contemporary affairs, and of social maturity and emotional stability.) The encouragement to personal and social development which had been given in the freer atmosphere of the schools which had dared to experiment had resulted in no reduction of ordinary academic standards, but had led to a greater degree of what can be described as mental health and a more satisfactory transition to the willing acceptance of adult status and mature responsibility of attitude.

REFERENCES

[1] For discussion of this see:
Mursell, J. L., *Successful Teaching*. New York: McGraw-Hill, 1954.
Fleming, C. M., *Teaching: A Psychological Analysis*. London: Methuen, 1958
and 1959; New York: John Wiley, 1958.

[2] See:
Fleming, C. M., *Research and the Basic Curriculum*. London: Univ. of London
Press, 1946 and 1952.
and, at the infant level:
Gardner, D. E. M., *Testing Results in the Infant School*. London: Methuen,
1942.

[3] Fleming, C. M., *The Social Psychology of Education*. London: Kegan Paul,
Trench, Trubner, 1944, 1959 and 1961.
Fleming, C. M., loc. cit., 1958 and 1959. [2].

[4] Information as to the California Growth Study may be found in:
Murphy, G., Murphy, L. B., and Newcomb, T. M., *Experimental Social
Psychology*. New York: Harper, 1937.
Jones, H. E., The California Adolescent Growth Study, *J. Educ. Res.*, XXXI,
8, 561–567, 1938.
Meek, L. H., *The Personal–Social Development of Boys and Girls with Implica-
tions for Secondary Education*. New York: Progressive Educ. Assoc.,
1940.
Jones, H. E., *Development of Adolescence*. New York: D. Appleton-Century,
1943.
Newman, F. B., *The Adolescent in Social Groups*. Studies in the Observation of
Personality. Stanford: Standford Univ. Press, 1946.

[5] For discussion of such processes of acculturalisation see:
Murphy, G., Murphy, L. B., and Newcomb, T. M., loc. cit. [4].
See also:
Kaplan, B. (ed.), *Studying Personality Cross-Culturally*. Evanston: Row Peterson,
1961.

[6] Tryon, C. M., Evaluations of Adolescent Personality by Adolescents, *Monogr.
Soc. Res. in Child Dev.* IV. 4. Washington: Nat. Res. Council, 1939.
This is summarised in Meek, L. H., loc. cit. [4].
Tryon, C. M., The Adolescent Peer Culture, in Jones, H. E., *et al.*, Adoles-
cence, *The Forty-third Yearbook Nat. Soc. Soc. Study Educ.* Chicago: Univ.
of Chicago, 1944.
With this may be compared:
Coleman, J. S., Johnstone, J. W. C., and Jonassohn, K., *The Adolescent
Society*. Glencoe: Free Press, 1961.

[7] A detailed case-study of the social relationships and the gradual maturing of
a physically and a physiologically retarded boy is given in:
Jones, H. E., *Development in Adolescence*. New York: D. Appleton-Century,
1943.
See also:
Cruickshank, W. M., and Johnson, G. O., *Education of Exceptional Children
and Youth*. New York: Prentice Hall, 1958.

[8] Tryon, C. M., The Adolescent Peer Culture in Jones, H. E., *et al.*, loc. cit.
[6].

[9] Stolz, H. R., and Stolz, *Adolescent Problems Related to Somatic Variations*, in Jones H. E., *et al.*, loc. cit. [6].

Stolz, H. R., and Stolz, L. M., *Somatic Development of Adolescent Boys*. New York: Macmillan, 1951.

[10] For an accessible discussion of leadership in its relations to a group see: Fleming, C. M., 1944, 1959 and 1961, loc. cit. [3].
See also:
Partridge, E. D., *Social Psychology of Adolescence*. New York: Prentice-Hall, 1939.

Fleming, C. M., 1958 and 1959. loc. cit. [1].

Klein, J., *Working with Groups*. London: Hutchinson, 1961.

[11] Meek, L. H., loc. cit. [4].

[12] Mead, M., and Wolfenstein, M., *Childhood in Contemporary Cultures*. Chicago: Univ. of Chicago, 1955.

Schneiders, A. A., *Personality Development and Adjustment in Adolescence*. Milwaukee: Bruce Publishing Company, 1960.

[13] Williams, G., *Women and Work*. London: Nicholson & Watson, 1945.

Klein, V., *The Feminine Character: History of an Ideology*. London: Kegan Paul, Trench, Trubner, 1946.

Luetkens, C., *Women and a New Society*. London: Nicholson & Watson, 1946.

Mueller, K. H., *Educating Women for a Changing World*. Minneapolis: Univ. of Minnesota Press, 1954.

[14] Mead, M., *Male and Female*. New York: William Morrow, 1949.

[15] For summaries see:
Terman, L. M., *et al.*, Psychological Sex Differences, in Carmichael, L., (ed.), *Manual of Child Psychology*. New York: John Wiley, 1954.

Anastasi, A., *Differential Psychology*. New York: Macmillan, 1958.

[16] Sheldon, W. H., and Stevens, S. S., *The Varieties of Temperament: A Psychology of Constitutional Differences*. New York: Harper, 1942.

[17] A useful description of methods of investigation is given in:
Campbell, E. H., The Social–Sex Development of Children, *Genet. Psychol. Monogr.* 21, 461–552, 1939.

[18] Ibid.
Comparable evidence from a group of six thousand members of girls' clubs in England showed (as a result of a questionnaire) that most girls of fourteen to sixteen had boy friends of the same age or not more than one year older. See:
Club Girls and their Interests. London: National Association of Girls' Clubs and Mixed Clubs. (n.d.)
For other studies of clubs in England see:
Basu, A., *A Descriptive Study of a Group of Adolescents at a Youth Club*. M.A. Thesis, Univ. of London, 1950.

Piercy, E. F., Boys' Clubs and Their Social Patterns, *Brit. J. Delinq.*, II, 3, 229–237, 1952.

Tawadros, S. M., *A Study of Group Treatment and Techniques with Special Reference to an Experience in a Therapeutic Social Club*. Ph.D. Thesis, Univ. of London, 1952.

Tawadros, S. M., Factors in Group Therapy, *Internat. J. Soc. Psychiat.*, II, 1, 44–50, 1956.

Ansari, G. A., *A Study of Attitudes and Relationships in a Group of Adolescents at a Youth Club*. M.A. Thesis, Univ. of London, 1953.

Jephcott, P., *Some Young People*. London: George Allen and Unwin, 1954.
See also:
Schneiders, A. A., loc. cit. [12].

[19] Hall, G. Stanley, *Adolescence. Its Psychology and its Relations to Physiology, Anthropology, Sociology, Sex, Crime, Religion and Education*. New York: D. Appleton, 1904.

[20] Brooks, F. D., *The Psychology of Adolescence*. Boston: Houghton Mifflin, 1929.
Campbell, E. H., loc. cit. [17].
See also:
Dennis, W., The Adolescent, in Carmichael, L. (ed.), *Manual of Child Psychology*. New York: John Wiley, 1946.
With this may be compared figures obtained by taking the breaking of the voice in boys as the criterion of maturity:
Scott, J. A., *Report on the Heights and Weights (and Other Measurements) of School Pupils in the County of London in 1959*. London County Council, 1961.

[21] A well-informed but inadequately annotated discussion of these topics may be found in:
Dunlap, Knight, *Civilised Life: The Principles and Applications of Social Psychology*. London: Allen & Unwin, 1925 and 1934.

[22] For a relevant description of the social behaviour of little children see:
Murphy, L. B., et al., *Personality in Young Children*. New York: Basic Books, 1956.

[23] Meek, L. H., loc. cit. [4].

[24] A somewhat similar conception is offered in:
Paneth, M., *Branch Street*. London: Allen & Unwin, 1944.
For discussion of the social values of club-work see:
Rogers, C. R., *The Clinical Treatment of the Problem Child*. Boston: Houghton Mifflin, 1939.
Macalister Brew, J., *Youth and Youth Groups*. London: Faber and Faber, 1957.
See also:
Observer, Young People's Colleges and Leisure Time, *Brit. J. Educ. Psychol.*, XIV, II, 80–84, 1944.
Bierer, J., *The Day Hospital*. London: H. K. Lewis, 1951.
Moreno, J. L., *Sociometry and the Science of Man*. New York: Beacon House, 1956.
Corsini, R. J., *Methods of Group Psychotherapy*. New York: McGraw Hill, 1957.
Liebermann, L. P., Joint-Interview Technique: An Experiment in Group Therapy, *Brit. J. Med. Psychol.*, XXX, 3, 202–207, 1957.
Slavson, S. R., *Child Centered Group Guidance of Parents*. New York: Internat. Univ. Press, 1958.

[25] For discussion of this in relation to problems in the United States of America:
Thayer, V. T., et al., *Reorganizing Secondary Education*. New York: D. Appleton-Century, 1939.
Blos, Peter, *The Adolescent Personality. A Study of Individual Growth*. New York: D. Appleton-Century, 1940.
Zachry, C. B., and Lighty, M., *Emotion and Conduct in Adolescence*. New York: D. Appleton-Century. 1940.
See also:
Everett, S. (ed.), *A Challenge to Secondary Education*. New York: D. Appleton-Century, 1935.
Goodykoontz, B., and Coon, B. I., *Family Living and Our Schools*. New York: D. Appleton-Century, 1941.
A not dissimilar approach in relation to the very different problems of French education may be found in:
Marcault, J. E., and Brosse, T., *L'Éducation de Demain*. Paris: Librairie Félix Alcan, 1939.

[26] Representative English experiments are described in:

Greenough, A., *Educational Needs of the 14–15 Group*. London: Univ. of London Press, 1938.

Kitchen, P. I., *From Learning to Earning*. London: Faber and Faber, 1944.

A not dissimilar approach is described in:

Glover, A. H. T., *New Teaching for a New Age*. London: Nelson, 1946.

Rowe, A. W., *The Education of the Ordinary Child*. London: Harrap, 1959.

See also:

Schreiber, D., Field Programs in Finding and Developing Talent, in Monro, J. U. (Director), *The Search for Talent*. New York: College Entrance Examination Board, 1960.

Extensive experimenting has also been undertaken in Comprehensive Schools in Sweden and in England:

Pedley, R., *Comprehensive Education: A New Approach*. London: Gollancz, 1956.

Husén, T., Interaction between Teacher and Pupil as a determinant of Motivation and Satisfaction with School Work, *Proc. XIII Congress. Internat. Assoc. Applied Psychol.*, 1958.

Husén, T., and Svensson, N., Pedagogic Milieu and Development of Intellectual Skills, *School Rev.*, 36–51, 1960.

Husén, T., *Educational Structure and the Development of Ability*. Paris: O.S.T.P., 1961.

Husén, T., *Problems of Differentiation in Swedish Compulsory Schooling*. Stockholm: Inst. Educ. Res. (n.d.).

Miller, T. W. G., *Values in the Comprehensive School: An Experimental Study*. Educ. Monogr. V. Edinburgh: Oliver and Boyd, 1961.

[27] An account of this is given in the five volumes entitled: *Adventure in American Education*.

Volume I. Aikin, W. M., *The Story of the Eight Year Study*. New York: Harper, 1942.

Volume II. Giles, H. H., *et al.*, *Exploring the Curriculum*. New York: Harper, 1942.

Volume III. Smith, E. R., Tyler, R. W., *et al.*, *Appraising and Recording Student Progress*. New York: Harper, 1942.

Volume IV. Chamberlin, D., *et al.*, *Did They Succeed in College?* New York: Harper, 1942.

Volume V. *Thirty Schools Tell Their Story*. New York: Harper, 1942. In comment on this see:

Redefer, F. L., The Eight Year Study . . . After Eight Years, *Progressive Education*, 28, 2, 33–36, 1950.

CHAPTER XII

GROUP MEMBERSHIP

Successful schooling is now admittedly defined in terms not merely of intellectual or physical growth but of personal and social development. Prowess in games and brilliance in scholarship are no longer the only acknowledged goals; but the task of the teacher is now generally believed to include the fostering of emotional and social maturity. This change of emphasis may be detected not only in discussion of curriculum-content and in comments on the attributes of a good teacher or the qualities of an admirable pupil but also in recent experimental study of the principles of grouping and the effects of group-membership upon learning.

It is hardly necessary to repeat that human beings are now recognised as being from their birth social in their nature and their attributes. Their personal development is also directly related, not only to their inherited potencies but also to the experiences they meet and the treatment they receive from day to day in the family, the school and the community.[1] Their social maturing is revealed by the degree of their toleration of others as well as by their attitude towards the role which they themselves can play in the complex functioning of the social patterns of which they form a part. They differ markedly in endowment. They are expected to play differing roles, and they wish to do so. Only in the light of some knowledge of their social relationships as well as their personal attributes can their behaviour be understood or modified.

Realisation of the importance of group membership came somewhat tardily to the schools; and much current discussion by parents and teachers is still in terms of a somewhat superficial study of the effect of membership of groups upon performances in school subjects or upon the output of new ideas after corporate discussion.[2] Investigations have, for example, been made into the relative effects of competition as contrasted with co-operation, individual activity as against team work, or isolated study as opposed to reading in the companionship of others. The effect of observers upon output has been studied in workshops and classrooms along with the modifications produced by the comparable incentives of reward, punishment, praise, blame, teasing or neglect.

It is known that companionship is not without its consequences, that work done in the presence of others is greater in quantity though often poorer in quality than that achieved alone, that the findings of group discussions are more varied in content and more voluminous than those resulting from private meditation—but not necessarily of better quality. There is evidence that work under close supervision tends to be more rapid but less accurate; and that any social increment is less for those of high intellect than of low and greater for slow workers than for those who are more swift.

The effect of competition is also known to result in greater output but in work of poorer quality; and evidence is accumulating that this is related to the fact that rivalry tends to distract the attention of the worker to anti-social and somewhat depressing thoughts. Co-operative learning appears to result in better social adjustment for both duller and brighter pupils. Accompanying it there seems to be greater satisfaction of the basic psychological needs and an obvious sequel of greater healthiness and happiness of outlook.

Awareness of success and the receiving of praise are a greater stimulation to learning than indifference and neglect on the part of one's associates; and discouragement or reproof, though they may lead to a sudden spurt, can be observed progressively to lose their effectiveness.

These findings are quite generally recognised as applicable to the deliberate use of social incentives in the conduct of class teaching in the secondary school. It is not so often realised that the same mechanisms form part of the group learning which is a universal accompaniment of the formal instruction of a classroom.

Adolescents are continuously learning through their contacts with their contemporaries. This influence of what has been called the "peer-culture" makes itself felt in fashions quite similar to those outlined above; and it is also powerful in proportion to the satisfaction it permits of the primary personal needs of the growing boy or girl.

Dominant individuals—whether adults or "peers"—make their influence felt upon a group through the prestige they win by superior prowess, by the confidence they establish and to the degree to which they commend themselves through their essential oneness or kinship with the aims and purposes of the group.

Groups in turn exert pressure through their control of admission to the inner circle of the elect, and through the signals of injury, abuse or ridicule by which they indicate their rejection of unacceptable members. By such devices they commonly limit their membership to those who are willing to conform to their code; and by similar means they retain their hold upon those who have once come within their influence. "You are one of us." "We do this." "You can't possibly do that." "None of us do that." "Good idea!" "Well done!" Praise and complimentary comments retain many members within the fold. Scorn or indifference suffice to exclude the undesired outsider.

The mechanisms have been extensively studied within the classroom. They are equally operative in playground, street, workshop or club.

Reactions to them, both in classroom and club, are now known to be attitudinally controlled. The youngster who is secure in his membership of an admired society is largely immune to the blandishments or the scorn of another social group. The requests of a teacher, a youth leader or an employer may meet with compliance, with indifference or with scorn, according to the position which he holds in the estimation of an individual or a group. Not all advice is accepted and not all instructions are followed. What will happen in any situation is related not merely to the quality of the suggestions made and the attributes of those to whom they are given, but to the group relationships subsisting within the total "field" of which any particular incident forms merely one part.

Some realisation of the complexity of these relationships and of the subtlety and sensitivity of educational processes has in recent years rendered the task of the enlightened teacher, parent or employer more difficult; but increasing awareness of the complexity of the social situation is also making more possible an appreciation of the flexibility, adaptability and modifiability of any such social relationship.

Partly because of this change in viewpoint, an understanding of methods by which desirable alterations can be wrought is more widespread than it was some years ago. Bullying and cruelty are less prevalent in classrooms or workshops. Negative reactions and hooliganism are less apparent in the streets of cities, towns or villages. There is greater understanding of the adolescent's need for acceptance, for adventure and for some share in responsibility; and in many parts of the world these requirements are to an increasing degree being met through improved attitudes in schools and factories and through extended provision for voluntary educational efforts in Youth Clubs and Evening Institutes of a variety of types.[3]

These changes are reflected in illuminating fashion in recent modifications both in the content of such discussions as to the nature of adolescence and in the expressed opinions of groups of teachers as to the relative seriousness of various forms of mis-behaviour. An investigation in the 1920s[4] into the attitudes of teachers revealed, for example, an emphasis on the desirability of silent and submissive behaviour on the part of pupils. The teachers showed that they regarded as very serious offences of an aggressive type, such as masturbation, talking, untruthfulness, truancy, impertinence, cheating, destroying school materials, dis-obedience, profanity, disorderliness in class and inattention; and they attached little importance to shyness, restlessness, sensitive-ness, over-criticism of others, unsociability and suspiciousness. (A comparable study of parental attitude a few years later[5] revealed a somewhat similar interest in the externals of conduct. The parents indicated that they considered that it was most unwise to allow aggressiveness or independence, to criticise accepted con-ventions in the presence of children or to permit children to make their own mistakes.)

Repetition of the same type of questionnaire fourteen years later[6] showed a definite shift towards closer agreement on the part of teachers with the views of those psychologists who had in 1927 emphasised the seriousness of conditions such as unsociability, suspiciousness, depression, resentfulness, timidity, discouragement, sullenness and domineering. In 1941 the teachers, with greater apparent realisation of the issues involved in social maturing and effective group membership, attached more significance to non-aggressive traits than did their predecessors in 1927.

A related increase of awareness of the significance of group relationships is revealed also in the study of the effects of variations in social climate which forms part of the subject-matter of "Field" or "Topological" psychology,[7] in the emphasis upon the varia-tions of patterns of friendliness whose investigation is included in the province of the Sociometrist[8] and in the realisation of the therapeutic effects of group discussion,[9] which appears likely to prove the most significant development in psychological interpre-tation brought to public notice by the experimental work of psychologists in the Second World War. All of these approaches have some relevance to the study of group relationships among adolescents in schools or in workshops. They may therefore briefly be considered here.

Adolescent behaviour is now recognised as a function not merely of the personal attributes and the physiological condition of an individual but also of the treatment given to him and the expectations held of him by parents, by teachers or by employers. This finding is supported by much of the evidence outlined in earlier chapters. Further experimental confirmation has also been given in an important series of studies of the changes in group tensions observable upon transition from one type of leadership[10] to another. A group of pupils was set to perform a similar series of tasks under three different types of handling—an autocratic, a *laissez-faire* and a democratic. They responded in different fashions to the three sorts of social climate. Their behaviour as a whole changed when the meaning of the task was modified. They adjusted themselves to the total "field" under each variety of educative influence.

The reality of these group relationships has not, in the past, been fully realised by teachers and administrators. Their significance has, however, probably at no point been underestimated by the pupils who have experienced their resulting tensions and who have lived within the range of their forces. Adolescents are continuously engaged in an assessment of the personal influences exerted by their elders; and they discuss these adults among themselves in no uncertain fashion. Their interest in social interactions is shown not only in such clear-sighted comments upon adult behaviour but also in a willingness to read books in which vivid distinctions are drawn between the tyrant, the fool and the friend and in which detailed descriptions are given of the sorrows and the joys of the youthful heroes and heroines who find themselves in turn neglected, appreciated, despised or persecuted. With the help of such discussion and such reading (in combination with the more deliberate educative influences of school and home), they may be observed to approach gradually to some conquest of that social maturity through which it becomes possible to accept oneself in relation to others and to accept others in relation to oneself.

Increasing realisation of the complexity of these inter-relationships between adolescents in groups—whether in schools, in clubs

GROUP MEMBERSHIP 169

or in factories—has been aided not only by group experiments of
the type described by the Field Psychologists but also by the careful
observation of personal contacts for which the term Sociometry has
relatively recently been coined.[11]

Moreno, for example, in studies of group formation reclassified
the pupils of an entire school after asking each pupil to name the
friend who was preferred as a room-mate, as a hiking companion
or as a fellow-worker in laundry, salesroom or classroom. Each
pupil was invited to express a first, a second and a third choice;
and an analysis was subsequently made of the networks of like,
dislike and indifference within each group.

Various patterns were found to emerge. There were, for example, the "isolates"—those who were chosen by no one either
as first, as second or as third choice. There were "mutual pairs",
in whose case the two individuals mentioned each other (not
necessarily in the same order of preference). There were "chains",
where A chose B, B chose C and C chose D. There were "stars",
who were asked for by several pupils at once, and there were
"triangles", where A wanted B, B chose C and C asked for A.

The pattern of preference differed for differing activities; and,
through the study of the resulting evidence of successful establishment of contacts, it became possible for the "Sociometrist" not
only to detect "isolates" who needed help in the development of
spontaneous participation in social living but also to understand the
paths taken by the suggestions and imitations which form the basis
for group action. Through such analysis of contacts light was also
shed on the functional and specific nature of leadership; and it
became possible to liberate immature personalities through permitting individuals to "find themselves" in the exercising of the
functions in which there was most promise of their becoming
socially accepted.

The importance of this work lies not only in the emphasis it
puts on the complexity of any social patterning but also in the significance it attaches to the effect of such patterning. Through a
fuller knowledge of the processes involved in inter-relationships
within groups[12] it may become possible to understand more fully
the relation of man to man and to permit free growth of social
participation not by attempting tuition or instruction from without
(with its resulting stimulation of negative reactions) but by re-
moving the barriers which, by their frustrating effects, limit the
possibility of healthy personal and social maturing.

M

The language and the procedures of Moreno's group of Socio-metrists carry with them also the implication that the leadership observable in any freely developing social pattern is not dictatorial or monarchic in its structure but democratic and diversified in its functioning. Different individuals become "stars" for differing social purposes; and any patterning within a group is not permanent but flexible.

Moreno's work, both in schools in the United States of America and in institutions for delinquent girls and camps for displaced persons in Austria at a much earlier date, implies also a faith in the primacy of the human need for friendliness of contact and a belief in the efficacy of such contact in the promotion of mental health and socialised living.

Such a faith likewise motivates an increasing number of teachers who·have come by differing routes to a knowledge of the superior effectiveness of the learning which takes place in an atmosphere of co-operative activity and trust, as contrasted with that resulting from old-fashioned classroom procedures based on an expectation of passivity on the part of pupils and of authoritarian instruction on the part of the staff.

A comparable conviction of the desirability of permitting ex-pression to pupils' judgments of and preferences for one another can be detected in many attempts at what used to be called "self-government"—the selection of school representatives by pupils and the discussion of school activities by the committees so formed. (It is observable also in the ratings of candidates for commissions by their comrades as well as by their officers which were invited in the later years of the war by British War Office Selection Boards.[13])

Human beings can be understood somewhat fully only if they are observed from many points of view. Corporate living is more successfully achieved in groups which are conscious of some degree of satisfaction for their basic psychological needs of acceptance and responsible contributing; and those institutions are more successful in which there is provision for a variety of what have been called "prestige pyramids".[14] Too often in the schools of the past there was opportunity for the experience of success only for those pupils who excelled in a limited range of school subjects or games. Too often prestige was accorded in the adult world only to those who were outstanding in the acquisition of money or of social status. Through a realisation of the existence of a variety of avenues of recognition, it is now, however, becoming possible to promote more widely the growth of mental health.

In the facilitation of such opportunities for diverse forms of leadership is to be found a further argument in favour of comprehensive secondary schools. Through the experiences of a curriculum in which a wide sampling of all human activities is given at the secondary level (as it is at the primary stage in the best present practice) it is possible not only to build more firmly an adherence to common loyalties on a basis of mutual understanding between pupils of different levels of attainment but also to fortify all pupils with the knowledge that there are many human avenues through which success and its resulting self-respect can be experienced.

Comparable with these findings from the field of the Sociometrists is the increasing efficacy now ascribed to the effect of group membership as an aid to mental therapy. Responsible contributing to the welfare of a group is an important ingredient in mental health. Fortified by experiences of such contributions in childhood and adolescence, adults are more able to withstand the shocks and sorrows of later life. Morale is highest among those who have known the satisfaction of this basic psychological need.[15]

Through deliberate utilisation of the healing effect of such contributory membership, psychologists have relatively recently come to an acknowledged awareness of the therapeutic consequences of group discussions and of group treatment which, while apparently organised by a group for other purposes, brings unsuspected benefits to the participating members.

The form taken by such group therapy varies somewhat under differing clinical conditions. It has been employed for many years in the guise of the mass instruction and "thought control" arranged by enterprising doctors for patients suffering from tuberculosis and allied diseases.[16] It has been used unofficially, and with positive or negative effects, in the waiting rooms of physicians and surgeons. "He'll soon put you right." "Her patients always get better." "I was just like that myself, but it didn't last long." "I've been coming here for years and nothing does me any good." It has been deliberately organised in the form of training for child-birth, of group discussion as a means of shortening analysis[17] and of clubs whose membership consisted of recovering patients (Recovery Inc.) who were pledged to pass on their experiences as an encouragement to their successors.[18]

Quite similar mechanisms have been observed in the benefits obtained from membership of co-operating groups of children in clinics[19] and institutions[20] and of neurotic patients in residential camps,[21] from the organised activities of prisoners of war[22] and from the deliberate acting out of disturbing situations in the life history (Psycho-drama) of perturbed patients or of problem children.[23] It has been proved that all such devices of discussion, enlightenment, encouragement, co-operation and dramatisation are of definite therapeutic effect in the establishment of mental health.

This form of therapy is not in itself new. (In certain of its forms it is not dissimilar from that implicit in any Socratic discussion.) It has long been employed by those churches which emphasise the intellectual content of their services; and it forms part of the influence of any well-balanced and active-minded community. Its relevance to a discussion of adolescent membership of school groups lies in the fact that such methods are directly in line with the therapeutic work which is daily being achieved by the skilful teacher of English, of Music, of Mathematics, of Language, of Dancing, of Science, of Art or of Handicrafts. These media are being used as a means of liberating pupils, of providing them with the satisfactions of achievement and of comforting them with the knowledge that they are not unique or peculiar but members of the great human family and compassed about with a great cloud of witnesses who share their aspirations and testify to the possibility of their triumphant living.

English as an aid to psycho-therapy;[24] literature as an aid to the exploration of life;[25] history as an occasion for the construction of life-dramas—through all of these the skilful educator is able to contribute to the personal and spiritual, as well as the intellectual and physical, maturing of the young people in his charge.

REFERENCES

[1] Fleming, C. M., *The Social Psychology of Education*. London: Kegan Paul, Trench, Trubner, 1944, 1959 and 1961.
[2] For useful summaries see:
Allport, F. H., *Social Psychology*. Boston: Houghton Mifflin, 1924.
Dashiell, J. F., in Murchison, C. (ed.), *A Handbook of Social Psychology*. Worcester: Clark Univ. Press, 1935.
Murphy, G., *et al.*, *Experimental Social Psychology*. New York: Harper, 1937.
Sprott, W. J. H., *Social Psychology*. London: Methuen, 1952.
Asch, S. E., *Social Psychology*. New York: Prentice-Hall, 1952.
Argyle, M., *The Scientific Study of Social Behaviour*. London: Methuen, 1957.
Sprott, W. J. H., *Human Groups*. London: Penguin, 1958.
Young, P. T., *Motivation and Emotion. A Survey of the Determinants of Human and Animal Activity*. New York: John Wiley, 1961.
[3] Progressive reduction in hooliganism is described in:
Lowndes, G. A. N., *The Silent Social Revolution: 1895–1935*. London: Oxford Univ. Press, 1937.
Giles, F. T., *Children and the Law*. London: Pelican Books, 1959.
For an account of youth organisations in England see:
Macalister Brew, J., *Youth and Youth Groups*. London: Faber and Faber, 1957.
For descriptions of conditions in the United States of America see the publications of the American Youth Commission.
Rainey, H. P., *et al.*, *How Fare American Youth?* New York: D. Appleton-Century, 1937. *Youth and the Future*. Washington; D.C.: American Council on Education, 1942.
and the reports of the Department of Health, Education and Welfare.
Coleman, J. S., Johnstone, J. W. C., and Jonassohn, K., *The Adolescent Society*. Glencoe: Free Press, 1961.
See also:
Gardner, J. W., *Excellence: Can We Be Equal and Excellent Too?* New York: Harper, 1961.
For discussion of industrial morale see:
Watson, Goodwin (ed.), *Civilian Morale*. Boston: Houghton Mifflin, 1942.
This may be compared with:
Brown, J. A. C., *The Social Psychology of Industry*. Penguin Books, 1954.
Paterson, T. T., *Morale in War and Work: An Experiment in the Management of Men*. London: Max Parrish, 1955.
Fogarty, M.P., *Personality and Group Relations in Industry*. London: Longmans, Green, 1956.
[4] Wickman, E. K., *Children's Behavior and Teachers' Attitudes*. New York: Commonwealth Fund, 1928.
See also:
Laycock, S. R., Teachers' Reactions to Maladjustments of School Children, *Brit. J. Educ. Psychol.*, IV, I, 11–29, 1934.
[5] Stogdill, R. M., Attitudes of Parents Towards Parental Behavior, *J. Abn. Soc. Psychol.*, XXIX, 293–297, 1934.
Stogdill, R. M., Experiments in the Measurement of Attitudes Toward Children, 1899–1935, *Child Dev.*, 7, 31–36, 1936.

[6] Mitchell, J. C., A Study of Teachers' and of Mental-Hygienists' Ratings of Certain Behavior Problems of Children, *J. Educ. Res.*, XXXVI, 292–307, 1943.

Schrupp, M. H., and Gjerde, C. M., Teacher Growth in Attitudes toward Behavior Problems of Children, *J. Educ. Psychol.*, 44, 4, 203–214, 1953.

See also:

White, M. A., and Harris, M. W., *The School Psychologist.* New York: Harper, 1961.

[7] Lewin, K., *et al.*, Patterns of Aggressive Behavior in Experimentally-created "Social Climates", *J. Soc. Psychol.*, 10, 2, 271–299, 1939.

See also:

Katz, D., *Gestalt Psychology.* Translated by R. Tyson. New York: Ronald Press, 1950.

Lewin, K., and Cartwright, D., *Field Theory in Social Science.* New York: Harper, 1951.

Escalona, S., The Influence of Topological and Vector Psychology upon Current Research in Child Development, in Carmichael, L. (ed.), *Manual of Child Psychology.* New York: John Wiley, 1954.

Fleming, C. M., *Teaching: A Psychological Analysis.* London: Methuen, 1958 and 1959; New York: John Wiley, 1958.

[8] Moreno, J. L., *Who Shall Survive?* Washington: Nervous and Mental Disease, 1934.

Moreno, J. L., *Sociometry and the Cultural Order.* Sociom. Monogr. 2, 1943.

Moreno, J. L., *Sociometry and the Science of Man.* New York: Beacon House, 1956.

Jennings, H. H., *Sociometry in Group Relations: A Work Guide for Teachers.* Washington, D.C.: Amer. Council on Educ., 1948 and 1959.

Northway, M. L., *A Primer of Sociometry.* Toronto: Univ. of Toronto Press, 1952.

See also:

Richardson, J. E., *et al.*, *Studies in the Social Psychology of Adolescence.* London: Routledge, 1951.

Moustaka, C., Sociometric Study of a Greek School, *Internat. J. Sociom. and Sociat.*, II, 1, 35–39, 1960.

Blyth, W. A. L., The Sociometric Study of Children's Groups in English Schools, *Brit. J. Educ. Studies*, VIII, 2, 127–147, 1960.

For a more abstract discussion on not dissimilar lines see:

Dodd, S. C., *Dimensions of Society. A Quantitative Systematics for the Social Sciences.* New York: Macmillan, 1942.

[9] Sutherland, J. D., and Fitzpatrick, G. A., Some Approaches to Group Problems in the British Army, in Moreno, J. L. (ed.), *Group Psychotherapy.* New York: Beacon House, 1945.

Powdermaker, F. B., and Frank, J. D., *Group Psychotherapy: Studies in Methodology of Research and Therapy.* Cambridge: Harvard Univ. Press, 1953.

[10] Lewin, K., loc. cit. [7].

See also:

Fleming, C. M., loc. cit. [1] and [7].

Anderson, H. H., *et al.*, Studies of Teachers' Classroom Personalities, *Applied Psychol. Monogr. Amer. Psychol. Assoc.*, 6, 8, 11, 1945, 1946.

Sherif, M., and Sherif, C. W., *Groups in Harmony and Tension.* New York: Harper, 1953.

Sherif, M., and Sherif, C. W., *An Outline of Social Psychology.* New York: Harper, 1956.

Jensen, G. E. (Chairman), *The Dynamics of Instructional Groups*. Chicago: Univ. of Chicago Press, 1960.
[11] Moreno, J. L., loc. cit. [8].
[12] For a very full discussion of this see:
Moreno, J. L. (ed.), *Group Psychotherapy*. New York: Beacon House, 1945.
See also:
Hamley, H. R., Training Leaders in Iraq, *Times Educ. Sup.*, March 18, 1944.
Flack, W. S., An Experimental Farming Camp School, *Brit. J. Educ. Psychol.*, XV, I, 41–54, 1945.
Cartwright, D., and Zander, A., (ed.), *Group Dynamics: Research and Theory*. New York: Row Peterson, 1953.
Thelen, H. A., *Dynamics of Groups at Work*. Chicago: Univ. of Chicago Press, 1954.
Klein, J., *Working with Groups*. London: Hutchinson, 1961.
[13] Sutherland, J. D., and Fitzpatrick, G. A., loc. cit. [9].
Experimentation with democratic methods of leadership is described also in:
Bavelas, A., and Lewin, K., Training in Democratic Leadership, *J. Abn. Soc. Psychol.*, 37, 1, 115–119, 1942.
Coch, L., and French, J. R. P., Overcoming Resistance to Change, in Swanson, G. E., *et al.*, *Readings in Social Psychology*. New York: Henry Holt, 1952.
Katz, D., and Kahn, R. L., Some Recent Findings in Human Relations Research in Industry, in Swanson, G. E., ibid.
[14] Warner, W. L., Havighurst, R. J., and Loeb, M. B., *Who Shall be Educated?* London: Kegan Paul, Trench, Trubner, 1946.
[15] Watson, G. (ed.), loc. cit. [3].
[16] Pratt, J. H., The Class Method of Treating Consumption in the Homes of the Poor, *J. Amer. Med. Assoc.*, 49, 755, 1907. Cited Bierer, J., Group Psychotherapy, *Brit. Med. J.*, 14, 214–217, 1942.
Pratt, J. H., The Group Method in the Treatment of Psychosomatic Disorders, in Moreno, J. L., (ed.), loc. cit. [12].
[17] For an accessible summary see:
Bierer, J., loc. cit. [16].
See also:
Schilder, P., The Analysis of Ideologies as a Psycho-therapeutic Method Especially in Group Treatment, *Amer. J. Psychiat.*, 93, 601–617, 1936.
Wender, L., The Dynamics of Group Psychotherapy and its Application, *J. Nerv. Ment. Dis.*, 84, 1, 54–60, 1936.
Snowden, E. N., Mass Psychotherapy, *Lancet*, 769, 770, 1940.
Jones, M., Group Psychotherapy, *Brit. Med. J.*, 276–278, 1942.
Blair, D., Group Psychotherapy for War Neuroses, *Lancet*, 204, 205, 1943.
Bion, W. R., and Rickman, J., Intra-Group Tensions in Therapy, *Lancet*, 678, 1943.
Bierer, J., A New Form of Group Psychotherapy, *Proc. Roy. Soc. Med.*, 208, 209, 1943.
Foulkes, S. H., and Lewis, E., Group Analysis. A Study in the Treatment of Groups on Psycho-Analytic Lines, *Brit. J. Med. Psychol.*, XX, 2, 175–184, 1944.
Rome, H. P., Military Group Psychotherapy in Solomon, H. C., and Yakovlev, P. I., *Manual of Military Neuropsychiatry*. Philadelphia: Saunders, 1944.
Strauss, E. B., Strom-Olsen, R., and Bierer, J., A Memorandum on Therapeutic Social Clubs in Psychiatry, *Brit. Med. J.*, 861, 1944.

For a comparable account from the United States of America see:
Katz, E., A Social Therapy Program for Neuropsychiatry in a General Hospital, *Psychol. Bull.*, 42, 10, 782–788, 1945.
See also:
Viets, H. R., Neuropsychiatric Experiences of the Foreign Armies as Reflected in the Current Literature, in Solomon, H. C., and Yakovlev, P. I., *Manual of Military Neuropsychiatry*. Philadelphia: Saunders, 1944.
Bierer, J. (ed.), *Therapeutic Social Clubs*. London: H. K. Lewis (n.d.).
Bierer, J., *The Day Hospital*. London: H. K. Lewis, 1951.
Jones, M., *Social Psychiatry*. London: Tavistock Publications, 1952.
Corsini, R. J., *Methods of Group Psychotherapy*. New York: McGraw Hill, 1957.
[18] Low, A. A., The Combined System of Group Psychotherapy and Self-Help as Practised by Recovery, Inc., in Moreno, J. L. (ed.), loc. cit. [12].
[19] Slavson, S. R., *An Introduction to Group Therapy*. New York: Commonwealth Fund, 1943.
See also:
Miller, C., and Slavson, S. R., Integration of Individual and Group Therapy in the Treatment of a Problem Boy, *Amer. J. Orthopsychiat.*, IX, 792–797, 1939.
Martin, A. R., Psychiatry in a Boys' Club, *Amer. J. Orthopsychiat.*, IX, 123–135, 1939.
Tawadros, S. M., A Study of Group Treatment and Techniques with Special Reference to an Experience in a Therapeutic Social Club, Ph.D. Thesis, Univ. of London, 1952.
Tawadros, S. M., Factors in Group Therapy, *Internat. J. Soc. Psychiat.*, II, 1, 44–50, 1956.
This may be compared with descriptions of the behaviour of deprived London children in:
Paneth, M., *Branch Street*. London: Allen & Unwin, 1944.
See also:
Fromm-Reichmann, F., and Moreno, J. L., *Progress in Psychotherapy*. New York: Grune and Stratton, 1956.
[20] Aichhorn, A., *Wayward Youth*. London: Putnam, 1936.
Rogers, C. R., *The Clinical Treatment of the Problem Child*. Boston: Houghton Mifflin, 1939.
See also:
Bender, L., Group Activities on a Children's Ward as Methods of Psychotherapy, *Amer. J. Psychiat.*, 93, 1151–1173, 1937.
Curran, F. J., The Drama as a Therapeutic Measure in Adolescents, *Amer. J. Orthopsychiat.*, IX, 215–231, 1939.
Durkin, H. E., Dr. John Levy's Relationship Therapy as Applied to a Play Group, *Amer. J. Orthopsychiat.*, IX, 583–597, 1939.
Axline, V. M., *Play Therapy*. Boston: Houghton Mifflin, 1947.
This may be compared with:
Dixon, C. M., *High, Wide and Deep*. London: Allen & Unwin, 1939.
See also:
Solomon, J. C., Group Psychotherapy for Withdrawn Adolescents, *Amer. J. Dis. Children*, 68, 2, 87–101, 1944.
Fleming, C. M., Participation as a Therapeutic Agent, *Internat. J. Soc. Psychiat.*, IV, 3, 214–20, 1958.
Fleming, C. M., Therapies in the School Situation, *Acta. Psychotherap.*, 7, Supplement, 117–123, 1959.
[21] Bion, W. R., and Rickman, J., loc. cit. [17].
Sutherland, J. D., and Fitzpatrick, G. A., loc. cit. [9].

[22] Jones, M., Rehabilitation of Forces Neurosis Patients to Civilian Life, *Brit. Med. J.*, 533–535, 1946.
See also:
Wilson, A. T. M., The Serviceman Comes Home, *Pilot Papers*, I, 2, 9–28, 1946.
Wilson, A. T. M., *et al.*, Transitional Communities and Social Re-Connection, in Swanson, G. E., *et al.*, loc. cit. [13].
[23] Moreno, J. L. (ed.), loc. cit. [12].
See also:
Jones, M., loc. cit. [17].
Hendry, C. E., Lippitt, R., and Zander, A., *Reality Practice as Educational Method*. Psychodrama Monogr. 9. New York: Beacon House, 1944.
Shoobs, N. E., *Psychodrama in the Schools*. Psychodrama Monogr. 10. New York: Beacon House, 1944.
Wilkinson, O. M., *First Report of Experiments in Drama Carried out in Community House, Glasgow*. Glasgow: Community House, 1946.
Moreno, J. L., *Psychodrama*. New York: Beacon House, 1946 and 1959.
Haas, R. B., (ed.), *Psychodrama and Sociodrama in American Education*. New York: Beacon House, 1949.
[24] Fleming, C. M., loc. cit. [7].
Fleming, C. M., Reading as an Aid to Psycho-Therapy, *Higher Educ. J.*, 23, March 1945.
Fleming, C. M., *Research and the Basic Curriculum*. London: Univ. of London Press, 1946 and 1952.
Wood, A. B., Psychodynamics through Literature, *Amer. Psychologist*, 10, 1, 32–33, 1955.
[25] Rosenblatt, L. M., *Literature as Exploration*. New York: D. Appleton-Century, 1938.
Wunsch, W. R., and Albers, E., *Thicker than Water*. New York: Appleton-Century, 1939.
Lenrow, E., *Reader's Guide to Prose Fiction*. New York: D. Appleton-Century, 1940.
Raushenbush, E. (ed.), *Literature for Individual Education*. New York: Columbia Univ. Press, 1942.
For a somewhat similar list see also:
Littérature Enfantine et Collaboration Internationale. Genève: Bureau International d'Éducation, 1932.
A description of comparable experimentation with younger pupils is given in:
Stevenson, E., *Home and Family Life Education in Elementary Schools*. New York: John Wiley, 1946.
For discussion of analogous topics, see also reports of committees of the Commission on Secondary School Curriculum of the Progressive Education Association (1934 to 1939); and publications of the National Council of Teachers of English (notably 1945 and 1950).

CHAPTER XIII

SOCIAL ENGINEERING IN THE SCHOOL SETTING

Not all pupils are to be found in the classrooms of the "skilled educators", and even the wisest of teachers may occasionally stumble in his treatment of the adolescents in his charge. Human relationships present difficulties in school as well as at home; and there are problems peculiar to the personal experiences of both adults and children within the school community.

Certain of these problems are related to the special task of the school as an institution in which learning is deliberately to be effected. In the earlier days in which emphasis was exclusively put upon the school as a place for intellectual stimulation there was special distress attached to scholastic failure; and it was most often in relation to individual differences in attainment that defeat[1] was met by pupils and the complementary temptation to contempt and scorn was experienced by teachers. Both continuous shame and too much awareness of superiority are damaging to mental health; and schoolrooms in consequence were often places in which "problem pupils" and "problem teachers" exasperated one another to an unnecessary degree.

The teacher can do what his pupils cannot do. The teacher knows and his pupils are ignorant. The adolescent in school, therefore, tends to be continuously in the position of the one who is duller, weaker, less well informed and the recipient of instruction; and there is thus a considerable measure of inadequacy and resulting insecurity inherent in the school pattern.

In schools, however (as in homes), this inescapable concomitant of youth need not lead directly to symptoms of distress if opportunities are provided for other forms of satisfaction of the basic human needs. The self-esteem which results from responsible contributing to group welfare can do much to redress the balance. Changes in the social climate of schools come only gradually, and it has to be admitted that all schools do not yet foster an atmosphere of tolerance, happiness and encouragement. On the whole, however, there has been an appreciable shift[2] from an emphasis on passive learning, on docility and on silence to an appreciation of the value of active co-operation and of willing acknowledgment of interest.

This has been accompanied by changes in the interpretation of the process of learning[3] from that which, in earlier centuries, laid stress on the "impressing" of ideas on a "blank tablet" through a Thorndikian insistence on the mechanisms inherent in the establishment of bonds and a "behavioristic" emphasis on habit-formation[4] to the more flexible interpretation which admits the adaptability and educability both of the individual and his human environment[5] and describes the subtleties of their interaction in terms of the complexities of a pattern, an object in a field or a figure seen over against its ground.

Adolescent pupils wish to learn. At the same time they wish to instruct. They desire to do new things, and at the same time they wish to go on doing the things which they have always done. They crave originality.[6] They think of themselves as unique. They are thrilled by their own ingenuity and initiative. At the same time they wish to be accepted as members of a group. They hope to be recognised as indistinguishable from the others—to be admittedly as clever, as smart, as handsome, as good, as correctly dressed, as socially polished as any one in the admired circle of their associates. "We do this." "We think this." "We wear this." "I am one of them—accepted by them."

The flexibility and complexity of this pattern is, however, not characteristic of adolescence alone. It is an attribute of all living; and changes in its content are not now believed to occur suddenly at any one age even in relation to the somewhat spectacular physiological development of puberty. As in the case of other forms of maturing, any modifications are gradual and any shift in emphasis is almost imperceptible. Careful observation of the same children over a number of years seems to indicate also that the experience does not merit the descriptions formerly given to it in terms of the emotionally toned and distressful concept of "conflict". It is less a matter of "warfare" either within an individual and his environment than a part of the process of social maturing—a development towards the blending of attitudes which characterises the mentally healthy adult who is able to accept himself as both follower and leader, teacher and learner, popular and unpopular, the same and different.

Efforts to modify the school so as to render more easy these processes of learning have taken various forms. Pupils admittedly differ in rate and degree of educability; and certain proposals to meet these differences have been made in most countries where widespread education has been attempted. (These have been referred to in Chapter IX and Chapter X above; but their recall here is not irrelevant.)

Pupils differ. These differences may be met by providing variety of stimulation and by arranging for such modifications of teaching methods as will permit each child to advance at his own rate within a framework of co-operative endeavour.[7] This is the type of solution which has, in most countries, had its origin in successful experiments by teachers and research workers. An alternative proposal came from those responsible for educational administration—to the effect that the differences might be neutralised by the device of classification into homogeneous groups. Selection of pupils to form these homogeneous groups was attempted by various means.[8] Separation was arranged in some districts in terms of mental age, and, in others, in terms of subject-age or of so-called aptitude for a specified type of learning. Deliberate modification of treatment at the age of eleven or twelve was also supported on the grounds that "psychological changes of profound significance" occurred at the time of puberty; and after such rearrangements and their accompanying segregation had been effected it was commonly supposed that pupils would remain in the categories in which they had been placed and that rapid class tuition of homogeneous groups would thereafter be possible.

As has been indicated above, these nineteenth-century assumptions have not found support in twentieth-century records of the behaviour of pupils who have been followed through the years of their adolescence. Pupils have not remained in the ability-groups into which they were put. Variations and variability have characterised their growth; and the process of maturing has proved to be describable rather as a gradual infiltration into adult territory than as a sudden assault, a new birth or the crossing of a rubicon. "Psychological changes of profound significance" are now no longer believed to occur at a specified date in the life of a child. Not a little of the distress which many adolescents have experienced in the school situation is now known to be attributable to misguided attempts at unjustifiable segregation and regimentation. The experiences of failure and disappointment which have been the frequent accompaniments of such classifying[9] have been proved to result in delinquency—as well as in habit disorders such as enuresis, persistent disobedience and lack of concentration. They have also in many instances been accompanied by sexual perversions of greater or lesser degree, since such experimentation (in word or deed) is, in quite comparable fashion, useful as a device for securing the social prestige denied to many duller members of an unhappy school community. It is not without significance that simple modifications of attitudes, methods and school organisation which resulted in greater experience of success and more confident participation in school activities have been followed by the disappearance of such symptoms in the lives of many adolescents.

Treatment of delinquency in earlier centuries took no other form than direct punishment for specified misdemeanours. Use of that method of direct assault was followed by a period in which psycho-analytic attacks were made upon the attitudes of the delinquents; and that, in turn, has been succeeded by an endeavour to interpret the behaviour of the individual in the light of his total history and all his social relationships. This social interpretation is now further supplemented by a species of "social engineering" exemplified by the work of topological psychologists, sociometrists, gestalt psychologists, and social psychologists. Adolescents at school are now being helped through awareness of the complexity of the interaction between them and their environment. Situational treatment and the therapy of groups (to use the language not of teachers but of psychologists) are being employed by many successful teachers; and the pupils of such teachers are finding too many opportunities for spontaneous participation in social living to have interest to spare for delinquencies, perversions and bad habits—many of which are now recognised as signals of distress from adolescents whose schooling is imperfectly adjusted to their needs.

Not least among the modifications of the school "situation" implicit in such environmental treatment have been apparently small changes in the attitudes of teachers.[10] An increase in the frequency of commendation, a reduction in the number of commands, a modification in teaching methods so that success instead of failure is possible, changes in textbooks so that some measure of self-instruction is achieved, a rearrangement of groups so that companionship with one's contemporaries is possible—all such apparently trifling changes have been proved in the life-history of some adolescent to produce such a modification of the total pattern that adjustment could occur and a more wholesome attitude became attainable.

Similar changes appear to have been effected through the sheer stimulus of a new experience—tuition by a new teacher, the unsupervised writing of a play or the development of a corporate enterprise, a school journey, a camping expedition, an interview by a stranger or a visit to a Child Guidance Clinic—especially where such social adventures have been impressively staged. The effect of such experiences (as of all others) depends again upon their meaning for the pupil. They may seem a mere continuance of undesirable interference and instruction. They may bring new hope to a child who has suffered from despair.

To the adult these things may appear small. To the adolescent who is as yet a learner they may make the difference between an environment in which his difficulties are too great to be faced and one in which he is able to believe in the general friendliness and adequate security of his life-space within the school.

The teacher who has learned to stop scolding, the school which has ceased to attach undue penalties to defeat (like the parent who is aware of the human need for success and responsible contributing) have gone far to improve the morale of the adolescent and to preserve for him a desirable absence of storm and stress in the years of his scholastic transition from the dependency of childhood to the personal responsibility for learning which is characteristic of maturity.

REFERENCES

[1] For summaries of research evidence relating to backwardness see:
Schonell, F. J., *Backwardness in the Basic Subjects*. Edinburgh: Oliver & Boyd, 1942.
Cruickshank, W. (ed.), *Psychology of Exceptional Children and Youth*. New York: Prentice-Hall, 1955.

[2] See:
Fleming, C. M., *Research and the Basic Curriculum*. London: Univ. of London Press, 1946 and 1952.

[3] For discussions of the psychology of learning see:
Morris, R., *The Quality of Learning*. London: Methuen, 1951.
Smith, F. V., *The Explanation of Human Behaviour*. London: Constable, 1951 and 1960.
Hilgard, E. R., *Theories of Learning*. New York: Appleton-Century, Crofts, 1958.
Broadbent, D. E., *Behaviour*, London: Eyre and Spottiswoode, 1961.
See also:
Magne, O., *Perception and Learning*. Uppsala: Appelbergs Boktryckeri, 1952.
Harris, T. L., and Schwahn, W. E., *Selected Readings on the Learning Process*. New York: Oxford Univ. Press, 1961.
Frandsen, A. N., *Educational Psychology. The Principles of Learning in Teaching*. New York: McGraw-Hill, 1961.

[4] Interpretations in terms of conditioning may be found in:
Miller, N. E., and Dollard, J., *Social Learning and Imitation*. New Haven: Yale Univ. Press, 1941.
Allport, F. H., *Theories of Perception and the Concept of Structure*. New York: John Wiley, 1955.
Bugelski, B. R., *The Psychology of Learning*. New York: Henry Holt, 1956.

[5] Interpretations in terms of a Gestalt or field psychology may be found in:
Katz, D., *Gestalt Psychology*. Translated by R. Tyson. New York: Ronald Press, 1950.
Lewin, K., and Cartwright, D., *Field Theory in Social Science*. New York: Harper, 1951.
Escalona, S., The Influence of Topological and Vector Psychology upon Current Research in Child Development, in Carmichael, L. (ed.), *Manual of Child Psychology*. New York: John Wiley, 1954.
See also:
Johnson-Abercrombie, M. L., *The Anatomy of Judgment*. London: Hutchinson, 1960.
Mowrer, O. H., *Learning Theory and the Symbolic Processes*. New York: John Wiley, 1960.

[6] For a clear statement on this see:
Debesse, M., *Essai sur la crise d'Originalité Juvénile*. Paris: Alcan, 1937. Cited Guillaume, P., *La Psychologie de l'Enfant*. Philosophie VII. 873, 1940.

[7] Fleming, C. M., *Teaching: A Psychological Analysis*. London: Methuen, 1958 and 1959; New York: John Wiley, 1958.

[8] Coxe, W. W., *et al.*, The Grouping of Pupils, *Thirty-fifth Yearbook Nat. Soc. Study Educ.* Part I. Bloomington: Public School Publishing Company, 1936.

Jensen, G. E., (Chairman), *The Dynamics of Instructional Groups.* Chicago: Univ. of Chicago Press, 1960.

9 Moodie, W., *The Doctor and the Difficult Child.* New York: Commonwealth Fund, 1940.

Plant, J. S., *Personality and the Cultural Pattern.* New York: Commonwealth Fund, 1937.

10 For a description of the development of such changes see:

Bavelas, A., and Lewin, K., Training in Democratic Leadership, *J. Abn. Soc. Psychol.,* 37, 1, 115–119, 1942.

Arbuckle, D. S., *Teacher Counseling.* Cambridge: Addison-Wesley Press, 1950.

Redl., F., and Wattenberg, W. W., *Mental Hygiene in Teaching.* New York: Harcourt-Brace, 1951.

Corey, S. M., *Action Research to Improve School Practices.* New York: Teachers College, Columbia Univ., 1953.

Oeser, O. A. (Ed.), *Teacher, Pupil and Task.* London: Tavistock Publications, 1955.

Moustakas, C. E., *The Teacher and the Child.* New York: McGraw-Hill, 1956.

See also:

Husén, T., Interaction between Teacher and Pupil as a Determinant of Motivation and Satisfaction with School Work, *Proc. XIII Congress Internat. Assoc. Applied Psychol.,* 1958.

Barnes, J. B., *Educational Research for Classroom Teachers.* New York: Putnam, 1960.

See also:

Hagan, M., and Wright, E., Psychodramatic Technique as a Teaching Device, in Moreno, J. L., *Group Psychotherapy: A Symposium.* New York: Beacon House, 1945.

French, J. R. P., Role-Playing as a Method of Training Foremen, in Moreno, J. L., ibid.

Moreno, J. L., *Psycho-drama.* Volume I. New York: Beacon House, 1946.

Rohrer, J. H., and Sherif, M. (ed.), *Social Psychology at the Crossroads.* New York: Harper, 1951.

Redl, F., and Wineman, D., *Controls from Within.* Glencoe: Free Press, 1952.

Sherif, M., and Sherif, C. W., *Groups in Harmony and Tension.* New York: Harper, 1953.

Bray, D. H., *A Study of Personal Attributes and Roles Favoured by Boys and Girls Aged Eleven to Thirteen Years,* Ph.D. Thesis, Univ. of London, 1961.

PART III
ON THE THRESHOLD OF MATURITY

N

CHAPTER XIV

EDUCATIONAL AND VOCATIONAL GUIDANCE

The Way Out of School

The route taken on the way out of school is determined in certain important respects by the experiences of a pupil within the school community. Success at later stages is related not merely to the initial ability shown in an entrance examination but to the type of training given in school, the encouragement received at home and in the classroom, the wishes of the pupil and the degree to which his basic psychological needs have received satisfaction within the school.

Pupils require acceptance in the school group. They need adventures in learning. They require opportunities for the exercise of responsibility. They need success; and they need assistance in the solving of the questions they ask as to the part their life may play in a wider scheme of existence. Their happiness and their healthy mental functioning appear to be related to the degree to which these requirements are met; and, other things being equal, the length of their continuance at school seems also to be directly connected with the extent of such basic satisfactions.[1] In countries in which free participation in continued schooling is encouraged, the age of leaving school has been shown to be more directly related to school experiences of success than to the occupation of the parents, to socio-economic level or to initial performance at the stage of an entrance examination. The type of employment which can be secured on leaving school is, to this extent, directly associated with the nature of the satisfactions provided in the school setting. It is also, of necessity, dependent upon the vocational opportunities available in the district, upon the economic status of the home and upon the attitude towards immediate earning which has been encouraged by parents, relatives and associates.[2]

Assistance in the choice of suitable employment is now in many countries coming to be recognised as an essential activity of the secondary school; and it is beginning also to be admitted that such assistance is intimately related to the treatment and the content of the courses attempted by the pupil in the last few years prior to the actual date of leaving.

A successful programme of vocational guidance in any district is necessarily dependent upon a careful analysis of the skills and attitudes required in each available occupation—coupled with a study of the present abilities and the personality of the candidates who are in search of employment.[3] Its problem is to match job analysis with personnel analysis in such a way that, through the fullest possible functioning, each individual may contribute most fully to the welfare of the group and secure most readily the personal satisfactions consequent upon such contribution.

Expressed in such terms, this seems a task beyond the powers and the resources of ordinary teachers in ordinary schools. In effect, however, the problem always narrows itself to the question as to whether Beth should train to be a doctor or a teacher, whether George should go in for engineering or enter a chemist's shop, whether John should become a telegraph boy or should go to sea.

A full consideration of the methods and the implications of vocational guidance is beyond the scope of this discussion. Evidence is, however, readily accessible as to the marked improvements in vocational adjustment effected by the application of skilled observation and expert testing to the study of the social circumstances, the physique, personal attributes, attainments and interests of boys and girls in search of a suitable career. The techniques of vocational guidance, like those of educational guidance, have passed in succession from the impressionistic methods of the unstandardised interview through the single testing or controlled interview at the end of a school career to an acceptance of the claim that vocational guidance can most fairly be given by a study of development over a number of years in terms of the findings of cumulative recording[4] of some kind and in the light of continuous remedial tuition.

Within the school setting it can readily be shown that a group which is homogeneous in September in respect of mental age, of subject age, of so-called aptitude or of physiological age will prove heterogeneous by December. Some pupils will have been absent. Some will have been ill. Others will have experienced bereavement. Some will have been emotionally upset. Others will have decided that they do not wish to learn. Some, for an apparently irrelevant reason, will have begun to find the topic supremely interesting. No exact prediction of any of these happenings is possible; but it is now generally admitted that, in view of the personal variability of human development, it is wiser to attempt a progressive adaptation of tuition to individual differences (and to encourage children by individualised activities to proceed as swiftly as they can) than it is to spend time first upon classifying according to ability and then upon mass teaching of supposedly homogenous groups.

In similar fashion the relevance of observable interests to the vocational guidance of adolescents is now being recognised[5] and

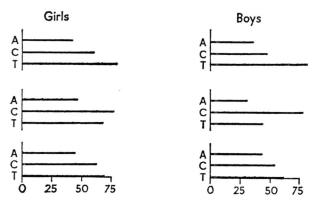

FIG. X. Interest profiles of three girls and three boys, Grammar School pupils, age 13 years. A: Interest in ideas; C: Interest in people; T: Interest in things. Fleming, C. M., Cotswold Personality Assessment: a test of adolescent interests. Glasgow: Robert Gibson. 1960.

emphasis is being put upon the part which is played in the later vocational success of adults by their social relationships, mental health, interests and wishes. While there is some positive correlation between the initial score of a group in a battery of analytic tests of aptitude and their later competence in the more complex skills demanded by entrance to a trade or to professional life, the exact degree of prediction for any one individual is not high.

Within the field of training the correlations between initial score in an individual performance test and technical school success four years later are, for example, of the order of + 0·15, + 0·01, + 0·28 for single tests, while those for batteries of performance tests range from + 0·30 to + 0·54. In contrast to this, the first-year grades within the training situation yield correlation coefficients of the order of $+$ 0·84. Similar findings come from University Colleges and from schools for dental students.[6] The predictive value of achievement tests applied after actual trial of the courses is higher than that of the most skilled single testing of so-called aptitudes. The explanation of this appears to be that the response to a working situation is affected by and is a reflection of the reactions of the person as a whole. Adjustment, if it is to be successful, must take account of this developing personality, and guidance, to be effective, must be both continuous and flexible.

These findings as to individual variability and susceptibility to training find support in the records of the inadequacy of mere ability testing and aptitude testing of the recruits who required allocation in the Army.[7] They are in line with recent developments in interpretation of the process of learning from an emphasis on the discrete activities of an individual to an awareness of the complexity and the interrelatedness of all forms of human functioning.

What, then, can be done at the stage of early adolescence when for many pupils there are economic and social as well as administrative reasons for making a vocational decision?

As has been indicated above in Chapter X, there is reason to believe that a solution to this problem is being found in the preliminary admission of all candidates to a wide variety of secondary courses followed at a later date by tentative decisions based both upon expressed vocational wishes and interests, upon vocational openings and upon success in the subjects so far attempted. This advance from selection and segregation at an early age to the provision of continuous many-sided educational stimulation for all pupils is comparable in certain respects to the development of the technique of officer selection in the British Army to which reference has already been made. The old-fashioned procedure in military circles was not dissimilar to the out-moded school technique of the face-to-face interview of an isolated pupil by a small panel of adults.[8] It left behind it the same sense of unfairness and a similar suspicion of injustice, and it resulted in a comparable number of misfits. Greater reliability and marked improvement in morale followed upon a fuller study of interests as well as of abilities coupled with observation over a longer period of the social reactions of the candidates as members of a leaderless group engaged upon corporate solution of a problem of the type which was later to challenge their powers in a real-life situation. This was combined with individual tests of ingenuity and enterprise, group discussions of relevant topics and experiments devised to provide opportunities for the exercise of organising ability and group leadership.[9]

In similar fashion, a child aged thirteen or fourteen after two or three years of exploratory activity in a well-balanced and comprehensive secondary curriculum is in a much better position both to know his own preferences and to reveal his personal reactions and his powers. His performance at thirteen or fourteen will also be nearer to his performance at fifteen or seventeen than it was at the early age of eleven. (It is probably largely for this reason that the degree of correlation with later success can usually be reported to be somewhat higher at thirteen or fifteen than at eleven.) If the years of schooling have been wisely employed—with due attention to the activities and the occupations of the society in which he lives—he will also have more idea as to what is required in the types of employment open to him; and it will become progressively more possible for his teachers to direct his attention to intelligent preparation for a "suitable" vocation.

Such guidance of interest and analysis of occupations, combined with supervised visits to local works and friendly discussions with representatives of various professions, are already among the devices by which certain teachers are assisting in the choice by their pupils of a suitable route out of school.[10] Fortunate are the children whose schools make provision for the possibility of such informed judgments upon the direction of their vocational decisions.

It is now, however, realised more fully than it was in the 1930s that vocational guidance does not end at this stage of allocation to a specific occupation. To be satisfactory, guidance must be a continuous process implying the co-operation both of employees and of management. Success in the activities of adult life (like success in schools or success in the Armed Forces) is related to the development and the co-operation of the whole person. It is affected by social relationships, by opportunities for responsible contributing and by insight into the meaning of that contribution. While the low degree of predictive certainty of a single testing is a reminder of the complexity of human functioning, the improvements in adaptation effected by skilled vocational guidance are an index to the educability of human beings and provide a justification for the emphasis on wholesome maturing which is beginning to characterise progressive industries as well as enlightened schools.[11]

REFERENCES

[1] McQueen, H. C., *et al.*, *The Background of Guidance*. New Zealand Council Educ. Res., 1941.
Similar findings as to completion of College Courses are reported in the studies from Sarah Lawrence College summarised in:
Murphy, L. B., and Ladd, H., *Emotional Factors in Learning*. New York: Columbia Univ. Press, 1944.
Pedley, R., *Comprehensive Education: A New Approach*. London: Gollancz, 1956.
McIntosh, D. M., *Educational Guidance and the Pool of Ability*. London: Univ. of London Press, 1959.
Husén, T., Interaction between Teacher and Pupil as a Determinant of Motivation and Satisfaction with School Work, *Proc. XIII Congress Internat. Assoc. Applied Psychol.*, 1958.
Husén, T., and Svensson, N., Pedagogic Milieu and Development of Intellectual Skills, *School Rev.*, 36–51, 1960.
Husén, T., *Educational Structure and the Development of Ability*. Paris: O.S.T.P., 1961.
Husén, T., Problems of Differentiation in Swedish Compulsory Schooling. Stockholm: Inst. Educ. Res. (n.d.).
Miller, T. W. G., *Values in the Comprehensive School: An Experimental Study*. Educ. Monogr. V. Edinburgh: Oliver and Boyd, 1961.

[2] See:
McQueen, H. C., *et al.*, loc. cit., for a discussion of the background of guidance in New Zealand and, for a comparable study of the challenge of unequal opportunities in the United States of America, see:
Warner, W. L., Havighurst, R. J., and Loeb, M. B., *Who Shall be Educated?* London: Kegan Paul, Trench, Trubner, 1946.
See also:
Floud, J. E., *et al.*, *Social Class and Educational Opportunity*. London: Heinemann, 1957.
Fraser, E., *Home Environment and the School*. Univ. of London Press, 1959.
Monro, J. U. (Director), *The Search for Talent*. New York: College Entrance Examination Board, 1960 (*passim*).

[3] On vocational guidance see:
Rodger, A., and Davies, J. G. W., Vocational Guidance and Training in *Chambers' Encyclopaedia*. London: Newnes, 1950.
Smith, M., *An Introduction to Industrial Psychology*. London: Cassell, 1952.
Arbuckle, D. S., *Student Personnel Services in Higher Education*. New York: McGraw-Hill, 1953.
Super, D. E., A Theory of Vocational Development, *Amer. Psychologist*, 8, 5, 185–190, 1953.

[4] Fleming, C. M., *Teaching: A Psychological Analysis*. London: Methuen, 1958 and 1959; New York: John Wiley, 1958.

[5] Strong, E. K., *Vocational Interests of Men and Women*. California: Stanford Univ. Press, 1943.
Emrys-Davies, W., *Experimental Work in Educational Guidance in a Mixed Selective Central School*. M.Ed. Thesis, Manchester Univ., 1943.

Berdie, R. F., Factors Related to Vocational Interests, *Psychol. Bull.*, 41, 3, 137–157, 1944.

Lambert, C. M., *A Study of Interest in School Subjects among Secondary School Pupils at Different Ages.* M.A. Thesis, Univ. of London, 1944.

Morris, B. S., and Phillipson, H., The Development of Research. Problems of Assessment and Guidance, *Times Ed. Suppl.*, February 9, 1946, and April 20, 1946. Transition from School to Work, *Times Educ. Suppl.*, June 1, 1946.

Strong, E. K., *Vocational Interests 18 Years after College.* Minneapolis: Univ. of Minnesota Press, 1955.

Thorndike, R. L., and Hagen, E., *Ten Thousand Careers.* New York: John Wiley, 1959.

See also:

Peel, E. A., Assessment of Interest in Practical Topics, *Brit. J. Educ. Psychol.*, XVIII, 1, 41–47, 1948.

Peel, E. A., Psychology and the Teaching of Science, *Brit. Educ. Psychol.*, XXV, III, 135–144, 1955.

Fleming, C. M., Preferences and Values among Adolescent Boys and Girls, *Educ. Res.*, II, 3, 221–224, 1960.

Stern, H. H., A Follow-up of Study of Adolescents' Views of their Personal and Vocational Future. *Brit. J. Educ. Psychol.*, XXXI, II, 1961.

[6] Brush, E. N., Mechanical Ability as a Factor in Engineering Aptitude, *J. App. Psychol.*, XXV, 300–312, 1941.

Harris, A. J., The Relative Significance of Measures of Mechanical Aptitude, Intelligence and Previous Scholarship for Predicting Achievement in Dental School, *J. App. Psychol.*, XXI, 513–521, 1937.

See also:

Stuit, D. B., The Prediction of Scholastic Success in a College of Medicine, *Educ. Psychol. Meas.*, I, 1, 77–84, 1941.

McDaniel, J. W., and Reynolds, W. A., A Study of the Use of Mechanical Aptitude Tests in the Selection of Trainees for Mechanical Occupations, *Educ. Psychol. Meas.*, IV, 3, 191–197, 1944.

Thorndike, R. L., and Hagen, E., *Measurement and Evaluation in Psychology and Education.* New York: John Wiley, 1955 and 1961.

See also:

Stuit, D. B., Construction and Educational Significance of Aptitude Tests, *Rev. Educ. Res.*, XX, 1, 27–37, 1950.

Mollenkoff, W. G., Development and Applications of Tests of Special Aptitude, *Rev. Educ. Res.*, XXIII, 1, 33–55, 1953.

Guildford, J. P., *et al.*, Development and Applications of Tests of Intellectual and Special Aptitudes, *Rev. Educ. Res.*, XXIX, 1, 26–41, 1959.

[7] Vernon, P. E., Research on Personnel Selection in the Royal Navy and the British Army, *Amer. Psychol.*, 2, 35–51, 1947.

Vernon, P. E., and Parry, J. B., *Personnel Selection in the British Forces.* London: Univ. of London Press, 1949.

Stouffer, S. A., *et al.*, *The American Soldier. Combat and its Aftermath.* Princeton: Princeton Univ. Press, 1949.

[8] For accessible evidence on the inadequacy of the traditional interview, see: Hartog, P., *et al.*, *The Marks of Examiners.* London: Macmillan, 1936.

See also:

Fleming, C. M., loc. cit. [5].

[9] Pratt, C. C. (ed.), Military Psychology, *Psychol. Bull.*, 38, 6, 309–508, 1941.

Loutitt, C. M., Psychological Examining in the United States Navy: An Historical Summary, *Psychol. Bull.*, 39, 4, 227–239, 1942.

The development of techniques may be traced in the series of articles in the *Psychological Bulletin* entitled Psychology and the War:

Britt, S. H. (ed), 1942–43.

Marquis, D. G. (ed), 1943–45.

Comparable accounts for the British forces will be found in:

Rees, J. R., Three Years of Military Psychiatry in the United Kingdom, *Brit. Med. J.*, 1–6, 1943.

Cunningham, K. S., The Use of Psychological Methods in War-Time in Australia, *Occup. Psychol.*, XVII, 3, 111–118, 1943.

Rodger, A., The Man and His Job: From War to Peace, *Occup. Psychol.*, XVIII, 2, 63–68, 1944.

Child, H. A. T., Industrial Planning and Vocational Guidance, *Occup. Psychol.*, XVIII, 2, 69–75, 1944.

Cockett, R., The Rationale of Scientific Selection I, *Occup. Psychol.*, XIX, 1, 20–27, 1945.

Blain, I. J., The Rationale of Scientific Selection II, *Occup. Psychol.*, XIX, 1, 28–34, 1945.

Garforth, F. I., de la P., War Office Selection Boards (O.C.T.U.), *Occup. Psychol.*, XIX, 2, 97–102, 1945.

Rodges, A., The Work of the Admiralty Psychologists, *Occup. Psychol.*, XIX, 3, 132–139, 1945.

Wilson, N. A. B., Interviewing Candidates for Technical Appointments or Training, *Occup. Psychol.*, XIX, 4, 161–179, 1945.

Harrisson, T., The British Soldier: Changing Attitudes and Ideas, *Brit. J. Psychol.*, XXXV, 2, 34–39, 1945.

Mercer, E. O., Psychological Methods of Personnel Selection in a Women's Service, *Occup. Psychol.*, XIX, 4, 180–200, 1945.

Oakley, C. A., *Men at Work*. London: Hodder and Stoughton, 1945.

Sutherland, J. D., and Fitzpatrick, G. A., Some Approaches to Group Problems in the British Army, in Moreno, J. L. (ed.), *Group Psychotherapy*. New York: Beacon House, 1945.

Misselbrook, B. D., The Short Personnel Selection Interview, *Occup. Psychol.*, XX, 2, 85–97, 1946.

Tuck, G. N., The Army's Use of Psychology during the War, *Occup. Psychol.*, XX, 113–118, 1946.

See also:

Harris, H., *The Group Approach to Leadership Testing*. London: Routledge and Kegan Paul, 1949.

Powdermaker, F. B., and Frank, J. D., *Group Psychotherapy: Studies in Methodology of Research and Therapy*. Cambridge: Harvard Univ. Press, 1953.

[10] For a description of methods see:

Davis, J. A. M., Social Studies and Vocational Guidance, *J. Educ.*, 79, 930, 14–16, 1947.

Hall, R. K., and Lauwerys, J. A. (ed.), *Yearbook of Education*, 1955.

Schneiders, A. A., *Personality Development and Adjustment in Adolescence*. Milwaukee: Bruce Publishing Company, 1960.

[11] Evidence on the improvement effected by recognition of the significance of human relationships is accessible in reports from the research division of the Hawthorne Western Electric Company. See:

Mayo, Elton, *The Human Problems of an Industrial Civilization*. New York: Macmillan, 1933.

Whitehead, T. N., *The Industrial Worker*. London: Oxford Univ. Press, 1938.

Mayo, Elton, *The Social Problems of an Industrial Civilization*. Boston: Harvard Univ. Press, 1945.

Rogers, M., Problems of Human Relations in Industry, *Sociometry*, IX, 4, 350–371, 1946.
See also:
Brown, J. A. C., *The Social Psychology of Industry*. Penguin Books, 1954.
Paterson, T. T., *Morale in War and Work. An Experiment in the Management of Men*. London: Max Parrish, 1955.
Moonman, E., *The Manager and the Organization*. London: Tavistock Publications, 1961.

CHAPTER XV

IN SEARCH OF WORK

Few boys and girls pass their entire adolescence in school or college. For most of them the later years of maturing are spent in industry, commerce or trade; and life in the classroom early becomes a fleeting memory.

Attitudes towards work vary with the traditions of the group in which an adolescent has been reared. They differ to some extent from one home to another, from one socio-economic level to another and—in very obvious fashions—from one type of society to another. In Samoa,[1] for example, where from the age of four or five little children perform definite tasks—graded according to their strength and intelligence—their attitude towards working appears to be similar in certain respects to that of the tiny shirt maker, the chimney sweet or the miner in the days when child labour was customary in western lands—with the important difference that in Samoa there is no leisured play-boy group to stimulate envy and that the tasks required are not discharged in an atmosphere of poverty, anxiety and strain.

In many homes in Europe and America a not dissimilar attitude is observable among children of somewhat greater age. Boys and girls look forward to the time when they (like their parents) will contribute to the family exchequer and win the prestige of membership in a group in which everyone is more or less fully employed.

In other circles (and in other communities, such as those of the Maori settlements in New Zealand[2]) there is no such point of view. No special emphasis is put on the choice of a career or the earning of an income, and no special honour is given to those who succeed in retaining a job.

The desire for a monetary reward is therefore not now believed to be an essential accompaniment of the process of maturing. It is demonstrably relative to group attitudes and wishes; and it may or may not accompany an adolescent's need for growth through fresh experiences or his desire to make an increasing and responsible contribution to the welfare of his group. It is very definitely modified by the point of view which the group happens to hold; and, like the desire for a definite occupation, it is observably absent in certain social circles and in certain cultural patterns.

Many surveys[3] have been undertaken of the nature of the employment available to adolescents and the character of their vocational decisions. The studies are of great local importance as a guide to those who have opportunities of influencing the choices made by young people within a specified area. Their details are, however, somewhat irrelevant to a consideration of more general problems. Suffice it to say that the choice of a career is determined not only by the personal attributes of an adolescent and the requirements of a district but also by the standards of the more intimate groups to which he thinks of himself as belonging. The choice of teaching,[4] for example, has been shown to be related more closely to a favourable attitude towards school or to admiration for a particular teacher than to the socio-economic level of the home, the intelligence or achievement of the pupil or the fact that other members of the family are already members of the teaching profession. Similar attitudinal controls can be detected in relation to recruiting for mining, for domestic service, for salesmanship, for engineering, for the ministry or for medicine. There are fashions in such things, and these fashions vary to some extent from one home to another; but, in all cases, the influence of personal and social relationships is now admitted to operate to a degree which was formerly unrecognised.

The extent of the employment of adolescents, like that of adults, varies from time to time and from place to place according to national and international circumstances. On the whole, however, it may be said that in periods of widespread unemployment, adolescents tend to suffer most severely.[5] The psychological damage consequent on loss of regular work is not unnaturally greatest in the case of those who have had the shortest experience of the satisfactions of such established and accepted contributing to group welfare.

Wastage of effort and injury to self-respect through selection of unsuitable work and undue frequency of change of occupation appear to be greatest among those groups who leave school earliest and among those who are least highly qualified. The extent of such maladjustment is now, however, less than it was even thirty years ago. Much is now known as to the qualities of ability, of interest and of personality which are required in differing occupations; and in most industrialised countries vocational guidance[6] is increasingly being given through the co-operation of schools or employers with research bodies such as the National Institute of Industrial Psychology in Britain or the Occupational Information and Guidance Services of America. The best results of such work are now known to be obtainable (as indicated in Chapter XIV) through a long-term study of the pupil in his response to school situations combined with an understanding of the requirements of industry and commerce; and it is now becoming recognised that at later stages the best results within industry or commerce can follow only from a skilful and continuous supervision of employees and adjustment of occupational demands to their abilities and their interests. Contemporary Vocational Guidance had its roots in the trade-testing undertaken in the armies and factories of the First World War. There is reason to believe that quite comparable improvements in the subsequent attitude and the well-being of workers have resulted from the knowledge won in the Second World War, both of methods of assessment of the entire personality in action and of the procedure necessary for the successful supervision of workers and the adequate maintenance of civilian morale. The skill which is known to be necessary for the rehabilitation[7] of returned prioners of war, for the resettlement of civilians, and for the after-care of the crippled and the neurotic has, when exercised in comparable fashion in the'more intelligent supervision of industry, resulted in undreamed-of improvements in social relationships within factory and workshop.

Adolescents in industry require satisfaction of their basic psychological needs to as great a degree as they did at earlier ages at home or in school; and it has been in the failure of industry to satisfy those needs that most of the unsatisfactory personal relationships within workshop and factory have had their origin.

Many adolescents nowadays leave school with the hopeful anticipation that they will find in the business world a kindliness and co-operativeness similar to those which they have met in the more or less child-centred school society of which they have formed a part. Disappointment often follows, and the transition to adult status is consequently, in many cases, unnecessarily difficult. Explanations of this again are to be found not merely in the personal attributes and the physiological condition of adolescents but in the structure and the social relationships of the group into which they enter. Variety of type among industrial communities is as great as anything that has been reported in families or in schools. Some are authoritarian in structure. Some are democratic. Some accept a *laissez-faire* philosophy. Some are small. Some are big. Some consist wholly of men. Others include women and girls (or boys). Some have a long tradition behind them. Others give no guidance as to what is expected or required.

The reactions of adolescents to these communities also vary as widely as did their responses to differing types of handling at home or in school. Under dictatorial control they work submissively enough while they are watched; but they show little initiative. They react by noisiness, bullying or destructiveness when supervision is slackened; and their manner and gestures show apathy or boredom. Under *laissez-faire* discipline they are restless and lacking in any understanding of the purpose of their work. When, however, intelligent co-operation is expected and democratic tuition is given,[8] the same adolescents have been reported to rise to quite unexpected heights of social maturity and purposeful activity.

Adolescent attitudes towards life as a whole differ as markedly; and in this connection also the facile generalisations of former years are therefore now suspect. In certain social circles and in the case of certain individuals attitudes may be like those often described in discussions of modern youth:[9]

"1. The natural world exists solely to be exploited by men. Smash and grab is the only law.

"2. The happiest person is he who has the most material possessions; the chief satisfaction in life is to get and get, more and more.

"3. The law of the world is competition; the only sensible way to act is to get on, climb up, and push someone else down.

"4. Work is a nuisance to be avoided by every device possible; the further up the tree you climb the less work you do, whilst the 'big toff' at the top of the tree does no work at all.

"5. The powers that rule this world—known as 'they'—are untrustworthy and arbitrary, to be tricked and outwitted as often, and obeyed as seldom, as possible."

Such attitudes, however, are not "modern" in the sense that they are unknown in earlier centuries, and they can best be assessed in the light of some knowledge both of the treatment which has made them possible and also of the ubiquity and reality of quite opposing sentiments. Many adolescents as a result of their experiences at home, in school or at work do suffer from a subtle and pervading sense of failure, of inadequacy and of rejection.[10] (This is reflected in attitudes of boredom, rebellion and expectation of defeat.) When they are handled more wisely and when it is expected that they will show loyalty, courage and magnanimity the same "ordinary" people rise to heroic levels. It is recorded, for example, in the cool wording of scientific journals that in the face of enemy brutality and starvation in prison camps "men in the extremity of fatigue and debility lined up to take the place or bear the burden of those in worse case . . . the weak supported or carried the weaker";[11] and in air-raids on the civilian population it was not unusual for an observer to report . . . "and then, in London I found myself helping to carry four people away from a burning house. And what did each one of them say? Each of the four actually said the same hackneyed or rather hallowed words: 'Don't bother about me. Look after the others.' Now I did rather suspect that this did not happen as much as people said. But the curious thing, without any cant, is, it does."[12]

Cruelty, brutality, cynicism, a sense of futility or an absence of a sense of purpose can be seen among adolescents as among adults; but under quite comparable physical conditions and at quite comparable ages the opposite qualities are also observable. Neither the one type of behaviour nor the other can fairly be said to be characteristic of any one stage of growth as such. The responsibility of the employer (as of the parent or teacher) is therefore now believed to include both an awareness of the types of treatment which tend to encourage the more desirable attitudes and a reorganising of personal relationships within industry or commerce in order that there may be provided within working hours some degree of satisfaction of the primary human needs of recognition, responsible contributing, adventure and insight.

Hope for the future is to be found in the fact that many industrial concerns are now awakening to a realisation of the fact that they share the responsibility of the community for the development and the fostering of the mental as well as the physical healthiness of their employees. This concern for individual welfare is not merely helpful to the morale of a whole workshop, but it serves to lessen for adolescents the shock consequent on the transition from the "discipline" or social structure of the home or the school to that of the adult working world.

Many schools also are becoming aware of the importance of

preparing adolescents for the difficulties of business or commercial life. This is being done both by pre-vocational visiting of factories and workshops, by discussion of the requirements of different available occupations and by interesting adolescents in those forms of social maturing which have to do with the tolerance of other people and with the development of some ability to see the point of view of the other person. Work comparable to this was attempted with great success in the Civil Resettlement Units[13] which prepared the way for the transition from army life to civilian responsibilities after the Second World War. These transitional societies retained some of the formalities of the Army but utilised the therapy of group discussions and group enterprises, of dramatisation, dancing and music, and of supervised reintroduction to the customs and requirements of the world of industry and commerce. They also revived the social interest of neurotic patients by demonstrating to them through corporate living that they were not alone in their inability to re-establish with ease the spontaneity of ordinary human contacts. From the testimony of those who experienced such group therapy, whether as patients or as co-operating staff, there is reason to believe that there has been some dissemination of a new attitude towards social relationships in employment.

A further protection against the unfriendliness of an outside group is to be found in awareness of one's acceptance by an admired inner circle. This may be the society of the school, the home or the street. "You are one of us." "We appreciate you." "We understand you." "We are all in the same boat." These group relationships, exemplified by the appreciative home, the friendly company of one's peers or the kindly interest of one's teachers, supply the warmth and comfort which too often are missing in the work-a-day world into which the adolescent has to make his entry.

The same mechanisms of group support continue to operate in the case of older workers through years of what to an outsider may seem monotonous and unsatisfying toil. Many jobs are in consequence not as dull as they appear. They can never be fully assessed in terms either of the physical movements required, the intellectual activity involved or the monetary reward they offer. Their real meaning can be glimpsed only when they are seen as the worker sees them in the total setting[14] of his life-space. Fortunate are the adolescents who are fortified by the position

O

they hold in the esteem of an admired group or who early find acceptance in a community of adults to whom the relatively simple tasks of the working day have social significance, meaning and purpose.

Even in such circumstances, the transition to work is not easy. New skills have to be learnt and insight into new situations has to be achieved. Patience and tolerance are required on the part of senior workers and employers; and courage and perseverance on the part of young people. The adolescent is a novice. He is clumsy. She is ignorant. He is an outsider in a new group. All the others know one another (or appear to the newcomer to do so). All the others know what is expected of them. The adolescent makes mistakes and experiences teasing as to clumsiness in work or inexperience in social relations. For all such reasons there is in the years of apprenticeship an element of insecurity and distress which is greater or less in proportion to the wisdom and the kindliness of all the members of the working community.

Reaction against such uncertainties may take the form of aggressiveness, noisiness, over-attention to dress, lack of vitality or physical ailments of various kinds. Treatment of such behaviour disorders is now recognised as falling into the same categories as treatment of similar distresses among pupils of school age. Provision of adequate food, ventilation, sitting accommodation, protection against accidents and the like are necessary, both in school and at work; but more important than all these is the recognition of the significance of attitudinal controls. "Much depends on you." "You do matter." "We are interested in you." "We need your help." "This is what we are trying to do." "You are one of us." "Entertaining things happen here." "This is worth doing." "You are learning very well." "You will soon be grown up."

Difficulties of a somewhat different type arise (from the point of view of the management of firms in which adolescents are employed) from the fact that there are marked differences in the nature of the responses made by individuals to learning of any kind.[15] Some human beings accept instructions, are prepared to listen and appear to find complete satisfaction in the carrying out of tasks which involve attention to detail. Others seem to win less excitement from what they see or what they hear and prefer occupations involving gross motor activities and bodily skill. Some appear to be unsatisfied unless they are expressing themselves or giving instructions. Others are secretive or possessive in attitude. And these cross-classifications of types of approach to learning are further complicated by distinctions which can be described as attributable to prevailing interests in ideas, in people or in things. For some individuals the activities of workshop or office appear to provide absorbing personal satisfactions. For others they are a mere stop gap in a life whose chief attention is turned outwards towards the skills or the attempted masteries of the hours of leisure.

Allied to these differences are the more general difficulties related to the various personal, social or physical experiences which affect the day-to-day behaviour of adolescents (as of adults) to an extent greater than is generally realised. Such complications (like those more commonly associated with learning in the narrower sense) have more often been studied in the lives of students at school or college than in the experiences of those adolescents who enter workshops, factories or offices at an early age. There is, however, no reason to suppose that the repercussions they produce are any less real in the life-histories of the latter group.

Boys and girls, by the time they reach adolescence, have lived through something. In a large group whose life stories had been thoroughly studied it was, for example, estimated that two-thirds had already confronted severely disturbing experiences which were producing observable effects upon their attitude and performance.[16] Some had known bereavement. Others had lived through family scandals or financial failure. Some had met hostility and rejection within their homes. Some had parents who were ill. Others had relatives of whom they were ashamed. Some were uncertain of their social status. Others believed that they had lost a social prestige which was formerly theirs. Some were perturbed because they had few friends or received few letters. Others suffered anxiety over their health or worried over their future likelihood of success.

Not all could talk of their difficulties. Many found some measure of healing in the fashions indicated in earlier chapters— through the relief and catharsis experienced in membership of apparently casual group discussions (at home, at work, in church or in a club), or through the reading of books in which the distresses experienced by others cast a revealing light upon their own problems.

Tensions were also reduced in other ways through behaviour which proved to be more usefully interpreted as an appeal for help rather than as evidence of an undesirable and fixed biological endowment. Some relieved the strain by excessive and compulsive social activities. They could not bear to be alone and must always be assertively noisy and the centre of attention. Others expressed their difficulties by too meticulous an attention to detail—fierce over-working or pathologically rigid concentration on one line of interest. Some were scattered in their activities and revealed their anxiety through inability to concentrate for long on any one topic. Others reacted by symptoms of bodily ill-health—by proneness to colds, gastric disturbances or easy fatigability. In every case help was most successfully given by adults who were prepared to show the tolerance, patience and belief in the possibility of improvement which become progressively more possible to those who are prepared to refrain from abrupt condemnation and to believe that undesirable conduct is rather a symptom of distress than an indication of irretrievable badness of nature or disposition.

During the years of more or less informal apprenticeship adolescents are fortified to the extent to which they meet such favourable attitudes; and almost unawares they begin to agree not only that they are willing to grow up but also that they are rapidly doing so.

Transition to adult status within the world of work cannot be said to take place at any clearly defined point (any more than at any specific age). Like social and personal maturing, it is more comparable to a journey through a borderland whose boundaries are unmarked than it is to the crossing of a rubicon or the experiencing of a new birth. From the point of view of economic maturity, however, there does come a time when it is realised that the wages obtained are as good as they are ever likely to be or that the salary is now sufficient for the discharging of adult responsibilities as a householder.

The age at which such an experience comes varies again from district to district and from one occupation to another. It is commonly followed more or less rapidly by social pressures which lead boys to decide that it is time that they "think about taking a wife". On the average, this occurs nowadays at an earlier age[17] than it did formerly; but, while for many adolescents there is no economic immaturity to prevent their setting up a home of their own in the late teens or the early twenties, there are also many for whom an extension of the time required for elaborate professional training has led to the postponement of the age of economic maturity to the late twenties or middle thirties.

The reactions of adolescent girls or boys to the attainment or postponement of such economic maturity form no inconsiderable part of the further experiences they are all the while meeting along lines which may be described as the learning how to live—in the circumstances and under the conditions of which their particular life-pattern forms a part.

REFERENCES

[1] Mead, M., and Wolfenstein, M., *Childhood in Contemporary Cultures*. Chicago: Univ. of Chicago, 1955.
  Kaplan, B. (ed.), *Studying Personality Cross-Culturally*. Evanston: Row Peterson, 1961.
[2] McQueen, H. C., *Vocations for Maori Youth*. New Zealand Council Educ. Res., 1945.
[3] Carr-Saunders, A. M., and Jones, D. C. *A Survey of the Social Structure of England and Wales as Illustrated by Statistics*. Vol. III. Oxford: Clarendon Press, 1927 and 1937.
  James, H. E. O., and Moore, F. T., Adolescent Leisure in a Working-Class District, *Occup. Psychol.*, XIV, 132–145, 1940, and XVIII, 1, 24–34, 1944.
  Barnes, L. J., *Youth Service in an English County*. London: King George's Jubilee Trust, 1945.
  See also the publications of the American Youth Commission such as:
  Youth and the Future. Washington, D.C.: Amer. Council on Educ., 1942.
  With this may be compared:
  Hurlock, E. B., *Adolescent Development*. New York: McGraw-Hill, 1955.
  Kuhlen, R. G., and Thompson, G. C. (ed), *Psychological Studies of Human Development*. New York: Appleton-Century, Crofts, 1952.
  Jersild, A. T., *Child Psychology*. Fourth Edition. New York: Prentice-Hall, 1954.
  Strang, R., *The Adolescent Views Himself*. New York: McGraw-Hill, 1957.
  See also:
  Evans, K. M., *Club Members Today*. London: National Assoc. Mixed Clubs and Girls' Clubs, 1960.
  Hemming, J., *Problems of Adolescent Girls*. London: Heinemann, 1960.
  Whyte, W. F., *Street Corner Society. The Social Structure of an Italian Slum*. Chicago: Univ. of Chicago Press, 1943.
  McQueen, H. C., *et al.*, *The Background of Guidance*. New Zealand Council Educ. Res., 1941.
  Barker, R. G., and Wright, H. F., *Midwest and its Children*. Evanston; Row Peterson, 1955.
  Peck, R. F., and Havighurst, R. J., *The Psychology of Character Development*. New York: John Wiley, 1960.
[4] Vernon, M. D., The Drives which Determine the Choice of a Career, *Brit. J. Educ. Psychol.*, VII, 302–316, 1937, and VIII, 1–15, 1938.
  Finch, F. H., and Odoroff, M. E., Sex Differences in Vocational Interests, *J. Educ. Psychol.*, 30, 151–156, 1939.
  Seagoe, M. V., Some Origins of Interest in Teaching, *J. Educ. Res.*, 35, 673–682, 1942.
  Evans, K. M., *A Study of Attitude towards Teaching as a Career*. M.A. Thesis in Education, Univ. of London, 1946.
  Evans, K. M., A Study of Attitude towards Teaching as a Career, *Brit. J. Educ. Psychol.*, XXII, 63–69, 1952.
  Evans, K. M., *A Study of Teaching Ability at the Training College Stage in Relation to the Personality and Attitudes of the Students*. Ph.D. Thesis, Univ. of London, 1952.

Evans, K. M., A Further Study of Attitude towards Teaching as a Career, *Brit. J. Educ. Psychol.*, XXIII, 58–63, 1953.

Evans, K. M., Is the Concept of "Interest" of Significance to Success in a Teacher Training Course?, *Educ. Rev.*, 9, 3, 205–211, 1957.

Evans, K. M., Research on Teaching Ability, *Educ. Res.*, 1, 3, 22–36, 1959.

[5] Edgar, W. M., and Secretan, H. A., *Unemployment among Boys.* London: Dent, 1925.

Men Without Work: *A Report Made to the Pilgrim Trust.* Cambridge: Univ. Press, 1938.

Lush, A. J., *The Young Adult.* Cardiff: South Wales & Monmouthshire Council of Social Service, 1941.

Disinherited Youth: A Survey, 1936–1939. A Report on the 18+ Age Group Enquiry prepared for the Trustees of the Carnegie United Kingdom Trust. Dunfermline, 1943.

Watson, G. (ed.), *Civilian Morale.* Boston: Houghton Mifflin, 1942.

Youth and the Future, loc. cit. [3].

Landis, P. H., *Adolescence and Youth.* New York: McGraw-Hill, 1945 and 1952.

[6] See, for example:

Thomas, M. W., *Young People in Industry, 1750–1945.* London: Thomas Nelson, 1945.

On vocational guidance see:

Rodger, A., and Davies, J. G. W., Vocational Guidance and Training, in *Chambers' Encyclopaedia.* London: Newnes, 1950.

Smith, M., *An Introduction to Industrial Psychology.* London: Cassell, 1952.

Arbuckle, D. S., *Student Personnel Services in Higher Education.* New York: McGraw-Hill, 1953.

Super, D. E., A Theory of Vocational Development, *Amer. Psychologist*, 8, 5, 185–190, 1953.

[7] Jones, M., Rehabilitation of Forces Neurosis Patients to Civilian Life, *Brit. Med. J.*, 533–535, 1946.

Sutherland, J. D., and Fitzpatrick, G. A., Some Approaches to Group Problems in the British Army, in Moreno, J. L. (ed.), *Group Psychotherapy.* New York: Beacon House, 1945.

Powdermaker, F. B., and Frank, J. D., *Group Psychotherapy: Studies in Methodology of Research and Therapy.* Cambridge: Harvard Univ. Press, 1953.

[8] Hall, P., and Locke, H. W., *Incentives and Contentment. A Study Made in a British Factory.* London: Pitman, 1938.

Hearnshaw, L. S., Industrial Relations in a New Zealand Factory, *Occup. Psychol.* XVIII, 1, 1–12, 1944.

Brown, W. B. D., Incentives within the Factory, *Occup. Psychol.*, XIX, 2, 82–92, 1945.

Viteles, M. S., War-Time Applications of Psychology. Their Value to Industry, *Occup. Psychol.*, XX, 1, 1–11, 1946.

Brown, J. A. C., *The Social Psychology of Industry.* Penguin Books, 1954.

Paterson, T. T., *Morale in War and Work. An Experiment in the Management of Men.* London: Max Parrish, 1955.

Moonman, E., *The Manager and the Organisation.* London: Tavistock Publications, 1961.

[9] Reeves, M., *Growing up in a Modern Society.* London: Univ. of London Press, 1946.

[10] This is well described in:

Van Waters, M., *Youth in Conflict.* London: Methuen, 1926.

See also:

Lush, A. J., loc. cit. [5].

Rowe, A. W., *The Education of the Ordinary Child*. London: Harrap, 1959.

Pedley, R., *Comprehensive Education*. London: Gollancz, 1956.

[11] Dunlop, E. E., Medical Experiences in Japanese Captivity, *Brit. Med. J.*, 481–486. 1946.

[12] Press Cutting, October 15, 1940.

[13] Jones, M., loc. cit. [7].

Sutherland, J. D., and Fitzpatrick, G. A., loc. cit. [7].

Wilson, A. T. M., The Serviceman Comes Home, *Pilot Papers*, I, No. 2, 9–28, 1946.

Wilson, A. T. M., *et al.*, Transitional Communities and Social Re-Connection, in Swanson, G. E., *et al.*, *Readings in Social Psychology*. New York: Henry Holt, 1952.

See also:

Bierer, J. (ed.), *Therapeutic Social Clubs*. London: H. K. Lewis. (n.d.).

Bierer, J., *The Day Hospital*, London: H. K. Lewis, 1951.

Jones, M., *Social Psychiatry*. London: Tavistock Publications, 1952.

[14] Oakley, C. A., *Men at Work*. London: Hodder and Stoughton, 1945.

[15] Examples of such differences at the College level may be found in the distinctions which can be drawn between students who "drink in", "master", "possess" or "release" knowledge.

See:

Murphy, L. B., and Ladd, H., *Emotional Factors in Learning*. New York: Columbia Univ. Press, 1944.

[16] Ibid., and

Munroe, R. L., *Teaching the Individual*. New York: Columbia Univ. Press, 1944.

See also:

Jersild, A. T., loc. cit. [3].

Strang, R., loc. cit. [3].

Schneiders, A. A., *Personality Development and Adjustment in Adolescence*. Milwaukee: Bruce Publishing Company, 1960.

Coleman, J. S., Johnstone, J. W. C., and Jonassohn, K., *The Adolescent Society*. Glencoe: Free Press, 1961.

[17] Landis, P. H., loc. cit. [5].

CHAPTER XVI

LEARNING HOW TO LIVE

Human beings are social in origin and attributes; and their learning how to live, like their search for a livelihood, can be understood only in its relation to the total setting of the life-dramas in which they find themselves expected to play a part. The issues encountered in this educative experience are not dissimilar to those discussed in Chapter XI under the heading of social and personal development. There is need for acceptance of one's position (strength–weakness, ignorance–knowledge, similarity–difference, popularity–unpopularity, or submission–dominance) in relation to one's contacts with other people and one's achievements at school or at work. There is also the continuing necessity for experiencing adventures, for attaining insight and for winning the satisfaction of success through the conviction that progress is possible and that more can probably be accomplished to-morrow than has yet been achieved to-day.

Alongside these, however, there are certain aspects of living which in all known societies come within the province of the "code". Discovery of this code has to be made by all adolescents, and much of their subsequent history is affected by the nature of their reaction to the traditions and the requirements of their community.

Respect for property, regard for the truth, kindliness towards other people, trustworthiness in business, chastity in social intercourse—on all such issues decisions are made, and these are enshrined in the beliefs of each community as a whole and also of each sub-group within any cultural pattern. All adults share the responsibility of passing on these traditions; and upon all children and adolescents is laid the burden of discovering as swiftly as possible the responses which they are required to make to the opportunities of the world as they find it.

The difficulties encountered in such learning are inevitably more acute in societies in which there are marked variations of interpretation as between one sub-group and another; and the ensuing bewilderment is greater for those adolescents in whose past experience there has been either an undue lack of knowledge of the existence of such differences or an excessively authoritarian attitude in the home* which has bred an unwillingness to be guided by any standards offered.

There is reason to believe that fewer of the problems consequent upon conflicting values arise in those societies or social groups where the rate of change in custom is slow and where the movement of population is slight. In many parts of Europe and America the growing child may, however, witness all gradations of sanctioned behaviour from organised robbery through petty pilfering to complete honesty, from open brutality through indifference to extreme kindliness or from promiscuous living through rare infidelities to genuine chastity.

Such divergencies of viewpoint are reported to an especial degree in the United States of America, where the patterns of socially acceptable behaviour vary not only with family traditions in different types of social states but also with the ethnic origin of the sub-groups. Social expectations on the part of adults and adolescents are therefore markedly different in family circles in New England, in the Middle West or in the Deep South, and also in city, small town or farm communities.[1]

The problem of discrimination and selection in such circumstances becomes a real one; and its difficulties are increased by the refusal of many adults to admit conviction of one type or another. "It's up to you." "Do as you please." "Nobody minds." "Go your own way." "Youth must choose." The consequences of decision are none the less unexpected in their magnitude; and many young people find that their experimental behaviour is branded as delinquency and visited by the severest penalties of ostracism or public disgrace.

The learning which takes place in relation to these issues is achieved by means similar to those which have been discussed in Chapters XI and XII above. The influence of a community reaches young people through what they see, what they hear, what they read, the understanding they win through group discussions and the identification with admired types which they achieve through dramatisation and through direct imitation. Probably the most efficacious of these methods—because the most omnipresent—is that dependent on observation. "How can I hear what you are saying, when what you are is thundering in

* Compare Chapter VIII above.

my ears?" Much of the refusal of young people to accept what they regard as pious platitudes is associated with their suspicion of the would-be guide who says, in effect, "Do as I tell you and not as I do."

Many of the delinquencies of adolescents originate in the attempt to play a role which they seem to have seen accepted without social condemnation by admired adults. Stealing from the ticket-collector, telling lies to the doctor, saying hard things to one's relatives—all these appear little different to the child or the adolescent from those forms of dishonesty, deceit or cruelty to which more severe social penalties are attached. In many cases their experimentation with such behaviour not unnaturally leads directly to conflicts with the standards of those other groups who are convinced of the desirability of a higher moral code.

Other delinquencies have their origin not so much in imitation of older people as in the attempt to secure prestige in the eyes of other boys or girls—the peer group. This appears to happen particularly in social situations in which official recognition or reward is given in one field only—to academic success in certain homes and schools, to athletic prowess in others. It is also associated with an absence of personal religious experience consequent on lack of contact with religiously minded adults. Self-despising is the lot of many, and in the absence of other forms of reassurance a measure of self-respect may be won through crimes of violence which to an outside observer may seem to lack any motivation.[2]

Redirection of the education of deviating adolescents takes the form of treatment (a) through modifications in the content of the exemplars and the attitudes to which they are exposed, (b) through the indirect commendation and the direct rewarding of other forms of behaviour, and (c) through permitting the discovery by the young person that basic satisfactions can better be won through responses of another kind.[3]

The problem of the educator is not so much that of "training" towards spontaneous kindliness, initiative, honesty or emotional sincerity as of permitting opportunities for these attributes to reveal themselves. The child, the adolescent or the adult is not merely a "savage" or a "beast" whose anti-social impulses towards self-assertion, cruelty or greed require to be restrained; but a human being—social in nature ("a son of God")—who is capable of evil as well as of good, but who can find satisfaction only in the "good".[4] In an atmosphere of frustration, aggression, discouragement and neglect he will appear aggressive, cruel, anti-social and inhibited; but removal of such influences will result in the revelation of a new creature.

Abundant evidence along these lines has been collected in many lands from experiments in the situational treatment of problem children,[5] and from observation of the re-education of Nazified youth[6] and the rehabilitation of neurotic ex-prisoners and displaced persons.[7] Human beings are social. They need to give affection, to exercise responsibility and to attain insight; and in the absence of imposed frustrations and the presence of the complementary affection, trust and patient encouragement of friendly and receptive groups, they have been observed to blossom into social virtues whose flowering appeared impossible under other sorts of husbandry.

Much (both good and evil) is learnt insensibly through informal educational media such as books read, films seen or stories or sermons heard; but the degree of effectiveness of all of these is again related, not merely to their content, but to the past history, present attributes and future intentions of the adolescents and to the attitudes which they have been led to adopt to the total situation of which these educational media form a part.

Statistics as to the type and the extent of adolescent misdemeanours or the age of their greatest incidence are of relatively local interest. They vary inevitably in content from one district to another;[8] and even within one area they are known to be related rather to the intrinsic characteristics of a social group[9] than to its external circumstances of size, equipment, prosperity or racial composition. Their nature fluctuates also with conditions of peace or war, employment or unemployment, official interference or casual acceptance of their relative harmlessness.[10] For these reasons no attempt is made to reproduce such findings here. Like a knowledge of preferrred occupations, personal earnings, or educational opportunities, the study of such surveys of juvenile delinquency is of assistance chiefly to those adults who are trying to help adolescents within a specific neighbourhood. For such workers they are indispensable. Their relevance to more general problems is light.

It may, however, be recalled that it is not now believed that there is much connection between physical maturation or glandular development and either mental or social behaviour. It is not now thought that delinquency is necessarily great during adolescence (any more than it is now associated with physiological states such as menstruation) or that adolescent misdemeanours are related to inevitable biological upsets associated with conditions within the organism—the uprising of instinctive urges, a recapitulation of a revolutionary period in the history of the race, sublime emotions, turbulent temperaments, maladjustments in organic balance and the like. Exploratory behaviour is a characteristic of all human beings; and most adolescent delinquents mature into inconspicuous citizens,[11] not because they have outgrown a period of storm, conflict or lack of emotional control, but because, having tried certain ways of behaving, they have decided (in response to the signals they have received) that further journeys along certain paths are not worth the disapproval they entail.

Such forms of social learning also do not begin or end in adolescence. They are an accompaniment of life as a whole; and in this respect likewise it is now known that the period of adolescence is both more complex and less distinct than theorists formerly appear to have believed. The behaviour of an adolescent is directly related to, and continuous with, his attitudes and his experiences as a growing child; and relatively little distress or difficulty is encountered by those children whose home life has been such that they approach adult status[12] with a background of reasoned acceptance of the essentials of a moral code and with the confidence which results from an absence of the fear or revolt which are engendered by inconsistent or tyrannical handling.[13] At the beginning of this century, when emphasis was put on the biological determinants of behaviour, it was supposed that damage was wrought by failure to permit self-expression of all the so-called human instincts. (This theory was, however, less often evoked in support of theft, flight or destructiveness than as a cover for unlicensed sexual indulgence.) Now it is believed that behaviour is a function not merely of innate forces but of the social conditioning of a variety of human potentialities; and, in consequence, emphasis is once again being placed on the inevitability of adult guidance and the desirability that it be as well informed and as wise as possible. Little encouragement, in discussions of human development, is therefore now given to *laissez-faire* theories which imply that deliberate suggestion is necessarily dangerous. A swinging of the pendulum of educative opinion is discernible. More parents and teachers are admitting that signposts should be erected, that social learning is universal and that there should, on this account, be deliberate social transmission of the finest accumulated wisdom both of the past and the present.

Especially is this the case in connection with the social issue of the discovery and the acceptance of one's sex role, and with the learning of the techniques of acceptable behaviour in relation to the other sex. It is not without significance that the topic of sex education is one to which it is now expected that serious consideration will be given by the parents and the teachers of adolescents.

Like other social learnings involved in the discovery of how to live, the attitudes adopted towards sex have their roots in the period prior to adolescence, and their development continues far into adult life. In the years of adolescence the matter, however, assumes a special urgency, since physiological changes commonly render procreation then for the first time possible and because, in most countries, social pressure suggests certain changes in the approved behaviour of girls and of boys. The exact nature of those changes (as has been indicated in Chapter III) is now known to vary so much from one cultural pattern to another that it is not now possible to believe that any one form of secondary sex role is either biologically determined, inevitable or universal.

The problem is in every case a social as well as a physical or an intellectual one. Little children early know that they must grow up. Adolescents are prepared to admit to themselves a greater or lesser willingness to do so. Information as to what is meant by being grown up is available on every side—through direct observation, through books and films, through conversation overheard, through the implications of fragments of traditional games in which the typical life-dramas of a community are enacted by tiny boys and girls. Children wish the acceptance and esteem of an admired group, and they therefore desire in this respect also to conform to the cultural pattern presented. Without initiation, however, there seems no reason to believe that human beings have any inborn awareness of the complex techniques made possible by their biological equipment. Their difficulties are, however, much reduced if they are fortunate enough to find themselves in a circle containing friendly and unperturbed adults who, in turn, are sufficiently mature to be able to answer adolescent questions with a serene absence of perturbation. Not all adults are, however, in this position; and the question therefore nowadays is being openly discussed as to how or by whom more deliberate instruction should be given. (Help in this matter is now available to an extent which was formerly unknown.[14])

Sex education is not a mere matter of giving information to the effect that surprising physiological experiences, such as nocturnal emissions or menstruation, come to most boys or girls in the years of their teens. Nor is it disposed of by showing films depicting the life history of the amoeba or the frog or diagrammatic portrayals of the route taken by human spermatozoa. Still less is it a matter of mere discussion of secondary sexual characteristics, such as changes in physical appearance and structure. It is not adequately discharged by the reassurance that the sensations experienced during masturbation or in erotic fantasies are relatively harmless and quite to be expected. Nor does it, on the other hand, need to include details of the techniques of courtship or the sexual act. (The latter vary widely from one couple to another, and they belong to the stage of a Marriage Guidance Clinic[15] rather than an adolescent's initiation.) It is, however, important that the adolescent be helped—often in apparently casual fashion—to realise that this problem is bound up with the much larger one of human relations in general and that the decisions made in connection with physical intercourse with the opposite sex are intimately linked with the establishment at later ages of satisfactory relations within a family.

The process of learning is rendered more difficult in this, as in all such issues, by the fact that the direction of educational treatment to the adolescent as an isolated individual is largely foredoomed to failure. The adolescent remains a member of a group and wishes so to remain. His answer to the adult advisor who says (by implication), "Do as I tell you and not as I do" is (again by implication), "How can I hear what you are saying when what you are is thundering in my ears?" It is therefore now coming to be realised that the concomitant education of parents and teachers, the clarifying of their thinking and, where necessary, the modification of their attitude is a more fruitful procedure than a so-called "sex education" addressed to adolescents and children alone. Learning is both social and incidental, and consists as much in the gradual building up of a point of view as in any spectacular or isolated enlightenment. That point of view in turn depends on a multitude of things heard and things observed in the behaviour of those adults who have attained some prestige in the eyes of youth.

In the case of sexual practice, the matter is also further complicated by the fact that such experiences are both a matter of more or less pleasurable physical sensation and a form of psycho-motor expression through which certain personal relationships can be expressed in ways unattainable by other means. They carry symbolic as well as literal values. (In an older terminology, they are a vehicle for both lust and love.) To the outsider—to the child or adolescent who witnesses the experience, overhears its echoes or reads of it in books devised for his perusal—only the former may be evident, and the overtones of satisfactions obtainable from the latter may remain unknown. In this connection it may be remarked that it is probably one of the social consequences of overcrowding that not only are opportunities lacking for privacy for the cultivation of friendships within the home but that, through premature exposure, there may be lost an expectation of anything other than the physical aspects of sexual relationships. Within such crowded homes, however, many adolescents have to work out most of the adjustments involved in their personal maturing and their social-sex development.

The subject is admittedly of such moment that in all cultural groups there are quite definite traditions as to the ideals which are to be inculcated.

Human nature being what it is, experimental infringement of such canons of behaviour is also observable in every society. This sexual experimentation is not new; and there is some doubt as to whether even the modifications attributable in the western world to the licence of the First and the Second World Wars have actually resulted in significantly greater deviations than did previous wars or the tacitly authorised irregularities of village life in earlier centuries. Individualistic behaviour is nowadays very freely advertised; but there have always been groups who disregarded tradition—even in so-called relatively simple societies such as those of Samoa or New Guinea.

In the western world tradition lends support to what can be described as chastity (emotional sincerity), as it does to honesty and to truthfulness (intellectual sincerity). This is partly on the philosophic grounds of the inconceivability of the opposite as a foundation for stable living and partly on the religious grounds of a passion for righteousness conceived as a cosmic faith. Human beings are, in theory, believed to be so constituted that they find satisfaction only in attitudes which are compatible with their need for something other than the transient gratification of an individualistic and hedonistic lust; and in spite of the promiscuity which occurs, most men and women do, in practice, seek to form permanent alliances and do appear to experience their greatest amorous satisfactions therein. Monogamous marriage and its continuance remain as ideals towards which men and women actually strive; and within that framework they most satisfactorily find both opportunities for sexual intercourse and also a reduction of anxiety consequent on the satisfaction of their basic human requirements of acceptance and appreciation as unique individuals. Support on experimental grounds for monogamy and extra-marital abstinence is now also being supplied through statistical analysis of the case-records of Marriage Guidance Clinics or Child Guidance Services. There is reason, in the light of this evidence also, for believing that sex experiences before or outside marriage render more difficult both later marital adjustment and the rearing of happy and healthy children.[16]

Human beings are more than mere individuals. They are essentially social and members of groups. They are more than mere bodies. The claim of the hedonists that they are crippled by any failure to gratify every passing impulse is countered by the plea that no such individualistic interpretation is adequate as a description of the actualities of human relationships.

Sex intercourse has been likened to an appetite[17]—linked with sensations of desire and repletion; but it differs from other appetites in that its physical gratification is not necessary for individual survival. Abstention is not physiologically harmful to men or to women. Coition cannot be proved to be inevitably beneficial.[18] The effect of either is attitudinally controlled. Expectation of damage or of benefit may lead to the losing or the gaining of a sense of well-being. Prostitutes and their clients are not the most healthy group in the community—either mentally or physically.

Some awareness of the social character of sexual relationships is indicated by the reactions of most adolescents. Their interest in the subject, if carefully observed, may be seen to be in the first place a matter of social convention. They know that they are expected to have boy-friends or girl-friends; and the quest for a

P

mate is a more or less open topic for discussion among them as well as a subject for innuendos and teasing.

Their attitude towards this form of sanctioned transition to adult status varies with their personality and their background. "How will I know him when I see him?" asks the socially secure girl; and she watches and criticises the boys and men in her circle. "Will he know me when he sees me?" thinks the less-confident member of a circle where the expectation is that she find him quickly and marry him early. And in order to attract his attention she studies the beauty hints in the illustrated papers and expends her small savings on clever clothes. "Will she have me?" says the somewhat similarly insecure male, and he proceeds to show his prowess in a fashion acceptable to his circle. "Is she as nice as she looks?" thinks the more discriminating possessor of what he believes to be an attractive manner, a good income or a secure job.

For most boys and girls who have had normal and wholesome opportunities of mixing in heterosexual groups and sharing in the activities of members of the opposite sex there is, during adolescence, less than is sometimes supposed of passionate attachment and awareness of emotional excitation. Relatively greater importance is given by them to the mere fact that they are like the others in their circle in that they can talk of their "friends" or their "dates" and, at somewhat later ages, that they have satisfied their intellectual curiosity as to what it is that adults do in this matter of sex. Many of the early associations of boys and girls carry with them, therefore, no thrill (when viewed from within) beyond that of the fulfilment of social expectations.

Probably representative of the attitude of very many adolescents is, for example, a careful study[19] of the replies given by more than two hundred young College girls to the question as to what they thought a girl should know before coming to College. Seventy-three per cent considered it was important to "know about sex"—"how to go about with boys"—and in descending order from that were such social skills as how to dance, how to behave in company, how to mix with other people, how to take care of one's person and one's clothes, how to cultivate social poise, the uses of money, the acceptance of responsibility, methods of study (eleven per cent) and enthusiasm for sports (ten per cent).

Similarly typical of a slightly younger group of boys and girls is another analysis[20] of the anonymous written replies of 1,904 high-school girls aged fifteen to eighteen as to the personal problems which occupied them most. Difficulties associated with relationships with teachers, the choice of a vocation, feelings of social inferiority and financial conditions at home were mentioned in forty-six per cent, thirty-four per cent, twenty-four per cent and nineteen per cent of the cases respectively. Only eleven per cent made any admission of awareness of troublesome emotional experiences. While such figures relate in the first place to the situation in which they were obtained, there is reason to believe that they represent the point of view of youth more accurately than an outmoded emphasis on the violence of the emotional life of the adolescent. They are also in accord with observations from co-educational schools in this country and from the mixed clubs of churches or communities. Boys and girls during adolescence become more interested in one another.[21] Some experience strong sexual passion;[22] but many form heterosexual associations and reach the threshold of marriage in terms of a somewhat dream-like satisfaction of their wish for social prestige and their desire to do as others do.

Learning along these lines, it may again be observed, is imitative in many respects. The best initiation is obtained by those boys and girls who are reared in the presence of happy married relationships within their own homes, and receive their schooling in places where wholesome relations are observable among members of a co-educational staff. Even for such boys and girls there may, however, be questions which still need deliberate answering —especially under the conditions of life in a city where information as to the processes of life, birth and death is withheld by accident or design. Most boys and girls desire to be "virtuous" in the sense that they are prepared to conform to the code of their group. They often wish, for example, for guidance through intimate talk or through illuminating reading as to the normal consequences of varying types of personal caressing. Information on such matters is, of course, obtainable both directly and indirectly in many ways. It is possessed in more or less detail by most children long before puberty; but youth leaders still occasionally meet young people who suppose that "You will get a baby if you kiss a man" and others who think that "There won't be a baby anyway and everyone is doing it".

As in the case of the acceptance or rejection of other forms of guidance, mere direct instruction or weighty warnings are here of less effect than the commendation which sets the act of sexual intercourse in its background of total living—without either morbid fears or exaggerated over-emphasis. Sex education, therefore, is increasingly being thought of as part of a wider guidance in the best accumulated wisdom as to the laws of inheritance, the care of the young, the complexities of family inter-relationships and the like. The romantic approach of the search for Lancelot or Elaine then becomes subordinate to a forward-looking consideration of the content of successful and permanent adjustments and the discovery of a mate who will be acceptable as a partner in one's whole life-drama.

Comparable in importance to the subject of relationships between men and women is the adolescent's questioning as to the meaning of life and of death. This also is not an issue in connection with which there is necessarily a sudden flowering of interest about the age of puberty. Any acuteness of onset is related to the attitude of the home and the community. It tends to occur at different points in the life-history of individuals in differing cultural patterns.[23] The frequency of reported conversion during adolescence is, for example, nowadays less than sixty years ago:[24] and the search for a philosophy of life can be noted among human beings from the age of four or five onwards. The metaphysical questionings of the little child—Why? How? By whom?—are directly continuous with the adolescent's concern[25] as to what one should believe about the universe; but the form which religious conviction takes is related closely to the trend of thought accepted in the home.[26] This often differs markedly from one group to another. Within one district it may range from an attempt to interpret existence solely in terms of mechanical laws and physical forces through an agnostic balancing of recent evidence on the complexity of cosmic structure to a fundamentalist acceptance of mediaeval forms of church service and ritual. (The conflict between such opposing points of view forms part of what has been called the "cultural shock" of emerging from the educative influences of the home to those of a wider world.) These topics are nowadays very actively discussed; but many young people in spite of lively interest suffer from lack of confident acceptance of a religious interpretation which through its satisfying of their basic psychological needs[27] would result in the healing of their self-despisings and the grasping of the anchor of an abiding faith. Many other adolescents, however, experience a religious certainty which is the more real because it is not so much a matter of fashionable expectation as the fruit of reasoned conviction and genuine emotional response.

Accompanying such adolescent attempts at discovery of the best way to fit life into the adult pattern go explorations of the many less crucial but none the less important smaller issues of daily living. Adolescents in our culture learn in a variety of ways how life is to be lived. Many receive initiation into the technique of entrance to a party or of behaviour in a bank, a pub, a hotel or a post-office through participation in the activities of a socially developed home-life. Others need to learn through dramatisation and through more hesitant imitation of strangers glimpsed through films seen, books read or stories heard. Where deliberate provision is not made for such learning, the boys and girls set themselves to organise it in the gang life of village or city. Such learning is important in their eyes, and where adult aid is withheld, they accept the alternative of instruction from their peers—the "other fellows" and the "girls in our street". Illuminating revelations of the social barrenness of some districts both in town and country is given by records of the devices adopted by young people to secure places in which to meet[28] and activities with which to occupy themselves. In certain respects small towns provide, as a consequence, greater problems for Probation Officers, Juvenile Courts and other preventive agencies than do great cities. Young people wish, not idleness and dependency, but responsible and active sharing in the vital interests of the adult world.[29] If these are not available, their energies are directed to the substitutes which adults describe as destructiveness and hooliganism.

Associated with this is their desire to learn codes of behaviour in relation to traditional leisure-time occupations. The nature of these activities varies somewhat with the circumstances of their lives; and in this connection also it is now believed that there is little necessary relation between social preferences and biological development. The topic of the exact character of preferred activities or interests prior to and after puberty or menstruation is therefore now believed to be of much less general relevance than was formerly supposed.[30] Like any change in dress, in choice of books or of occupation, the selection of a hobby is now admittedly considered to be a reflection of contemporary and local interpretation of the social role which the girl or boy is to play; and a knowledge of its character is held to be of importance chiefly to those concerned with the taking of definite action in a specific situation.[31] It used to be thought, for example, that the making of collections was a phenomenon as typical of childhood everywhere as is growth in length of limb. There is now reason to believe that, while it is a potential form of behaving for all human beings, it shows itself at different ages and in differing degrees with variations in the traditions of the group and the opportunities for alternative activity which are available. This observation (based, in the first place, upon the study of different cultural groups) has been recently supported by differences in the reported percentage of children engaging in such activities at differing periods. The percentage who attach importance to collecting appears to have fallen with the increase in competing interests of other kinds (and possibly also with changes in type of building and in amount of storage space).[32]

No longer, therefore, even in connection with such a comprehensive activity as collecting, can the coiner of generalisations be as confident in the accuracy of his statements as he was some years ago.

REFERENCES

[1] See:

Miller, N. E., and Dollard, J., *Social Learning and Imitation.* New Haven: Yale Univ. Press, 1941.

Davis, A., Socialization and Adolescent Personality, in Jones, H. E., *et al.*, Adolescence, *Forty-third Yearbook Nat. Soc. Study Educ.* Part I. Chicago: Univ. of Chicago. 1944.

Landis, P. H., *Adolescence and Youth. The Process of Maturing.* New York: McGraw-Hill, 1945 and 1952.

Warner, W. L., Havighurst, R. J., and Loeb, M. B., *Who Shall be Educated?* London: Kegan Paul, Trench, Trubner, 1946.

Havighurst, R. J., and Taba, H., *Adolescent Character and Personality.* New York: John Wiley, 1949.

Hollingshead, A. B., *Elmtown's Youth.* New York: John Wiley, 1949.

Peck, R. F., and Havighurst, R. J., *The Psychology of Character Development.* New York: John Wiley, 1960.

See also:

Barker, R. G., and Wright, H. F., *Midwest and its Children.* Evanston: Row Peterson, 1955.

Kaplan, B. (ed.), *Studying Personality Cross-Culturally.* Evanston: Row Peterson, 1961.

See also:

Oeser, O. A., and Hammond, S. B., *Social Structure and Personality in a City.* London: Routledge, 1954.

Oeser, O. A., and Emery, F. E., *Social Structure and Personality in a Rural Community.* London: Routledge, 1954.

Connell, W. F., *Growing up in an Australian City.* Melbourne: Austral. Council Educ. Res. Series 72, 1957.

Vereker, C., *et al.*, *Urban Development and Social Change: A Study of Social Conditions in Central Liverpool.* Liverpool: Univ. Press, 1961.

[2] Discussions of the social origin of delinquency may be found in:

Healy, W., and Bronner, A. F., *New Light on Delinquency and its Treatment.* New Haven: Yale Univ. Press, 1936.

Plant, J. S., *Personality and the Cultural Pattern.* New York: Commonwealth Fund, 1937.

Cohen, A. K., *Delinquent Boys: The Culture of the Gang.* London: Routledge & Kegan Paul, 1956.

Andry, R. G., *Delinquency and Parental Pathology.* London: Methuen, 1960.

Fyvel, T. R., *The Insecure Offenders: Rebellious Youth in the Welfare State.* London: Chatto and Windus, 1961.

See also:

Goodman, P., *Growing up Absurd. Problems of Youth in the Organised System.* London: Gollancz, 1961.

Coleman, J. S., Johnstone, J. W. C., and Jonassohn, K., *The Adolescent Society.* Glencoe: Free Press, 1961.

See also:

Making Citizens: A Review of the Aims, and Achievements of the Approved Schools in England and Wales. London: H.M.S.O., 1945.

Gittins, J., *Approved School Boys.* London: H.M.S.O., 1952.

Herbert, W. L., and Jarvis, F. V., *Dealing with Delinquents*. London: Methuen, 1961.
Hsu, F. L. K., Watrous, B. G., and Lord, E. M., *Culture Patterns and Adolescent Behavior*, Internat. *J. Soc. Psychiat.*, VII, 1 33–53, 1960–61.
Pinto-Jayawardana, W. D., *A Comparative Study of Certain Selected Groups of Delinquent Boys*. M.A. Thesis, Univ. of London, 1957.
³ For accessible discussions of the processes involved in such learning see:
Fleming, C. M., *The Social Psychology of Education*. London: Kegan Paul, Trench, Trubner, 1944, 1959 and 1961.
Fleming, C. M., *Teaching: A Psychological Analysis*. London: Methuen 1958 and 1959; New York: John Wiley, 1958.
⁴ In the partial contradiction of this dual character lies the basic problem as to the essential nature of man. For discussion of this see:
Niebuhr, R., *The Nature and Destiny of Man. A Christian Interpretation*. Vol. I. London: Nisbet, 1941.
Ashley-Montagu, M. F., *On Being Human*. London: Abelard-Schuman, 1957.
⁵ Moreno, J. L., *Who Shall Survive? A New Approach to the Problem of Human Interrelations*. New York: Nervous Diseases Pub. Co., 1934.
Aichhorn, A., *Wayward Youth*. London: Putnam, 1936.
Rogers, C. R., *The Clinical Treatment of the Problem Child*. Boston: Houghton Mifflin, 1939.
Slavson, S. R., *An Introduction to Group Therapy*. New York: Commonwealth Fund, 1943.
Healy, W., and Alper, B. S., *Criminal Youth and the Borstal System*. New York: Commonwealth Fund, 1941.
Merrill, M. A., *Problems of Juvenile Delinquency*. Boston: Houghton Mifflin, 1947.
Strang, R., *The Adolescent Views Himself*. New York: McGraw-Hill, 1948 and 1957.
Eissler, K. R., *Searchlights in Delinquency*. London: Imago, 1949.
Powers, E., and Witmer, H., *An Experiment in the Prevention of Delinquency*. New York: Columbia Univ. Press, 1951.
Stott, D. H., *Saving Children from Delinquency*. London: Univ. of London Press, 1952.
Wills, W. D., *Throw Away thy Rod*. London: Gollancz, 1960.
⁶ Hamley, H. R., Training Leaders in Iraq, *Times Educ. Suppl.*, March 18. 1944.
⁷ Bion, W. R., and Rickman, J., Intra-Group Tensions in Therapy. Their Study as the Task of the Group, *Lancet*, 678–681, 1943.
Sutherland, J. D., and Fitzpatrick, G. A., Some Approaches to Group Problems in the British Army, in Moreno, J. L., *Group Psychotherapy*. New York: Beacon House, 1945.
Wilson, A. T. M., The Serviceman Comes Home, *Pilot Papers*, I, No. 2, 9–28, 1946.
⁸ Burt, C., *The Young Delinquent*. London: Univ. of London Press, 1925.
Brill, J. G., and Payne, E. G., *The Adolescent Court and Crime Prevention*. New York: Pitman, 1938.
Shaw, C. R., and McKay, H. D., *Juvenile Delinquency and Urban Areas*. Chicago: Univ. of Chicago Press, 1942.
Neumeyer, M. H., *Juvenile Delinquency in Modern Society*. New York: D. van Nostrand, 1949, 1955 and 1961.
⁹ Fleming, C. M., loc. cit. [3].
Nye, F. I., *Family Relationships and Delinquent Behavior*. New York: John Wiley, 1958.

[10] Ackerson, L., *Children's Behavior Problems. A Statistical Study Based upon 5,000 Children Examined Consecutively at the Illinois Institute for Juvenile Research. I. Incidence, Genetic and Intellectual Factors.* Chicago: Univ. of Chicago Press, 1931.

Glueck, S., and Glueck, E. T., *One Thousand Juvenile Delinquents.* Cambridge: Harvard Univ. Press, 1934.

Ackerson, L., *Children's Behavior Problems. II. Relative Importance and Inter-relations among Traits.* Chicago: Univ. of Chicago Press, 1942.

Carr-Saunders, A. M., *Young Offenders.* Cambridge: Univ. Press, 1942.

Norwood-East, W., *et al., The Adolescent Criminal.* London: J. & A. Churchill, 1942.

See also:

Muhl, A. M., *The ABC of Criminology.* Austral. Council Educ. Res., 1941.

Hughes, E. W., An Analysis of the Records of some 750 Probationers, *Brit. J. Educ. Psychol.,* XIII, III, 113–125, 1943.

Dawson, W. M., An Investigation into Social Factors in Maladjustment, *Occup. Psychol.,* XVIII, 1, 41–51, 1944.

Banister, H., and Ravden, M., The Environment and the Child, *Brit. J. of Psychol.,* XXXV, 3, 82–87, 1945.

Mannheim, H., *Juvenile Delinquency in an English Middletown.* London: Routledge and Kegan Paul, 1948.

See also:

Pearce, J. D. W., *Juvenile Delinquency.* London: Cassell, 1952.

Mannheim, H., and Wilkins, L. T., *Prediction Methods in Relation to Borstal Training.* London: H.M.S.O., 1955.

Schneiders, A. A., *Personality Development and Adjustment in Adolescence.* Milwaukee: Bruce Publishing Company, 1960.

[11] Glueck, S., and Glueck, E. T., *Juvenile Delinquents Grown Up.* New York: Commonwealth Fund, 1942.

See also:

Rogers, C. R., loc. cit. [5].

Glueck, S. and E., *Criminal Careers in Retrospect.* New York: Commonwealth Fund, 1943.

Glueck, S. and E., *Unraveling Juvenile Delinquency.* New York: Commonwealth Fund, 1950.

[12] Taylor, K. W., *Do Adolescents Need Parents?* New York: Appleton-Century, 1938.

See also:

Harms, E. (ed.), Difficulties of Adolescence in the Girl, *The Nervous Child,* 4, 1, 3–99, 1944.

and

Difficulties of Adolescence in the Boy, *The Nervous Child,* 4, 2, 111–171, 1945.

Yudkin, S., *All Our Children.* London: Max Reinhardt, 1956.

[13] Van Waters, M., *Youth in Conflict.* London: Methuen, 1926.

Dollard, J., *et al., Frustration and Aggression.* New Haven: Yale Univ. Press, 1939 and 1961.

Fleming, C. M., loc. cit. 1958 [3].

[14] For useful statements see:

Keliher, A. V., *Life and Growth.* New York: Appleton-Century, 1938.

Bibby, C., *Sex Education.* London: Macmillan, 1944 and 1957.

Henriques, R. L., *Girls and their Boys.* London: The Bernhard Baron Settlement, 1944.

Hacker, R., *Telling the Teenagers.* London: Andre Deutsch, 1957.

[15] Wright, H., *The Sex Factor in Marriage*. London: Williams & Norgate, 1930.
Plant, J. S., *Personality and the Cultural Pattern*. New York: Commonwealth Fund, 1937.
Sargent, W. E., *The Psychology of Marriage and the Family Life*. London: Independent Press, 1940.
[16] Taylor, K. W., loc. cit. [12].
Stern, B. J., *The Family Past and Present*. New York: Appleton-Century, 1938.
Mace, D. R., *Does Sex Morality Matter?* London: Rich and Cowan, 1943.
Bibby, C., loc. cit. [14].
Schneiders, A. A., loc. cit. [10].
[17] See, for example:
Blatz, W. E., *Understanding the Young Child*. London: Univ. of London Press, 1944.
[18] A good summary may be found in:
Bacsish, M. D., Sharman, A., and Wyburn, G. M., The Effects of the Injection of Human Semen into Female Animals, *Obstet. Gynaecol. of the British Empire*, LII, 334–338, 1945.
See also:
Contraception and Infertility, Leading Article, *Brit. Med. J.*, 438–439, 1946.
[19] Leonard, E. A., *Problems of Freshman College Girls*. New York: Teachers College, Columbia Univ., 1932.
See also:
Lunger, R., and Page, J. D., Worries of College Freshmen, *The Ped. Sem. and J. of Genet. Psychol.*, 54, 457–460, 1939.
Rose, A. A., Insecurity Feelings in Adolescent Girls, in Harms, E. (ed.), *Difficulties of Adolescence in the Girl. The Nervous Child*, 4, 1, 46–59, 1944.
Gallagher, J. R., *Emotional Problems of Adolescents*. New York: Oxford Univ. Press, 1958.
Evans, K. M., *Club Members Today*. London: National Assoc. Mixed Clubs and Girls' Clubs, 1960.
Comparable evidence from a slightly older group may be found in:
Heath, C. W., *et al.*, *What People Are: A Study of Normal Young Men*. Cambridge: Harvard Univ. Press, 1945.
Havighurst, R. J., *Human Development and Education*. New York: Longmans, Green, 1953.
Peck, R. F., and Havighurst, R. J., *The Psychology of Character Development*. New York: John Wiley, 1960.
Coleman, J. S., Johnstone, J. W. C., and Jonassohn, K., *The Adolescent Society*. Glencoe: Free Press, 1961.
Schneiders, A. A., loc. cit. [10].
[20] Pope, C., Personal Problems of High School Pupils, School and Society, 57, 443–448, 1943. Cited Landis, P. H., loc. cit. [1].
Hemming, J., *Problems of Adolescent Girls*. London: Heinemann, 1960.
[21] Careful records on this may be found in:
Campbell, E. H., The Social–Sex Development of Children, *Genet. Psychol. Monogr.* 21, 461–552, 1939.
Meek, L. H., *The Personal-Social Development of Boys and Girls*. New York: Progressive Educ. Assoc., 1940.
Strang, R., *The Adolescent Views Himself*. New York: McGraw Hill, 1957.
Macalister Brew, J., *The Young Idea*. London: Nat. Assoc. Mixed Clubs and Girls' Clubs. (n.d.).
[22] Mannin, E., *Commonsense and the Adolescent*. London: Jarrolds. Revised Edition. (n.d.).

Useful references and bibliographies are given in:
Taylor, K. W., loc. cit. [12].
See also:
Leitch, A., A Survey of Reformative Influences in Borstal Training, *Brit. J. Med. Psychol.*, XX, 1, 77–95, 1944.
Herbert, W. L., and Jarvis, F. V., *Dealing with Delinquents*. London: Methuen, 1961.

23 Mead, M., and Wolfenstein, M., *Childhood in Contemporary Cultures*. Chicago: Univ. of Chicago, 1955.
See also:
Landis, P. H., loc. cit. [1].

24 Starbuck, E. D., *The Psychology of Religion*. New York: Charles Scribner's Sons, 1899.
Hall, G. Stanley, *Adolescence*. New York: Appleton, 1904.
See also:
Moreton, F. E., Attitudes to Religion among Adolescents and Adults, *Brit. J. Educ. Psychol.*, XIV, II, 69, 1, 79, 1944.
Loukes, H., *Teenage Religion*. London: Student Christian Movement, 1961.

25 Macalister-Brew, J., *Youth and Youth Groups*. London: Faber & Faber, 1957.

26 For evidence as to attitudes see also:
Vernon, P. E., *Personality Tests and Assessments*. London: Methuen, 1953.
Remmers, H. H., *Introduction to Opinion and Attitude Measurement*. New York: Harper, 1954.
Brewster Smith, M., Bruner, J. S., and White, R. W., *Opinions and Personality*. New York: John Wiley, 1956.
Hovland, C. I., and Janis, I. L., *Personality and Persuasibility*. New Haven: Yale Univ. Press, 1959.
Hovland, C. I., and Rosenberg, M. J., *Attitude Organization and Change*. New Haven: Yale Univ. Press, 1961.

27 For discussion of and evidence as to the psychological benefits of religious belief see:
Brown, W., *Psychological Methods of Healing*. London: Univ. of London Press, 1938.
Yeaxlee, B., *Religion and the Growing Mind*. London: Nisbet, 1939.
Watson, G. (ed.), *Civilian Morale*. Boston: Houghton Mifflin, 1942.
Brown, W., *Personality and Religion*. London: University of London Press, 1946.
See also:
Fromm-Reichmann, F., and Moreno, J. L., *Progress in Psychotherapy*. New York: Grune and Stratton, 1956.
Pinto-Jayawardana, W. D., loc. cit. [2].
Fleming, C. M., Participation as a Therapeutic Agent, *Internat. J. Social Psychiat.*, IV, 3, 214–220, 1958.
Simey, T. S., *The Concept of Love in Child Care*. London: Nat. Children's Home, 1960.

28 Thrasher, F. M., *A Study of 1313 Gangs in Chicago*. Univ. of Chicago Press, 1927.
Brill, J. G., and Payne, E. G., *The Adolescent Court and Crime Prevention*. New York: Pitman, 1938.
Thrasher, F. M., The Boys' Club and Juvenile Delinquency, *Amer. J. Sociol.*, XLII, 66–80, 1936.
Mays, J. B., *Growing up in the City*. Liverpool: Univ. Press, 1954.
Cohen, A. K., loc. cit. [2].

[29] *Men Without Work*. Cambridge: Univ. Press, 1938.
See also:
Hanna, P. R., *Youth Serves the Community*. New York: Appleton-Century, 1936.
Rainey, H. P., *et al.*, *How Fare American Youth?* New York: Appleton-Century, 1937.
Lush, A. J., *The Young Adult*. Cardiff: South Wales & Monmouthshire Council of Social Service (Inc.), 1941.
Canfield-Fisher, D., *Meaning for Life in Youth and the Future*. Washington: Amer. C. on Educ., 1942.
Disinherited Youth: A Survey 1936–1939. A Report on the 18+ Age Group Enquiry prepared for the Trustees of the Carnegie United Kingdom Trust. Dunfermline, 1943.
Macalister-Brew, J., loc. cit. [25].
Wall, W. D., *Child of Our Times*. London: Nat. Children's Home, 1959.
Fyvel, T. R., loc. cit. [2].
Goodman, P., loc. cit. [2].
[30] Stone, C. P., and Barker, R. G., The Attitudes and Interests of Pre-menarcheal and Postmenarcheal Girls, *Ped. Sem. and J. Genet. Psychol.*, 54, I, 27–71, 1939.
Dennis, W., The Adolescent, in Carmichael, L. (ed.), *Manual of Child Psychology*. New York: John Wiley, 1946.
Jones, M. C., and Bayley, N., Physical Maturing among Boys as Related to Behavior *J. Educ. Psychol.*, 41, 129–148, 1950.
Davidson, H. H., and Gottlieb, L. S., The Emotional Maturity of Pre- and Post-menarcheal Girls, *J. Genet. Psychol.*, 86, 261–6, 1955.
Mussen, P. H., and Jones, M. C., Self-Conceptions, Motivations, and Inter-personal Attitudes of Late- and Early-maturing Boys, *Child Dev.*, 28, 243–256, 1957.
Mussen, P. H., and Jones, M. C., The Behavior-inferred Motivations of Late- and Early-maturing Boys, *Child. Dev.*, 29, 61–67, 1958.
Faust, M. S., Developmental Maturity as a Determinant in Prestige of Adolescent Girls, *Child Dev.*, 31, 173–184, 1960.
Representative discussions of the nature of interests will be found in:
Fryer, D., *The Measurement of Interests in Relation to Human Adjustment*. New York: Henry Holt, 1931.
Strong, E. K., *Vocational Interests of Men and Women*. Stanford: Stanford Univ. Press, 1943.
Strong, E. K., *Vocational Interests 18 Years after College*. Minneapolis: Univ. of Minnesota Press, 1955.
See also:
Adolescence. Current Affairs Bulletin, 20, 3. Sidney, 1957.
Terman, L. M., *et al.*, *Genetic Studies of Genius. Mental and Physical Traits of a Thousand Gifted Children*. Stanford: Stanford Univ. Press, 1925.
Burks, B. S., *et al.*, *The Promise of Youth: Follow-up Studies of a Thousand Gifted Children*. Stanford: Stanford Univ. Press, 1930.
Terman, L. M., and Oden, M. H., *The Gifted Child Grows Up. Twenty-five Years' Follow-up of the Superior Child*. Stanford: Stanford Univ. Press, 1947.
Terman, L. M., and Oden, M. H., *The Gifted Group at Mid-Life. Thirty-five Years' Follow-up of the Superior Child*. Stanford: Stanford Univ. Press, 1959.
[31] For an introduction to representative surveys see:
Shakespeare, J. J., An Enquiry into the Relative Popularity of School Subjects in Elementary Schools, *Brit. J. Educ. Psychol.*, VI, 147–164, 1936.

Boynton, P. L., The Relationship of Hobbies to Personality Characteristics of School Children, *J. Exper. Educ.*, 8, 363–367, 1940.

Hotoph, W. H. N., Some Characteristic Interests of Schoolboys, *Occup. Psychol.*, XV, 3, 133–144, 1941.

Rallison, R., The Interests of Senior School Children in Non-Scientific Subjects, *Brit. J. Educ. Psychol.*, XIII, I, 39–47, 1943.

Eid, N., *An Investigation into the out-of-school Activities of a Group of Adolescents*. London: M.A. Thesis, 1948.

Meyer, G. R., Factors Accompanying the Scientific Interest of a Selected Group of English Secondary Pupils, *Austral. J. Educ.*, 5, 1, 27–40, 1961, and 5, 2, 105–115, 1961.

Relevant British enquiries:

MacAlister-Brew, J., *Club Girls and their Interests*. London: Nat. Assoc. of Girls' Clubs and Mixed Clubs. (n.d.).

Ibid., *Interests of Boys in Mixed Clubs*, 1949.

Smaller surveys are represented by:

The Welfare of Youth: A City Survey. the Univ. of Bristol, 1945.

The Needs of Youth in Stockton-on-Tees. Stockton-on-Tees Service of Youth Office, 1946.

and a similar report from workers in Luton in the same year.

See also:

Brooks, F. D., *The Psychology of Adolescence*. Boston: Houghton-Mifflin, 1929.

Cole, L., *Psychology of Adolescence*. New York: Farrar and Rinehart, 1942.

Valentine, C. W., Adolescence and some Problems of Youth Training, *Brit. J. Educ. Psychol.*, XIII, II, 57–68, 1943.

Ausubel, D. P., *Theory and Problems of Adolescent Development*. New York: Grune and Stratton, 1954.

Jersild, A. T., *Child Psychology*. Fourth Edition. New York: Prentice-Hall, 1954.

Wattenberg, W., *The Adolescent Years*. New York: Harcourt-Brace, 1955.

Hurlock, E. B., *Adolescent Development*. New York: McGraw-Hill, 1955.

Strang, R., *The Adolescent Views Himself*. New York: McGraw-Hill, 1957.

Evans, K. M., *Club Members Today*. London: Nat. Assoc. Mixed Clubs and Girls' Clubs, 1960.

[32] Beaglehole, E., *Property: A Study in Social Psychology*. London: Allen & Unwin, 1931.

Waites, J. A., An Inquiry into the Attitudes of Adults towards Property in a Lancashire Urban Area, *Brit. J. Psychol.*, XXXVI, 1, 33–42, 1945.

CHAPTER XVII

ADOLESCENTS WITH PROBLEMS

The difficulties of adolescents (like those of all human beings) are very directly related to the experiences they meet in the various groups in which they find themselves members. Their power of reacting to these situations and the type of response they make is, however, a consequence of their inherited potentialities as well as of their environmental treatment.

It is not now thought that identity of nurture will result in uniformity of response; but at the same time it is not considered that the nature of all later reactions is fixed at birth.

In similar fashion there is reason to believe that, while the actions of the group produce marked effects upon the behaviour of its members, the individual in turn is not without influence upon the activities of the group.

The evidence which has accumulated from long-term studies has served to increase rather than to diminish both this realisation of the consequences of group membership and an awareness of the reality of individual differences. It is now established that there is not only a wide range of differences among human beings at any given age but also that these variations are accompanied by variabilities in the life-history of individuals, the nature of whose predisposing circumstances are as yet only imperfectly understood.

Many of the problems of adolescents are traceable to this fact of individual differences, and many adolescents can be helped to solve their problems by the serene acceptance by parent or teacher of the actuality of such differences and their relative unimportance.

On the side of physical maturing, such differences, if over-emphasised or greeted with anxiety or scorn, may lead to unhappiness which could have been avoided by an attitude of greater nonchalance.

Precocious puberty is, for example, more frequent than is commonly supposed.[1] Early menstruation may result from tumours of certain endocrine glands or from lesions of the brain, but it has also been reported in children ranging in age from fifteen months to seven years without any detectable abnormality of this kind.

Such sexual precocity may, however, have unfortunate social consequences through the self-consciousness which results from the child's awareness of the differences between herself and her contemporaries or from the shame-faced attitude of the parents at the appearance not only of primary but also of secondary sex characteristics. In certain social circles care has to be taken to protect such children from impregnation by mature boys or men who are attracted by their precocious physical charms. In some groups the fears of the parents may lead to invalidism and neurotic distress. In other families it may, however, be realised that such girls are, by the age of nine or ten, not appreciably different from many of their contemporaries, and in such homes their unusual maturity may lead to no undesirable consequences. The actual differences between these girls and their associates may or may not prove modifiable by medical or surgical means. The personal consequence of the idiosyncrasy is, however, definitely determined by the attitude of the social group.

Comparable personal problems may arise from the fact that human beings, like other animals, are not exclusively of one sex or the other, but carry potentialities in which one set of characters predominates. The relative preponderance of male and female sex hormones (detectable through examination of the blood and the urine) varies somewhat from one individual to another and from one time to another; and in this variation may be found a concomitant of certain individual differences in sensitivity to and interest in the presence of members of the opposite sex. Not all adolescents (or all adults) are ready for heterosexual activities at the same age or to the same extent. The absence of heterosexual interest is, in some cases, related to cultural pressure or to undue segregation in youth. In other instances it is accompanied either by marked deficiency[2] or by definite excess of one type or other of the sex hormones. The matter is complicated by the fact that there is no correspondence between such conditions and either mental or physical strength or outward bodily form; but the adults in contact with adolescents can again help them to meet reality without dismay or shock through an absence of teasing and critical comment—an admission that it takes all sorts to make a world and that very useful contributions can be made by individuals whose point of view on such issues is not identical with that of the majority of their contemporaries.

Of simpler form, and often more transient nature, are many of the difficulties mentioned in earlier chapters. Adolescence is a period of physiological learning, and the rate of bodily adjustment varies from one individual to another. Some children are acutely disturbed at any change which makes them markedly different from their neighbours. Others encounter with apparent equanimity the inevitable alterations in length of leg, width of shoulders or hips, size of trunk, formation of nose or chin, and the less-obvious changes of distribution of face or of hair. Some adolescents, in similar fashion, meet the more abrupt changes in their genitalia (and the sequels of ovulation in girls and discharge of motile spermatozoa by boys) with an absence of perturbation very different from the fear and anxiety which the same physical phenomena induce in others of like age. The exact character of physical maturation differs from one child to another, and the attitudes of the children also vary. The distresses consequent on all such changes can be much reduced by contact with adults who are aware of the extent of adolescent variability and its insignificance.

Special problems following upon this growth from the state of children to that of men or women are experienced by adolescents in social groups in which the cultural nature of secondary sex roles is not recognised. The expectations entertained by society as to the vocational and occupational parts to be played by women and by men very often run counter to the wishes and the preferred skills of the individuals concerned. Evidence as to the conventionality[3] of such expectations and their variation from country to country as well as from one generation to another renders it now more possible for sympathetic adults to assist children—by the casualness of their attitude—to adequate acceptance of their role and also to encourage them to believe that its present form need not be final. It is much less damaging to the self-esteem and wholesome development of a boy to be debarred from certain activities on the ground that it is a matter of convenience or custom that his sister or mother should do those things than it is to be told that "Boys can't . . ." "Boys are no use at . . ." "We'll need to get a woman to do that!"

Less modifiable problems are encountered by those boys and girls who, for one reason or another, are ashamed of their homes. In many circles this occasions more emotional distress than does a direct revolt against parental control. Especially is this the case in districts into which migration is recent and in settings in which social climbing is associated with very marked divergencies in the techniques of ordinary living. The rich boy in the company of children from poor homes, the foreigner, the city child in the country and the son of a drunkard or of an acknowledged thief may suffer acutely from the knowledge that their homes require apology in the presence of their peers. Their problem is the more severe if a compensatory home life does not supply for them the support of a preferred inner group. Such difficulties of reputation are not peculiar to adolescence as such, but adolescents who are seeking to establish their place in the world of their contemporaries are in these respects more vulnerable than they were as little children or than they will be as adults. The same observation may be made in connection with the not dissimilar problem faced by the physically handicapped—the blind, the deaf or the crippled.

Somewhat comparable difficulties are faced by children of sub-normal mentality.[4] Such children in the home, at school or at work may meet defeat so regularly that they fail to secure the acceptance, the recognition and the opportunity for responsible contributing which they require for healthy functioning. Their dullness may lead to quite inadequate satisfaction of their basic psychological needs. In their case also the kindliness and serenity of informed adults may prevent undue damage and distress.

Of slightly different type are the inadequacies directly attributable to the treatment given to adolescents in their groups. These are somewhat difficult to detect; and to some extent they are to be found in all human beings. (At all stages human performance is probably less than human potentialities.) The limits set by inheritance always operate; but their exact nature can become clear only under the best environmental conditions.[5] With recent advances in the understanding of the accompaniments of success it is, however, becoming possible to be more hopeful as to the uses of remedial treatment than it was formerly.

Certain information is, for example, now available as to the types of nurture which produce certain sorts of behaviour at various stages of growth. It is known that stimulation combined with acceptance and encouragement at an early age can improve measureable intellectual performance so much that the mental ratio or intelligence quotient may be significantly raised. The dull foster child may, after residence in a good foster home, approximate more closely in what is commonly called intelligence to the level of his foster-parents than to that of his true parents. In

Q

similar fashion, the temperamental responses of children have been observed to change under differing treatment or in association with different ensamples. The foster children of unusually aggressive adults in New Guinea,[6] for example, developed mannerisms and attitudes more like those of their foster-parents than those of their true parents. The pupils in American classrooms[7] became measurably less assertive and noisy under handling which was tolerant, controlled and calm. The hooligan adolescents in factories or streets lost their roughness[8] when treated as intelligent adults and given satisfaction of their needs of acceptance and adventure in groups which trusted them to share in their responsibilities.

Pupils in whom dullness and scholastic retardation increase from year to year and adolescents whose anti-social tendencies become more obvious with increasing age are children whose symptoms proclaim aloud their need for treatment. They are not so much problem adolescents as adolescents with problems; and their objectionable behaviour is less an inevitable consequence of their inheritance than a result of the experiences which they have been permitted to encounter.

Chief among such problems are those which have been described as the sex problems of the adolescent. Formerly these were attributed to the sudden birth or the increased activity of a sex instinct which was peculiarly the accompaniment of adolescence. Closer study of groups of different types has, however, indicated that there are greater variations in the incidence and the nature of such sexually toned experiences than can be accounted for in terms of such a physiological interpretation. In consequence, it is now believed that these difficulties in their more acute form are not so much difficulties of adolescence as such but are rather the distresses consequent on an adolescence lived under certain conditions.

It is not without significance, for example, that the most lively descriptions of their forcefulness come from social settings where adolescent boys and girls are educated apart and trained for distinct activities and with very different emphasis. The ecstasy or the distaste with which the green tunics of the girls from the girls' school are viewed by the boys from the boys' school[9] is remarkably different from the quality of any adolescent experience of boys of similar age who have been accustomed to continuous association with girls from Infant School to College. The somewhat exotic and hot-house fierceness of the longings of the cloistered boy or girl are quite unlike the strong attachments and open friendliness of adolescents whose experiments in love-making have been conducted in the atmosphere of a school where interest in the opposite sex is held to be normal, unremarkable and permissible. Descriptions of sexual frustrations and their reverberations in the lives of such segregated adolescents do not apply to tribes or families, states or schools in which the pattern of living is fashioned on quite different lines.[10]

Adolescent sex difficulties deserving of the name are also found among those whose home life has been lacking in satisfaction of the basic human needs. Prostitutes and sexual perverts (when case studies are made of their history) are, for the most part, individuals from broken homes, from family groups where mother or father was unduly possessive, or from homes where the children were unwanted. Homosexual perversions also reach the dimensions of a problem chiefly in the artificial segregation of single-sex establishments; and on evidence such as this, the promiscuity of the prostitute, the unattached student in Bohemia or the less-intelligent soldier in a foreign land is now believed to have its origin in loneliness and lack of social interests rather than in strong sexuality.[11] It is paralleled by the longing for approval of the adolescent girl who has had no father to pay her attentions and no satisfactory home life with opportunities for joyous sharing in many activities.[12]

Present-day treatment of such difficulties is turning, therefore, to an interpretation based upon the safeguards of a social interest which can be developed by competent organisation of group friendlinesses rather than to an acceptance of the older viewpoint that "it is as difficult for some individuals to escape the hands of the law as it is for them to add one cubit to their stature".[13]

An extension of wholesome heterosexual contacts in genuinely co-educational day schools or clubs is now known to be more efficacious as an aid to healthy maturing than the violent exercise formerly advocated for boys or the parental whippings administered to girls. In this connection also it is coming to be believed that wiser situational treatment can reduce many of the problems of adolescent behaviour.

The responsibility of adults—parents, teachers or employers—with regard to all such problems is, nowadays, not lighter but heavier than it was in the years when inescapable distresses and biologically determined turmoils were believed to be an inevitable characteristic of a certain stage of growth. Human beings are both individual and social. They differ in potentialities; but the capacities of all can be realised to an extent which was formerly unknown. The task of the educator is, therefore, the hard but fascinating one of diagnosing and treating the special difficulties of those adolescents who by misdemeanours of various kinds signify that they are human beings in distress—adolescents with personal problems which cry aloud for solution.

REFERENCES

[1] Greenhill, J. P., *Year Book Obstet. and Gynec.* Chicago: Year Book Publishers, 1959.

[2] Solomon, H. C., and Yakovlev, P. I., *Manual of Military Neuropsychiatry.* Philadelphia: Saunders, 1944.

Kinsey, A. C., *et al.*, *Sexual Behavior in the Human Female.* Philadelphia: Saunders, 1953.

[3] Mead, M., *Male and Female.* New York: William Morrow, 1949.

Benedict, R., *Patterns of Culture.* London: Routledge, 1935.

Lynd, R. S., and Lynd, H. M., *Middletown in Transition.* New York: Harcourt, Brace, 1937.

Williams, G., *Women and Work.* London: Nicholson and Watson, 1945.

Klein, V., *The Feminine Character. History of an Ideology.* London: Kegan Paul, Trench, Trubner, 1946.

Luetkens, C., *Women and a New Society.* London: Nicholson and Watson, 1946.

Mueller, K. H., *Educating Women for a Changing World.* Minneapolis: Univ. of Minnesota Press, 1954.

[4] Abel, T. M., and Kinder, E. F., *The Subnormal Adolescent Girl.* New York: Columbia Univ. Press, 1942.

Cleugh, M. F., *Psychology in the Service of the School.* London: Methuen, 1951.

Cruickshank, W. (ed.), *Psychology of Exceptional Children and Youth.* New York: Prentice-Hall, 1955.

[5] Summaries of evidence on inheritance and environment may be found in:

Stoddard, G. D., *et al.*, Intelligence: Its Nature and Nurture, *Thirty-ninth Yearbook Soc. Study of Educ.* Bloomington: Public School Publishing, 1940.

Waterhouse, J. A. W., Heredity and Environment in Relation to Education, in *Yearbook of Education.* London: Evans, 90–116, 1950.

David, P. R., and Snyder, L. H., Genetic Variability and Human Behavior, in Rohrer, J. H., and Sherif, M., *Social Psychology at the Crossroads*, 53–82. New York: Harper, 1951.

Vernon, P. E., *Intelligence and Attainment Tests.* London: Univ. of London Press, 1960.

[6] Mead, M., *Growing Up in New Guinea.* London: Penguin Books, 1942. (First published New York: William Morrow, 1930.)

[7] Arbuckle, D. S., *Teacher Counseling.* Cambridge: Addison-Wesley Press, 1950.

Redl, F., and Wattenberg, W. W., *Mental Hygiene in Teaching.* New York: Harcourt, Brace, 1951.

Corey, S. M., *Action Research to Improve School Practices.* New York: Teachers College, Columbia Univ., 1953.

Moustakas, C. E., *The Teacher and the Child.* New York: McGraw-Hill, 1956.

[8] Lowndes, G. A. N., *The Silent Social Revolution: 1895–1935.* London: Oxford Univ. Press, 1937.

Brill, J. G., and Payne, E. G., *The Adolescent Court and Crime Prevention.* New York: Pitman, 1938.

Giles, F. T., *Children and the Law.* London: Pelican Books, 1959.

[9] Iovetz-Tereschenko, N. M., *Friendship–Love in Adolescence.* London: Allen & Unwin, 1936.

[10] Suttie, I. D., *The Origins of Love and Hate*. London: Kegan Paul, Trench, Trubner, 1935.

Adler, A., *Understanding Human Nature*. London: Allen & Unwin, 1930.

Ganz, M., *The Psychology of Alfred Adler and the Development of the Child*. Translated by P. Mairet. London: Routledge and Kegan Paul, 1953.

Way, L., *Alfred Adler*. Pelican Books, 1956.

Dell, Floyd, *Love in the Machine Age*. London: Routledge, 1930.

Horney, K., *New Ways in Psycho-analysis*. London: Kegan Paul, Trench, Trubner, 1939.

Mowrer, O. H., *Learning Theory and the Symbolic Processes*. New York: John Wiley, 1960.

[11] Rees, J. R., *The Shaping of Psychiatry by War*. New York: Norton, 1945.

For comparable discussions of the complexity of sexual behaviour see also:

Plant, J. S., *Personality and the Cultural Pattern*. New York: Commonwealth Fund, 1937.

Harding, D. W., *The Impulse to Dominate*. London: Allen & Unwin, 1941. and

Marcault, J. E., and Brosse, T., *L'Education de Demain*. Paris: Librairie Felix Alcan, 1939.

Plant, J. S., *The Envelope: A Study of the Impact of the World upon the Child*. New York: Commonwealth Fund, 1950.

[12] Fleming, C. M., *The Social Psychology of Education*. London: Kegan Paul, Trench, Trubner, 1944, 1959 and 1961.

Macalister Brew, J., *Youth and Youth Groups*. London: Faber & Faber, 1957.

Macalister Brew, J., *The Young Idea*. London: Nat. Assoc. Mixed Clubs and Girls' Clubs (n.d.).

[13] Cited:

Maguinness, O. D., *Environment and Heredity*. London: Nelson, 1940.

CHAPTER XVIII

A BRIEF SUMMARY

Adolescence may be defined in general terms as the period of transition from childhood to maturity. It usually includes the experiences of physical growth which precede the onset of puberty; but the word "adolescent" has a wider connotation than the word "puberal".

Both premature and delayed pubescence are more frequent than is generally supposed; but the years of adolescence are commonly a time of physiological learning in which an individual's physical structure and bodily functions alter from those peculiar to little children to those characteristic of adult human beings. They are also a time of social learning in which adjustments are made both to these changes in physique and to accompanying alterations in social expectations and personal ambitions. The nature of these expectations and the forms which this adaptation must take vary markedly from one home to another and differ still more widely from one district or one country to another.

Widespread interest in the experiences of adolescents and serious concern with their problems are of relatively recent origin. They appear to be concomitants of modern increases in the length of economic infancy, of periods of widespread adult unemployment and of postponement of the admission of younger people to the satisfactions of responsible contributing to the welfare of their groups.

Discussion of the attributes of the adolescent (like the science of psychology itself) has passed from a reliance on introspection and theorising through a study of individuals in laboratories or consulting rooms to an awareness of the complexity of human interrelationships and of the adaptability and variety of human behaviour. Philosophic fiction in earlier centuries (influenced by traditions of ceremonial initiation or ritual rejoicing) emphasised the discreteness of the stages of human growth; and generalisations based upon the experiences of adolescents in western Europe or the United States of America at the end of the nineteenth century contributed to an exaggerated expectation of emotional turmoil, of mental ferment and of the occurrence of many psychological changes of profound significance in the life-history of all children during the early years of their adolescence. This expectation has exercised a regrettable influence upon the educational and vocational guidance of pupils in many secondary schools.

More recent studies, with better sampling, long-term observation of the same individuals, more adequate statistical techniques and greater attention to group relationships, have shown the inadequacy of many of the findings, both of theorists such as Rousseau and of early observers such as Stanley Hall or Freud. Careful reports from anthropologists have also drawn attention to the variations in intellectual, emotional and social behaviour which are found in differing types of society; and the challenge presented by this evidence has further directed the attention of psychologists to the differences observable from one home to another and from one social circle to another, as well as from one district to another. Many earlier generalisations can, for these reasons, now no longer be accepted; and attention is being redirected to the continuity of human growth, the gradualness and irregularity of human development, and the extent of human educability and adaptability.

The task of the educator, the parent or the employer is, therefore, both harder and more interesting than it was in the opening years of the twentieth century, when storm and stress, conflict and rebellion, moodiness and apathy were the legendary experiences of all adolescents.

It is now no longer possible to attribute to adolescence as such the difficulties experienced by those individuals who fall behind in their school work, rebel against adult standards, reveal sudden changes of interest, show signs of acute hero-worship, experiment with homosexual perversions, appear to be too highly-sexed, show anti-social or delinquent tendencies, or suffer from minor ailments of a physical kind.

It is now no longer supposed that, in the early teens, the growth of intelligence ceases, that the power of memorising deteriorates, that logical thinking and socialised living become, for the first time possible, or that there is a universal awakening of imagination, of sexual sensitivity and of religious awareness.

There is now no reason to believe that all adolescents pass through an observably negative phase, that they all require an opportunity of earning money and achieving economic independence or even that all girls mature earlier than all boys.

Careful estimation of the average performance and the deviations from the mean of the same individuals in successive years from infancy to maturity has shown both the degree of overlapping from one age-group to the next and the prevalence of variability and irregularity of development in the life history of each individual.

While children tend to remain within one group over a series of years (if classification is made into five or six broad categories) the growth of each individual appears to follow its own course in relation to the average of the group. Relative size (of any kind) or performance (of any type) proves not fully prognostic of later relative size or performance; and attempts at exact prediction are especially hazardous during the years of adolescence.

The physiological experiences of pubescence are now believed to be similar in average age of onset and in the variety and variability of their rate of development in human beings all over the world—without regard to race or climate and with a variation of about six months as the difference between the average age of maturation of girls and of boys. (With certain criteria of maturity there appears to be no significant difference between the sexes in average age of genital maturing.)

The social experiences of adolescence (which for most boys and girls includes the period of the onset of puberty) vary in their details from one home or school to another and from one country to another. In some cultural settings there is much strain and anxiety associated with the transition from the dependence and irresponsibility of childhood to the independence and responsible contributing of adult status. This storm and stress, with its resultant emotional instability and intellectual ferment, is not, however, biologically determined but socially conditioned. It is neither a universal nor an inevitable accompaniment of adolescent growth; and its occurrence presents a challenge to enquiry and indicates the desirability of some change in treatment and modification of group tensions.

The years of transition from childhood to maturity bring with them the necessity for certain personal adaptations. The growing child has to learn to accept himself—his size, appearance, strength, genital structure and functioning. He has to discover how to adjust his expectations and his wishes to his own capacity relative to his peers and also to the secondary sex roles which society expects him to fill. To the degree to which he develops social maturity he must also learn some acceptance of the variability of human nature—the unexpectedness of much human behaviour, the range of differences in attitude and points of view in the world at large, and the relativity of friendship and of the means by which human beings make themselves acceptable to one another. He requires to develop both flexibility and steadfastness in relation to all of these. And at the same time he is expected to learn the traditions of his group with regard to personal and sexual relationships.

All this brings with it a certain measure of insecurity and uncertainty which varies in amount with the nature of the child and the character of the experiences he has met at home or in school. The transition from the relatively narrow circle of the child to the wider group membership of the adult is most marked in the case of segregated children from self-centred homes and from single-sex boarding schools or residential institutions. The necessary change of outlook and modification of "time-perspective" or planning is greater among children who have been treated as toys or irresponsible dependants than it is among those who have enjoyed the friendship and shared the interests and anxieties of their parents. The distress consequent upon changes in physical structure and bodily functioning is greater among children who have been led to attach undue importance to personal appearance and among those who have met attitudes of disgust and shame in connection with their enquiries into the meaning of sexual maturity. The sense of personal inadequacy resulting from ignorance of adult social techniques or from lack of knowledge of the information required for participation in the adult life of a community varies also in degree with the nature of the activities, the type of social intercourse and the variety of group memberships which have been permitted to the child in earlier years. No generalisation as to the nature of these is valid; and collection of data as to their extent is admittedly of only local interest.

Uncertainty and insecurity in face of the unknown lead in the case of adolescents (as of adults or little children) to a certain tension and to fluctuations between aggressiveness and timidity. These, however, are not biological accompaniments of the adolescent years of physical growth so much as social consequences of certain sorts of experience. They vary in their incidence and their extent. In some social circles they are very marked. In others they are absent. The task of the educator, the parent or the employer is now not so much to provide for certain inevitable attitudes and inescapable conflicts as to provide opportunities for the gradual and wholesome maturing of intelligent and sociable children into intelligent and socially mature adults.

Results of thorough testing and prolonged observation of the personal and social development of large numbers of adolescents have served to emphasise the extent of individual differences, the overlapping of age-groups and sex-groups, and the variability which characterises the growth of each individual.

Attempts to evade the social and intellectual consequences of this variety and variability through the ability-grouping of pupils or the analytic testing of their "aptitudes" have led to fuller awareness of the complexity of nature observable in all human beings.

Thorough statistical analysis of the results of the testing of abilities (like careful anthropometric measurements of physical attributes) have proved the impossibility of classifying children or adults into a small number of discrete types. The relationship between physical and mental development at any age has been shown to be low; and the improvements which can be effected by better environmental treatment are now known to be demonstrably greater than was formerly supposed.

It is, therefore, not now possible to believe that there is any psychological justification for a change in the educational treatment of all pupils at about the age of eleven. There is no evidence that all children mature in any one direction at the same time, that the sequence of growth is the same in all or even that the development of any individual is quite regular in its rate.

Segregation in terms of any one form of maturity consequently finds no support from recent researches. There is no reason to believe that early vocational decisions (and consequent limitation of educational opportunities) can wisely be made in terms of an assumed divisibility into human types; and recent emphasis on the importance of social maturing indicates also the undesirability of any segregation based upon sex, upon chronological age or in terms of socio-economic level.

The interest of investigators has turned from the classifying of individuals in terms of single attributes, such as age, sex, intelligence or performance, to a study of human beings in active membership of the groups of which they form a part. Attention is therefore being given in many schools and workshops to a study of optimal conditions for the social and personal maturing of all adolescents. Cognisance is being taken of the effect of their attitudes, their interests and their wishes, and there is increasing awareness of the significance of group tensions, of the therapeutic effects of group discussions or the dramatising of human problems, and of the importance both of varied and stimulating intellectual activities and of ample opportunities for social-sex development in co-educational settings.

This concern with the successful maturing of the whole person is associated with a study of basic psychological needs; and it is now widely believed that the distressing behaviour which characterises some adolescents is neither an inevitable accompaniment of a certain stage of growth nor the inescapable consequence of the maturing of certain animal-like instincts.

Conflict, defiance or unhappiness have been observed to result from certain social antecedents and certain sorts of situational treatment. Problem adolescents are, therefore, now thought of as adolescents with difficulties which cry aloud for attention; and it is now known that many of their problems can be solved through more adequate satisfaction of their basic requirements of acceptance in society, an opportunity for responsible contributing to the welfare of some group and some measure of insight into and toleration of the complexities of human existence.

The behaviour of adolescents is in direct sequel to their behaviour and their experiences in earlier phases of growth. Development is gradual rather than saltatory in character. The mental health of a community is indivisible; and its foundations in adolescence, as in maturity, rest upon that mutual consideration, love and goodwill which are rendered possible by the essentially social nature of the human beings whose inter-relationships form the life-drama in which all adolescents are learning to play their part.

EPILOGUE

Homes in which interesting things happen and in which the co-operation of children is welcomed. Parents who have attained some measure of emotional maturity and an awareness of their own religious experience. A corner for some treasured possessions and a certain measure of responsibility for some part of the common welfare. An atmosphere of courtesy and consideration. The security which follows upon the consciousness of family affection. These are the requirements of youth in the home.

Schools in which meaningful activities occur and in which the willing participation of pupils is encouraged. Teachers who are themselves emotionally and socially mature. A measure of acceptance and recognition by an admired group. Opportunities for adventures in learning and a chance to contribute deliberately to the corporate life of the whole. These are the needs of youth in the school.

Communities in which attractive enterprises are undertaken and in which there is an acknowledged part for every child to play. Opportunities for recognition, adventure and responsibility. An atmosphere of friendliness and kindliness. Provision for the opening of windows upon the communal heritage of religion, philosophy, art, music and literature. This is the setting in which adolescents may mature to healthy adult living.

Factories and workshops in which even small tasks can be understood in their relation to the whole. Courtesy and consideration on the part of adult co-workers. Encouragement of youthful endeavour and deliberate provision for the acceptance of newcomers into the companionship of the whole—these are some of the needs of youth in its working hours.

A closer approach to the satisfaction of such requirements is not impossible. It can be achieved without undue interference with the needs of adults or of little children. Mental health is indivisible. A stable life for older men and women rests upon the same foundations of love and goodwill as does the building of a world which shall be suited to the adolescents in their midst.

APPENDIX

SOME STATISTICAL TERMS

Investigations in the field of human behaviour often take the form of intensive observation of a group of individuals chosen as a sample from a larger population.

The notes which follow give a simple introduction to the meaning of certain statistical terms in common use in the assembling and evaluation of such studies.

The reporting of a sampling study usually involves the presentation of a number of scores. These scores, when arranged in order, may be observed to show a certain concentration or central tendency as well as a dispersion, scatter or spread. In general, the "average" or "mean" is the measure of central tendency most frequently mentioned, and the standard deviation is commonly accepted as the most useful means of describing the dispersion or spread.

STANDARD DEVIATIONS

The standard deviation is obtained by finding the deviation of each score from the mean, squaring each deviation and calculating the square root of the average value of such squared deviations. It is commonly reported with the words "standard deviation" printed in full. On other occasions the abbreviation "S.D." is used, but sometimes the Greek word Sigma (or the symbol σ) is given instead. (See for example page 12 above.)

STANDARD SCORES

The position of any score in relation to the total distribution may conveniently be described by saying that its deviation from the mean is so many times the standard deviation of the distribution. If, for example, a pupil scored 122 on an occasion in which the mean score for his group was 90 and the standard deviation of the distribution was 16 his relative position could be given unambiguously by saying that he scored at the level of two standard deviations or sigmas above the mean or, in other words, that his "standard score" was +2. A standard score of −2 would be made by a pupil in the same group on the same occasion whose mark was 58 (two standard deviations below the mean), while a standard score of +1·5 would describe the relative position of a pupil scoring 114 (and one a half standard deviations above the mean).

PERCENTILES

A second method of describing the relative position of any score is in terms of its percentile rank. The word "percentile" may be understood in terms of the division of a group of pupils arranged in order of merit into one hundred numerically equal sets. Each such set of pupils can then be said to have a "percentile" rank. A percentile score of 75 is then the average score of the set of pupils holding the 75th "percentile" rank.

STANDARDISED SCORES

When attempts are made to evaluate results, it is important that it be realised that the distribution of scores depends not only upon the ability of the individuals forming the experimental population, but also upon the intrinsic difficulty of the test and the marking scheme used to evaluate results. When two sets of scores are to be compared or combined, it is therefore usually desirable to standardise them. This may be done by expressing them both as standard scores. Since however, when the distribution of scores is normal, two thirds of the standard scores fall between −1 and +1, it is often found more convenient to rescale two such sets of scores so that they have the same mean and the same standard deviation.

If test results showing a normal distribution have been adjusted so that the standard deviation of the distribution is 15, and if their mean is called 100, the relationship shown in Fig. III on page 94 holds between percentile ranks, standard scores and such standardised scores. The pupil mentioned above, who scored 122 in a group the standard deviation of whose scores was 16 and the mean of whose scores was 90, could then be described as having a standardised score (with standard deviation 15) of 130, or an approximate percentile rank of 98.

CORRELATIONS

On many occasions it is desirable to assess the degree of correspondence between two sets of measures. This relationship is conveniently expressed by a correlation coefficient. Some understanding of the degree of correspondence implied by correlations of +0·1, +0·3, +0·5, +0·8 and +0·9 may be obtained from a study of the scatter diagrams shown in Fig. XI–XV below. (The values chosen are those frequently referred to in discussions relating to adolescent development.)

Perfect correlation is represented by the value +1·00. This would be found between scores in spelling and reading in the case of a group of pupils in which the best speller was the most successful in reading, the child second in spelling was second in reading, and so on for the entire group. It is evident from the scatter diagrams given below that the relationships described by correlations of +0·1 or +0·3 are relatively slight, that a correlation of +0·5 expresses a fairly low degree of conformity between two measures, and that correlations as high as +0·8 or +0·9 describe the correspondence between two assessments which include cases of definite divergence.

PROBABLE ERRORS

In attempting to assess the significance of such correlations—whether they appear to be relatively high or relatively low—it is desirable also to remember that each one is obtained from a mere sample. The nature of this sample changes to some extent from one occasion to another, and the size of the probable error (even under the best conditions) varies with the size of the sample. For this reason considerable caution has to be exercised in the interpretation of findings based upon small samples; and it is well to remember that by chance

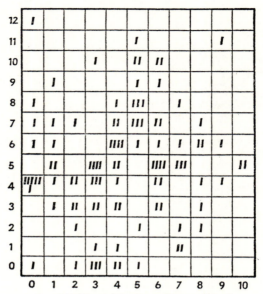

Fig. XI. Scatter Diagram. Correlation of
approximately +0·1.

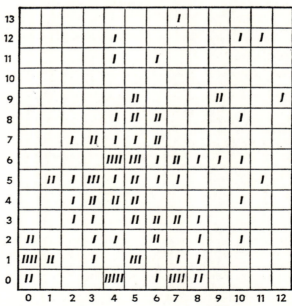

Fig. XII. Scatter Diagram. Correlation of approximately +0·3.

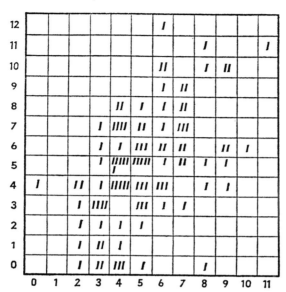

FIG. XIII. Scatter Diagram. Correlation of
approximately +0·5.

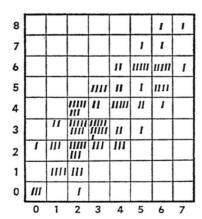

FIG. XIV. Scatter Diagram. Correlation
of approximately +0·8.

R

alone correlations might appear up to the limits expressed by three times the "probable error". The size of the "probable error" is commonly indicated by the symbols ± after a correlation coefficient (as, for example, +0·15 ±0·03 on page 96 above). For methods of calculating probable errors and discussion as to their significance reference may be made to books on statistical methods.

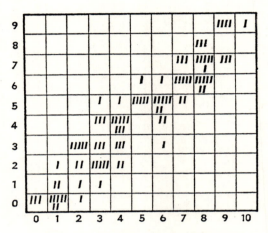

Fig. XV. Scatter Diagram. Correlation of approximately +0·9.

INDEX TO TEXT

224, 241, 244; therapy, 141, 171, 172, 175, 176, 181, 201, 207
Growth, 47, 48, 50, 103, 104, 106, 110; (bodily), 5–17, 95, 96, 142, 164; of abilities, 117–135; of intelligence, 89–99, 119–121, 142, 164, 240; spurts, 8–11, 93, 97, 103

Hair, 14, 156, 232; hairiness, 7, 12, 14
Handicrafts, 172
Hands, 13, 17
Harvard (long-term study), 10–12, 93, 97, 104, 106
Height, 8–11, 13, 14, 22, 95, 96, 97, 104, 154, 156
Hero-worship, 240
Hippocrates, 6
History, 99
Home, 2, 5, 30, 32, 49, 69, 70, 72, 75, 79, 146, 151, 196, 201, 203, 210, 233, 245; homes, 22, 53–61, 66, 72–81, 143, 203, 232, 235
Hormones, 13, 154, 156, 231
Hostility, 24, 28, 77

Imagery, 99
Imagination, 34, 45, 118, 240
Inadequacy, 178, 200, 233, 242
Incentives, 165
Independence, 28, 31, 68–70, 72, 205, 241
Individual differences, 6, 8, 9, 12, 14, 15, 21, 25, 39, 75, 81, 87–89, 110, 131, 133, 143, 148, 151, 152, 164, 178, 189, 202, 203, 230, 243
Industrial exploitation, 95; industry, 191, 196–205
Inferiority (sense of), 17, 77
Inheritance, 63, 109, 110, 219, 230, 233, 237
Initiative, 58, 79, 179, 199, 211
Insecurity, 16, 46, 178, 242
Insight, 47, 48, 74, 119, 191, 200, 209, 212, 244
Instincts, 38, 41, 45, 46, 212, 213, 234, 244; sexual, 40, 41, 235
Instruction (class), 91, 118, 141, 180; (individualised), 89, 150, 181, 189
Intellect, 34, 35
Intelligence, 89, 90, 92–95, 118, 119, 120, 142, 240; intelligence quotient, 96, 105, 107–110, 118, 233
Interests, 5, 21, 55, 59, 69, 78, 96, 108, 117, 119, 120, 125, 134, 142, 143, 144, 152, 153, 168, 188–191, 197, 198, 221, 222, 231, 240, 244

Interview, 142, 190
Isocrates, 87

Kant, 35
Kwakiutl, 24

Laissez-faire (social climate), 168, 199, 213
Languages (study of), 120, 133, 134, 141, 172
Leadership, 24, 150, 160, 169, 170, 175, 191
Learning, 179, 183, 202, 203; adult, 93, 120, 134; physiological, 16, 147, 232, 239; social, 16, 141–159, 209, 210–217, 223, 239
Linguistic skill, 99
Locke, 34, 87
London, 21, 45, 200
Long-term studies, 10–12, 92, 95, 97, 109, 117, 119, 142–147, 152, 155, 156, 158, 198, 230, 240
Love, 46, 48, 49, 50, 64–66, 69, 148, 216, 242, 245
Loyalty, 48, 49, 171, 200
Lying, 24

Marginal (man), 84
Marriage, 23, 26, 28, 63, 216, 217; marriage guidance, 215, 217
Masturbation, 167, 215
Mathematics, 99, 100, 133, 172
Maturing, early, 12, 13, 97, 104, 121, 123; genital, 14, 155, 241; maturity, physical, 12–14, 15, 21, 23, 25; social, 2, 61, 242; urge to, 24
McDougall, 45
Mead, 23
Mechanical ability, 118, 122, 123, 124, 130, 131, 134
Membership of groups, 2, 5, 23, 46, 151, 164–172, 179, 196, 203, 215, 230
Memorising, 119–120, 130, 240; memory, 34, 45
Menstruation, 12, 14, 15, 21, 27, 156, 213, 215, 221, 230
Mental age, 90, 105, 155, 188
Mental ferment, 240, 241
Mental health, 47, 63, 66, 81, 159, 165, 170, 171, 172, 178, 187, 189, 200, 244, 245
Mesomorphic, 7
Morale, 47, 48, 54, 171, 173, 182, 190, 198, 200
Moreno, 169, 170

INDEX TO REFERENCES

ARTICLES, PUBLICATIONS, REPORTS, ETC.